Teacher Development

Teacher Development

ROBERT F. McNERGNEY

University of Virginia

CAROL A. CARRIER

University of Minnesota

MACMILLAN PUBLISHING CO., INC.
New York

COLLIER MACMILLAN PUBLISHERS
London

Macmillan Publishing Co., Inc.
866 Third Avenue, New York, New York 10022

Collier Macmillan Canada, Ltd.

Library of Congress Cataloging in Publication Data

McNergney, Robert F
  Teacher development.

  Includes bibliographies and index.
  1. Teachers, Training of.   I. Carrier, Carol A.,
joint author.   II. Title.
LB1715.M3155   1981   370'.7'1   80-19444
ISBN 0-02-379600-6

Printing: 1 2 3 4 5 6 7 8   Year: 1 2 3 4 5 6 7 8

To *Maggie, Dick, Erin,* and *Carrie*

✦ Preface ✦

TEACHING is an honorable profession—indeed, a distinguished one. Teachers who in no sense can be said to have been ordinary have shaped our lives. We have been born to them, raised by them, disciplined and occasionally shamed by them, loved by them, bored by them, and excited by them. That we have also learned from them, there is no doubt.

The profession of teaching has always been vulnerable to its critics. Teachers have been accused of stifling young minds by demanding compliance and conformity; at the same time, they have been charged with contributing to lawlessness and moral decay by permitting students to direct their own learning. They have been criticized for declining achievement test scores, for both teaching and not teaching students about sex, for allowing and even perpetrating violence in the classroom, and, in general, for the alleged physical, mental, and moral flabbiness of youth. We do not suggest that teachers are exempt from responsibility for the tensions and failures of organized education, but we also do not believe that it is right to indict teachers for all our social ills.

It is not our intent to argue that teachers have been accused unjustly. Instead, *we propose that the support of teacher growth and innovation can best be accomplished by accepting the fact that teachers are unique in needs and abilities and should be viewed as individuals*, not just in theory or research, but as the real Miss Corrins, Mr. Zentics, and Mrs. Boydens we have known.

This book tries to integrate research and theory on individual differences with work in the area of in-class observation of instruction and methods of feedback to teachers. It also attempts to do this in a way that may be useful to the practitioner. This text seeks to encourage teacher educators—professors, principals, staff developers, supervisors, and teachers—to support the personal and professional growth of individual teachers in multiple ways. Because of the long-standing interest and contribution of supervisors in supporting teacher effectiveness, we draw upon examples from the area of supervision, but we stress that this book is not about supervision; it is about *teacher development*.

We distinguish between supervision and teacher development for several reasons. Supervision has traditionally been caught in the apparent dilemma of evaluating teachers versus supporting teachers. This has often resulted in what might be generously termed supervisory mishmash: "sort of" supporting and "sort of" evaluating. Genuine teacher growth is not possible without evaluation, but evaluation is not sufficient in and of itself to effect teacher growth. We believe the major emphasis of teacher development activities must be placed on deliberate, positive support of teachers to achieve richer and more effective personal and instructional skills.

Those who regard supervision as only evaluation have on occasion held it to be a means of admitting only the best teachers to the profession and excluding the less worthy. This attitude is especially appealing in a tight job market, and if life were always predictable and fair, this might not be a bad plan. We believe, however, that selective retention of teachers is largely a bogus issue today. Whether teacher educators care to admit it or not, entrance to and exit from the profession are controlled mainly by supply and demand, as well as by factors that are unrelated or only indirectly related to teacher competence, such as having children, moving, and changing professions. It is crucial for teacher educators to be concerned about selecting and retaining strong teachers, particularly when there are fewer new people assuming teaching positions. The public and the profession have a right to expect—and even demand such action. We suspect, however, that there will never be a short-age of those willing to determine who should be admitted and who should be excluded from teaching. In the meantime, while some people are preoccupied with these issues, we risk losing many talented, creative teachers because of failure to support their continued growth. It is urgent, therefore, to nurture the development of teachers as persons and as classroom instructors.

By directing this book also to teachers, we hope to shift the focus of teacher development away from those who have traditionally been identified as teacher educators and toward teachers themselves. Although many teacher educators have had teaching experience at one time or another, they are often not teachers, but they hold the keys to teacher evaluation and growth. Most often, teacher educators are curriculum or staff developers, principals, profes-sors, supervisors, and harried graduate students. Their interests in promoting teacher development, although perhaps no less sincere or admirable, may be quite different from the motivations of teachers. Teachers must share the major rights *and* responsibilities for their own development. When teacher development becomes a process of mutual teacher support rather than the ex-clusive province of supervisors, administrators, and colleges of education, the chances should improve for attaining greater teacher personal satisfaction and enriched teaching performance. And when teachers can encourage each other to be stimulating, thinking, feeling, risk-taking, fun people, the chances should greatly improve for them to help students grow in similar ways.

For this book, we have modified Lewin's well-known interaction statement in which he proposes that behavior is a function of the person and the environment, or $B = (f)P,E$. This formula suggests that neither personal abilities nor environmental factors are the sole determinants of behavior. Instead, different persons combine or interact with environments in different ways to yield behavior. We borrow from Lewin to underscore what we believe is the importance of viewing the behaviors of teachers in a similar way. That is, we suggest that teacher behavior (B) is a function (f) of the characteristics of the teacher or person (P), the teacher developmental environment (E), and the tasks (T) in which the teacher engages, or $B = (f)P,E,T$. This text explores the terms in this equation and suggests the implications that such a view holds for teachers and those who support them.

Chapter 1 reviews some of the past and present practices of teacher education and lays a conceptual base for matching teacher developmental environments with teacher abilities and needs. Chapter 2 discusses the goal of supporting personal and professional growth of teachers in terms of the tasks they might undertake and the behaviors they might demonstrate to accomplish these tasks. Chapter 3 concentrates on specific systems of classroom observation to provide a repertoire of methods for examining teacher and student behaviors. Chapter 4 reviews various conceptions of teacher characteristics from which prescriptions for developmental environments may be formulated. Chapter 5 encourages research and development activities related to the needs of teachers by presenting a selection of instruments designed to assess some of the teacher characteristics discussed in Chapter 4. Chapter 6 discusses the concept of a teacher developmental environment, or an approach to organizing learning experiences for teachers. Chapter 7 describes, step by step, a clinical environment, or process of teacher development, that may be adapted to the needs and abilities of teachers. Chapter 8 discusses the possible implications of working with different teachers in different ways by exploring the potential obstacles and promises of teacher development as we envision it.

We have drawn ideas from many sources—our own work as well as the experiences, research, and writing of others. We have leaned most heavily on the work of David E. Hunt and his colleagues on matching models because we have found his thinking to be not only sound and exciting but practical as well. We assume full responsibility for any misinterpretations of the work of others that might result because of our writing.

We thank all those who provided thoughtful criticism, technical assistance, and moral and financial support while we wrote this book; in particular, Lloyd Chilton and his associates at Macmillan Publishing Company, William Gardner, Robert Dykstra, Berj Harootunian, David Wetzel, Carla Hill, Marian Handy; and Ellen Garfinkel. Most of all, we thank our families.

R.F.M.
C.A.C.

❧ Foreword ❧

TEACHERS of teachers spend much of their time, energy and effort trying to make their charges more aware of individual differences in their pupils. What is most refreshing about this book is the simple and elegant idea it puts forth: teachers are individuals, too, and should be treated as such. But Robert McNergney and Carol Carrier have not just presented a theoretically interesting treatise on teacher development; they have included in this volume much that is immediately practicable in the real world of teaching. By developing and explicating the concept of teacher development as the interaction of teacher behavior, teacher characteristics, environments, and teaching tasks, the authors have dramatically pointed out the inadequacy of more simplistic conceptions of teacher education and teacher training.

Teacher education has assigned priority to a wide variety of teacher outcomes, ranging from a list of specific narrow behaviors to what may be termed "humanistic self-actualized individuals." In the former instance, the problem has and continues to be one of integrating the behaviors in a meaningful pattern of teaching; in the latter, the inability to distinguish between the ideal teacher and the ideal human being has led to confusion between general and professional education. McNergney and Carrier acknowledge and discuss these and other approaches to teacher development and present a way of helping teachers become more successful in their professional lives that is at the same time theoretical and practical. In this book they have demonstrated the validity of Kurt Lewin's words that there is nothing so practical as a good theory.

Hence, this is more than a "how-to-do-it" book. By bringing together theory, research, and practical applications, the reader is presented with a solid foundation for understanding what teaching is all about and, more importantly, for helping teachers in what they do and need in their daily endeavors in the schools of America. In turn, the theoretical and evidential base for each of the components of their paradigm is presented and discussed in sufficient detail before specific suggestions and principles are proposed. These principles are based, as well, on the personal experiences of the two authors who have taught courses and worked extensively with teachers in school settings.

Teacher education is at a peculiar crossroad. While there will continue to be formal programs of teacher education offered by colleges and universities, many more initiatives for teacher development will be coming from those who work in the field. For the immediate future, schools will no longer have the large influx of new teachers that has characterized most schools over the last two decades. As the insights and enthusiasm of these new members of the profession become unavailable, teacher development becomes more crucial. For any individual who would help improve teaching and teachers, *Teacher Development* has blazed a significant path for the future. Those individuals whose goal is to make teaching a true profession have been given a great assist by this volume and would do well to take it seriously.

BERJ HAROOTUNIAN
Professor and Director
Division for the Study of
   Teaching
Syracuse University

~&Contents &~

ᴥ 1 ᴥ

Responding to Teachers
as Individuals

T HE purpose of teacher education should be to encourage the growth of
teachers as persons and as professionals. Teachers who are growing are
becoming more open, more humane, more skillful, more complex,
more complete pedagogues and human beings. They are fulfilling their own
unique potentials or doing for themselves what others expect them to do for
students. But often teacher educators fail to recognize that teachers, like
students, have different needs and abilities.

Although teacher educators have long championed the idea of the individual in their rhetoric, they have shown only minimal concern for teachers as individuals in practice. They act at times as if they had the best set of methods
to enable all teachers, regardless of individual differences, to become effective
and personally satisfied professionals. No one, of course, possesses a magic
method for educating all teachers.

Not all teacher educators have used the same set of methods for preparing
teachers. Traditionally, the best preparation for teaching was thought to be a
strong liberal education with an emphasis in a particular discipline or spe-
cialty. Many colleges and universities have translated this philosophy into
programs of liberal arts education, followed by training for teachers in educational basics, then in courses on how to teach, and, finally, a brief appren-
ticeship in teaching. Some believe that the best approach to the preparation
of teachers is to train people as scientists or problem solvers who will discover
and apply laws of teaching and learning. Others have emphasized humanistic
approaches that concentrate on developing personal teacher growth and expression in the hope these values will in turn be transmitted through teachers
to students. There have also been teacher educational technicians, or systems

1

designers, who stress skill development, and there have been change agents who sought to educate teachers through social action. Variations on these themes are myriad. One does not have to look far to conclude that theory, research, and practice reveal no general-effects model or single set of best methods to enable all persons to become teachers. Teacher educators will take a positive step toward supporting teacher competence, independence, and satisfaction in teaching when they explicitly consider and respond to teachers as unique in needs and abilities.

This affirmation is based on three assumptions. First, there is no one superior method that can either support the growth of all teachers or meet all objectives of teacher growth. It is only reasonable and humane, therefore, to act differently with different people when sufficient prima facie evidence indicates that linear thinking and action are ineffective or stifling. Second, if a single approach to developing teachers is inappropriate, it logically follows that those who intend to encourage growth in different teachers must build a repertoire of diverse strategies. These strategies can be called upon as conditions warrant. Third, effective teacher education is strategic or systematic. It is not superficial or random.

Although systematic support of individual teachers is necessary and worthwhile, teacher educators cannot effect sweeping educational reform by themselves. They do not possess a ready store of solutions to the troubling problems facing the educational community and society at large. Teacher educators alone cannot force improvement in schools and schooling, nor should they be expected to do so. They can, however, help teachers to learn and develop independently and thus encourage teachers to do the same for their students.

Although teacher education can and should be a supportive process, it would be naive to suppose that teacher educators could divest themselves of their responsibility for teacher evaluation. Whether teacher educators are college/university people, school administrators, or members of professional teachers' associations, the responsibility for critical appraisal of teaching remains. The processes of support and evaluation may seem to be in conflict at times, but they are not as contradictory as one might suppose. Without a genuine attempt to look critically at what does and does not work in teaching, teacher support is more likely to degenerate into anomalous glad-handing than it is to refine instructional abilities and nurture self-esteem.

This view of teacher education as a process of responding to the needs of individual teachers might best be defined by comparing it to some of the common conceptions of teacher education and noting their philosophical strengths and weaknesses. Therefore, we turn to an examination of current ideas about teacher education that focuses on the diversity of roles played by teacher educators. Once this examination is completed we present an alternative approach to teacher education, which we call *teacher development*, and try to show how its goals agree and disagree with the conventional goals of teacher education.[1] Finally, we project the general form that teacher development might take in practice and discuss its potential strengths and limitations in relation to the individual needs and abilities of teachers.

Teacher Education as Supervision

In varying degrees, supervisors have usually functioned as teacher educators. Nowhere is this idea more clearly reinforced than in Lucio and McNeil's (1962) overview of the evolution of supervision. They trace the beginnings of supervision in America, for example, from colonial times. It was not long after the Massachusetts Bay Colony passed a law establishing public schools that local civil and religious officers began serving as supervisors. These early supervisors presided over the practice of teaching and inspected the conduct of teachers in the overall operation of schools. Thus the town elders were the first people to assume responsibilities for "educating" teachers in the ways of teaching, often in a paternalistic and severe fashion.

Two centuries later, in contrast, supervisors functioned as specialists in particular areas of curriculum. For quite different reasons than their early counterparts, these teacher educators also played a direct part in school operation. They saw a need to address particular problems raised by the addition to the curriculum of such new subjects as music, drawing, manual training, home economics, and physical education. Because teachers and superintendents were unfamiliar with these subjects, specialists were needed to provide methodological leadership. Following this curriculum-specialist period, supervisors attempted to discover laws of education through research and measurement and to apply these laws through teachers. The scientific supervisors focused on the ends of training, that is, the growth of the pupil. In so doing, they set themselves up as the early behaviorists of the teacher education movement.

In the 1930s and 1940s, supervision began to be characterized in terms of democratic human relations rather than as processes of administrative inspection. These democratic supervisors assumed that teachers possessed the requisite interests and abilities to function effectively, so their emphasis was on self-analysis, self-criticism, and self-improvement. The supervisor acted as a sort of guidance counselor who attempted to appeal to the feelings and emotions of teachers in order to assist their development. By the 1960s, the pinnacle of supervisory development, according to Lucio and McNeil, was supervision through "reason and practical intelligence." These twin objectives were translated into attempts to bring about the wide participation of teachers in the process of inquiry and the assessment of outcomes.

[1] The term *teacher development* has been used by others—most notably Mosher and Purpel (1972).

Today, supervision is practiced much as it was in the past and it incorporates many of the traditional functions: supervisors serve as overseers, human relations specialists, and instructional leaders. The contributions of supervisors as teacher educators have been and are considerable, but much of what passes for supervisory practice is marked by obvious drawbacks. Supervisors too often function in an orthodox role as paternalistic inspectors who watch over teachers. This has led to the characterization of supervision as "super vision" and "snooper vision"—indications of the low esteem in which supervisors are held by many teachers. In addition, supervisors are hampered by an apparent absence of theoretical support for their reasoning, a deficiency that has done little to buttress their credibility with researchers and practitioners. The most notable exception is in the area of clinical supervision (Goldhammer, 1969; Cogan, 1973; Acheson and Gall, 1980). Because of its focus on observable classroom practices, as opposed to other more general approaches to supervision, clinical supervision will be discussed when we examine the role of teacher educator as clinician.

Teacher Education as Administration

Any person involved in activities directed toward the improvement of educational programs might be characterized as a teacher educator. Perhaps the most familiar model of teacher educator, next to the college or university professor, is that of the public school administrator, particularly the building-level administrator. It is not surprising that most of the administrators who are simultaneously teacher educators function more as managers bent on evaluating and improving the total educational setting than as educators intent on directly assisting the growth and effectiveness of teachers.

The administrator as a teacher educator often looks upon the improvement of the instructional program primarily as a matter of organizational support rather than as direct involvement in classroom teaching. That is, if administrators hire appropriate personnel, provide information and materials, coordinate schedules, and outline procedures, they believe they are making schools more efficient and satisfying places in which to work. Largely because of their training, administrators as teacher educators seem to be motivated almost exclusively by a concern for creating and maintaining a workable educational system—one that concentrates mainly on the utilization of time, deployment of materials, organization of space, and the like. Even the most well-planned and efficiently organized system still depends for its success upon the people within it. That even the smoothest operating system often fails to yield happy, productive teachers and students lends support to the idea that teacher education must focus directly on the people in the system as well as on the educational programs and procedures of schools.

Teacher Education as Counseling

The humanistic or personal approach of many modern teacher educators has its roots in the works of such noted psychologists as Abraham Maslow and Carl Rogers. The development of this person-centered view of teacher education has taken place concomitantly with the growth of T-groups, encounter sessions, and other associated activities supported by such organizations as the National Training Laboratories in Washington, D.C., and the Center for Studies of the Person in La Jolla, California. In teacher education—as exhibited by Mosher and Purpel's (1972) work in ego counseling, the supervisory work of Blumberg (1974) and associates, and Gordon's teacher effectiveness training (1974)—person-centered approaches stress the importance of the teacher as a person and the dynamics of interpersonal relationships.

Teacher educators who adopt a counseling orientation usually do not subscribe to a laissez-faire attitude of teacher growth; nevertheless, they accede to individual differences in their acceptance of the teacher education environment as they believe it exists. This is an environment in which the goals and objectives for teaching are established and controlled primarily by the teacher. Person-centered or humanist teacher educators thus draw upon individual differences, such as perceptions of teacher warmth and openness, to minimize teacher frustration or failure and to look for abilities and aptitudes that determine successful teaching. Such teacher educators view growth and development mainly as the responsibility of the teacher.

Because they perceive people as unique in their abilities and needs, teacher educators who function as counselors try to respond differently with each individual. The premium such an approach places on uniqueness is a strength of this orientation and, in many cases, a professional life-saving technique for teachers seeking personal contact. Person-centered approaches, however, concentrate mainly on the personal needs of the teacher, not on the teacher's technical skills of delivering instruction. In addition, because teacher educators who function as counselors typically use nondirective approaches, they may frustrate teachers seeking more direct advice and guidance.

Teacher Education as Curriculum Development

Although curriculum development is concerned with the design of educational programs, it often influences the processes of teaching as well. Frequently, however, curriculum developers identify educational goals, create technological support systems, and design methods of evaluation without considering the process of instruction. They place major emphasis on the control and management of content rather than on the act of teaching. In attempts to reduce the role of the teacher, "teacher-proof" curricula of the 1960s also revealed the pessimism of some curriculum developers about the abilities of teachers to stimulate learning.

Other curriculum developers, however, have tried explicitly to build the teacher into the educational program. In their writing on curriculum development, for instance, Joyce and Weil (1980) have advocated an optimal balance, or a one-to-one relationship among educational objectives, curriculum design, and instructional strategy. They suggest an approach to curriculum development that addresses teachers and teaching, not only content.

Persons who function as resource teachers are excellent examples of curriculum developers whose concern lies not only with content and programs but also with teachers and teaching. Resource teachers seek to support other teachers in the creation, adoption, or adaptation of special kinds of educational programs in the classroom. They serve as resources to other teachers for developing objectives, making and organizing materials, and formulating methods of monitoring student progress. They may also demonstrate the use of a program in their own classroom or that of another teacher. In this sense, they are specifically concerned with the delivery of instruction.

The role of the teacher educator as resource teacher has certain advantages, but it is not without its limitations as well. Although these teacher educators are not usually stigmatized as administrators who try to force new programs on teachers, or as supervisors who see that teachers comply with the dictates of the program, they must often struggle to divest themselves of the "model teacher" mantle so as to make contact with other teachers. It is assumed that because these teacher educators come from the teacher ranks they can identify with other teachers, and it follows that they may be among the better persons to recognize and attend to teachers' needs. But this assumption may be unwarranted. Although they may be closer to teachers and teaching than are administrators, the resource teacher or curriculum developer, like the administrator, is expected typically to concentrate on the conditions surrounding teachers rather than on teachers as persons. Moreover, the conditions on which they concentrate are curricular, not instructional; that is, the role tends to exclude responsibilities for the systematic study of teaching behavior, thereby limiting the importance of instruction in the educational program.

Teacher Education as Science

Teacher education has also been regarded as a science—a matter of analyzing and quantifying behavior, and feeding results back to teachers. Modern analysis of teaching performance in behavioral terms was pioneered by Anderson and associates (1945, 1946a, 1946b) just after World War II and extended most notably through the early work of such persons as Withall (1949), Medley and Mitzel (1958), Bellack, Kliebard, Hyman, and Smith (1966), and Flanders (1960).

These early efforts in the design and development of classroom observation schemes have been followed by a proliferation of systems that have been referred to as *sign systems*—behaviors the observer usually checks only once when they occur during an observation period—and *category systems*—classifications of behaviors the observer learns and notes at regular intervals during the observation period (Medley and Mitzel, 1963). Some idea of the depth and range of these observation instruments is provided by Simon and Boyer (1974). They have assembled a compendium of ninety-nine observation instruments, focusing on such diverse areas as teacher management of misbehavior (Kounin, 1970), nonverbal behavior (Galloway, 1968), and affective and psychomotor dimensions of behavior (Spaulding, 1967). More recently, Borich and Madden (1977) published a book of instruments available for evaluating classroom instruction from an even greater variety of perspectives to encourage use of multivariate approaches to investigating teaching and learning. Other books (Brandt, 1972; Cartwright and Cartwright, 1974) also review various observation systems.

In spite of this substantial scientific literature on teaching, most of the work on analysis of instruction has been undertaken to learn *about* teaching, not to promote the improvement of teacher performance directly. Because these systems are part of the repertoire of many modern teacher educators, however, they are being used for training and evaluation of teaching performance. Even scientific approaches to teaching-learning yield striking anomalies when results are translated into practice. Rosenshine and Furst, for example, pointed out in 1971 that while the Far West Regional Laboratory was training teachers to repeat student answers less often, the Northwest Regional Laboratory was giving teachers the opposite advice.

In contrast to counseling-type teacher educators, those who work analytically tend to prefer the hard, quantifiable facts of teaching and learning that observation systems yield. If scientific teacher educators haphazardly apply these observation systems to complex and dynamic teaching-learning situations, the result may be a narrow translation of this information. Furthermore, the "facts" of teaching and learning as revealed through scientific observation can de-emphasize the importance of the teacher as a person. Attempts by teacher educators to use scientific methods, however, have introduced systematic thought to a process that has heretofore been largely a matter of folklore.

Beyond the use of observation systems, the most visible attempt to improve teaching directly through scientific methods has been performance- or competency-based teacher education (P/CBTE). Performance- or competency-based programs have been characterized by (1) specification of learner objectives in behavioral terms; (2) specification of the means of determining whether performance meets the indicated criterion levels; (3) provision for one or more modes of instruction pertinent to the objectives, through which the learning activities may take place; (4) public sharing of the objectives, assessment by criteria, and alternative activities; (5) assessment of the learning experience in terms of competency criteria; and (6) placement on the learner of accountability for meeting the criteria (Houston and Howsam, 1972). As Houston and Howsam point out, the use of modules, educational technology, and guidance and management support systems relate to the notion of individualized approaches to teacher education. In the main, however, proponents of these programs have not determined which educational methods are most appropriate for which teachers and for which objectives.

Teacher Education as Clinical Intervention

In recent years, many teacher educators, acting as clinicians, have focused on in-class techniques for the improvement of instruction. This interest in working directly with a teacher or team of teachers in the classroom has been stimulated by several developments. There are now more sophisticated ways to examine activities that occur in the classroom. Many clinicians have been guided by these systems in their work with teachers. In the past, such direction was largely unavailable. The simultaneous demand for relevance and accountability in higher education during the 1960s and 1970s, particularly in teacher training, has contributed to the idea that teacher educators must strive to integrate theory and practice. This is perhaps best illustrated by concepts of performance- and competency-based teacher education. Many have stressed early and continuing field experience and have relied heavily on the demonstrated performances of students as indications of teaching ability. Consequently, new teacher educator roles have emerged, such as the clinical professor and clinical supervisor who are concerned with in-class activities of teaching and learning.

Clinical supervision as conceived by Cogan (1973) and Goldhammer (1969) is of particular interest because its focus is not only on analysis of instruction but on in-class methods for supporting teachers. These educators differentiate clinical supervision from general supervision, which takes place primarily outside the classroom and involves writing and revising curriculum, preparing materials, and developing processes and instruments for reporting to parents, by narrowing the focus to classroom activities.

Cogan defines clinical supervision as

the improvement of the teacher's classroom instruction. The principal data of clinical supervision include records of classroom events: what the teacher and students do in the classroom during the teaching-learning process. These data are supplemented by information about the teacher's and students' perceptions, beliefs, attitudes, and knowledge relevant to the instruction. Such information may relate to states and events occurring prior to, during, and following any segment of instruction to be analyzed. The clinical domain is the interaction between a specific teacher or team of teachers and specific students, both as a group and as individuals. Clinical supervision may therefore be defined as the rationale and practice designed to improve the teacher's classroom performance. It takes its principal data from the events of the classroom. The analysis of these data and the relationship between teacher and supervisor form the basis of the program procedures and strategies designed to improve the students' learning by improving the teacher's classroom behavior.

Clinical supervision is important because it has taken a step toward thinking about both the people and the processes involved in teacher education. It is perhaps most important, however, because it has drawn attention to the need for rational thought and predictable action in classroom teacher educational situations. Clinical supervisors in particular (and clinicians in general) have begun to develop and refine their methods of observation and feedback, but they have not offered much substantive direction for considering the needs and abilities of individual teachers. Cogan, for example, has encouraged treating teachers as individuals but has provided little direction on how this might be accomplished. As Harris (1976) and Sergiovanni (1973) have implied or expressed, one of the major limitations of clinical supervision is that it is too narrowly defined and needs a broader conceptual base. Accordingly, such a conceptual base might usefully try to provide for teachers' individual needs.

An Alternative: Teacher Education as Teacher Development

There is currently no single best approach for preparing and sustaining all teachers. We urge, therefore, that theorists, researchers, and practitioners of teacher education reject the search for one single, all-purpose approach and, instead, formulate, apply, and examine different approaches with different teachers. Specifically, we propose that teacher education be guided by the Behavior-Person-Environment (B-P-E) conceptual scheme as set forth by Kurt Lewin (1935) and extended most notably by David Hunt (1971) and Hunt and Sullivan (1974). Cronbach (1957, 1975), and Cronbach and Snow (1977) have used the label ATI (aptitude-treatment interaction) to describe essentially the same approach, but we prefer Hunt's B-P-E scheme because of the practicality of his conceptual formulations. The B-P-E approach provides a way of understanding (1) the complexity of interactions among student learning behavior, the student as a person, and the environment created by the teacher, and (2) the complexity of interactions among teaching behavior, the teacher as a person, and the environment created by the teacher educator.

According to Lewin's (1935) interaction statement, behavior (B) is a function of the person (P) and the environment (E), or $B = (f)P, E$. Behavior, then, is a complex, dynamic, interactive phenomenon that is influenced or explained in different ways, depending upon the learners involved and the kinds of environments they inhabit. Essentially, this formula means that behavior is determined neither by the environment alone nor solely by the characteristics of the learner. It is, instead, dependent upon the person in combination with the environment. Figure 1–1 depicts the interactive relationship of persons and environments in a classroom setting, as discussed by Hunt and Sullivan (1974); in classroom terms, this illustrates the idea that student behavior (B) is produced by the student's or person's (P) abilities or aptitudes in combination with the environment (E) created by the teacher. Students behave in certain ways not because they are bright or dull, interested or uninterested, creative or conventional, or because they are exposed to the best or worst teaching; students behave as they do because of combinations of the influences of their personal characteristics and the environments of which they are a part.

If one accepts the idea that people are different in terms of interests, abilities, traits, or aptitudes, then it is reasonable to expect that the best educational environment for one student may not be equally effective for another. Hence it is necessary for the teacher to be able to create a range of educational environments to meet the needs of different learners. It is the job of the teacher educators to help teachers create educational environments that can be rich and responsive to various student needs. That might best be accomplished by their treating teachers in the same way that teachers are expected to treat students, or by extending the B-P-E conceptual scheme to the relationship between teacher and teacher educator.

Figure 1–2 represents an interactive relationship between teacher and teacher educator that is analogous to the relationship of teacher and students in Figure 1–1. Figure 1–2 differs from the original Lewinian formula, however, in that we have added a task (T) dimension in order to begin to address the complexities in teacher development. It may be read as follows: Teacher behaviors (B) are a function of the characteristics of the person who serves as teacher (P), the educational environment (E) that is created by the teacher educator, and the tasks (T) in which the teacher engages, or $B = (f)P,E,T$.

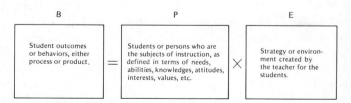

FIGURE 1–1.   Interactive Relationship Between Teacher and Student. Adapted from Hunt, D. E. and E. V. Sullivan. *Between Psychology and Education*. [Hinsdale, Ill.: The Dryden Press, 1974], p. 277.

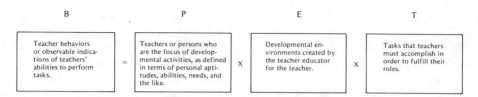

FIGURE 1–2.   Interactive Relationship of Teacher Behaviors, Teacher Characteristics, Teacher Developmental Environments, and Teacher Tasks.

The formula assumes, therefore, that teacher behavior, like the behavior of students, is influenced independently as well as interactively by several critical variables. Before one can understand the key concept of interaction of variables in the teacher-teacher educator relationship, however, one must first understand the terms *teacher behaviors* (B), *teacher-person characteristics* (P), *teacher developmental environments* (E), and *teaching tasks* (T).

Teacher behaviors are observable indications of teachers' abilities to accomplish the tasks in which they engage. There are many immediate and long-term outcomes or behaviors that teacher educators should be helping teachers demonstrate. One general set of behaviors might be characterized as instructional, or those that relate to the successful accomplishment of classroom teaching. For instance, as teachers plan or formulate an educational environment within a typical classroom, they must be able to perform such behaviors as diagnosing student needs, establishing instructional groups, setting appropriate goals and objectives, and selecting materials. Once planning has been completed, teachers must meet the demands of delivering instruction to students. The behaviors or interpersonal transactions associated with the delivery of instruction, however, are quite different from the teaching behaviors associated with planning. Encountering students face to face and attending to their needs by asking appropriate questions, reinforcing responses, and keeping them actively engaged are behaviors considerably different from planning. Behaviors demonstrated as teachers engage in planning and delivering instruction, as well as many behaviors pertinent to other instructional activities, are central to effective classroom teaching.

Another general set of teacher behaviors that teacher educators should encourage is more personal than classroom teaching behaviors. This complex of teacher behaviors is associated not only with the growth of teachers as teachers, but with the growth of teachers as persons. For example, as teachers confer with parents on a child's progress or interact with peers and administrators on the formulation of school philosophy and curriculum, they must function independently yet cooperatively, cope with stress, and understand and tolerate—if not accept—others' values, attitudes, and opinions. Teacher educators must be ready to support these teacher behaviors within and out-side the classroom from moment-to-moment and over a long period of time. In general, growth as a teacher and as a person is a matter of stretching one's own repertoire of instructional and personal behaviors.

The phrase *teacher characteristics* refers to the needs, abilities, traits, or aptitudes of teachers. The challenge for the teacher educator with respect to teacher characteristics is twofold: the teacher educator must first identify those teacher characteristics most salient for particular individuals and then design environments to complement or supplement such characteristics. For the teacher educator, then, the most important characteristics of teachers to understand are those that provide some direction for offering the right kind of support to the individual teacher (Hunt and Sullivan, 1974). Hunt's own ac-cessibility channels offer some direction for matching personal characteristics with educational environments. For example, he shows how people can be described in terms of their *motivational* orientation and how the appropriately matched environment can be described in terms of its form of *feedback*. French (1958), for example, found that people with high affiliative needs per-form better when given "feeling feedback," whereas those with high achieve-ment needs function better with "task-oriented" feedback. Unfortunately, the quantity and quality of evidence supporting such matching of people to envi-ronments, vary greatly. As noted in later chapters, teacher educators must draw upon a variety of sources of knowledge about teacher characteristics to guide the formulation of supportive environments for teachers. Such characteristics as general ability, cognitive style, values, attitudes, and concerns may be par-ticularly useful for describing teachers and guiding teacher educators as they work toward personalized support.

A *teacher developmental environment* is an educational approach created by a teacher educator for a teacher. We describe and differentiate among teacher developmental environments in terms of the following five characteristics: purpose, procedures, management strategy, support system, and provision for evaluation.

Purpose. All teacher developmental environments are designed to encour-age teacher growth. Beyond that, however, different teacher developmental environments may have different specific objectives. For instance, one envi-ronment may be intended to accomplish a goal as broad as supporting teachers to involve a greater range of human and material resources in curric-ulum planning, and another may focus on something as narrow as supporting a teacher in managing a particular behavior problem more effectively.

Procedures. A teacher developmental environment has an identifiable proce-dure or sequence of events for implementation. Although some environments may be more highly structured or predictable in terms of procedures than others, none are random. We use the concept of procedures to indicate that teacher educators follow a systematic progression of events as they create supportive educational environments.

Management Strategy. Management strategy refers to the locus of control for decision making in a teacher developmental environment. In some situations it may be appropriate for a teacher educator to decide what a teacher needs to work on and how such work should proceed. In other situations, the teacher might make such decisions. Most often, however, the decisions about the focus and flow of teacher developmental activities will be shared or negotiated between the teacher and teacher educator.

Support System. In order to establish some teacher developmental environments, it may be necessary to provide certain material support. This could take the form of books, films, recording equipment, money for released time to visit an exemplary program, or some other tangible good without which the environment would be impoverished. Beyond material support, a support system connotes teacher developmental environments that may also require special human skills. One environment may require special technical expertise such as the ability to operate video tape recording equipment. A different teacher developmental environment, such as one that uses nondirective counseling procedures, may demand special human relations skills.

Provision for Evaluation. As with any instructional process, a teacher developmental environment must provide the means for its evaluation. Processes of evaluation may vary greatly in sophistication and methods. Some kinds of assessment may be as simple as seeking teacher reactions; other kinds may look to measures of teacher performance. Still others may provide different methods and criteria for judging the value of environmental support.

Teacher developmental environments may be further differentiated in terms of their size or scope (See Chapter 6). Some are quite narrow, focusing on discrete, short-term, teacher-determined objectives. Others, more encompassing, may concentrate on a variety of objectives and extend over longer periods of time.

Teacher tasks are activities that teachers must accomplish to fulfill their roles (See Chapter 2). They may be characterized generally in terms of their focus (personal or instructional) and the demands they place on teachers (simple or complex). For now, however, perhaps the best way to explain tasks is by way of an analogy. Athletes, like teachers, must accomplish certain tasks. Those who compete in a decathlon, for example, engage in ten separate and very different physical tasks, including the shotput, javelin throw, 100-meter sprint, pole vault, high jump, and five other very different and individually demanding activities. In spite of the variety of demands they place on the athlete, however, these tasks have certain things in common: all require, for example, strength, agility, and concentration if they are to be performed with any degree of proficiency.

Similarly, the teacher must accomplish certain variable tasks. Teaching tasks, of course, are much more diverse in number and complexity of requirements than those in the decathlon. Organizing a field trip demands that a teacher arrange transportation, identify adult sponsors, coordinate schedules, provide background information to students, to name only a few responsibilities. In contrast, planning a mathematics lesson may necessitate, among other things, diagnosing student abilities, establishing objectives, and selecting appropriate materials. Organizing field trips and planning mathematics lessons are in some ways similar activities. Yet, they are sufficiently different from one another to expect that teachers' behaviors will be modified as they try to accomplish each task.

Interaction

The idea of the interaction of variables is not new. As noted earlier, Lewin's (1935) formula B = f(P,E) suggests that behavior is dependent upon a connection or combination of persons and environments. The recent interest of educators and psychologists in interaction, particularly person-environment interactions has been generally traced to Cronbach's (1957) presidential address to the American Psychological Association. He proposed that correlational psychology (with its concern for individual differences) and experimental psychology (with its emphasis on environments or treatments) be coordinated to study the interactive effects of persons and environments on behavior.

As researchers and theorists have responded to Cronbach's recommendation, the terms *interact* and *interaction* have taken on various meanings. Sometimes they are used to connote the combination, interdependency, or reciprocal action of personal characteristics and environmental variables. At other times *interact* and *interaction* are defined as the amount of statistical variance explained by the interaction term in analysis of variance or multiple regression (Olweus, 1977). As Hunt (1973) asserts, the concept of interaction is much too important to be limited to any narrow definition. Instead, it must be elaborated in a variety of ways as it is used in everyday educational practice, laboratory or classroom experiments, and psychological and educational theory.

Regardless of whether interaction is defined in terms of interdependence, reciprocal action, or the amount of variance explained statistically, the implications of this way of thinking are important for teacher education. In order to examine some of these implications, the components in Figure 1–2 are rearranged to show that the environment created by the teacher educator for the teacher as certain tasks are undertaken yields teacher behavior (E:P:T = B). This transformation facilitates an examination of the teacher educational environment as it relates first to the teacher, next to the teacher's task, and finally to teachers and tasks simultaneously.

Environments × Persons

Research on the interaction of environments and persons is referred to by various terms: *aptitude-treatment interaction* (ATI) (Cronbach and Snow, 1969, 1977); *trait-treatment interaction* (Hills, 1971; Berliner and Cahen, 1973), *attribute* or *achievement-treatment interaction* (Tobias, 1969, 1976) and *person-environment interaction* (Hunt, 1971; Hunt and Sullivan, 1974). Regardless of terminology, when person (P) and environment (E) are said to interact, the implication is that what is an appropriate environment for one person may be inappropriate for another.

A study by Domino (1971) illustrates the idea of person-environment interaction in a college teaching situation. Domino hypothesized an interaction between a student's achievement orientation and the style of teaching to which he or she was exposed in a psychology class. As shown in Figure 1–3, he reported that students who were high on the Achievement via Conformance scale of the California Psychological Inventory (CPI) performed better when taught by an approach that stressed discipline, attendance, clearly defined homework, and class lectures as a means of acquiring course material. Students who were high on the Achievement via Independence scale of the CPI, on the other hand, performed better when taught by an approach that emphasized class discussion and de-emphasized discipline, attendance, and homework. Student achievement on multiple choice and essay tests, their evaluation of the course and of the teacher, and their final course grade were maximized when teaching style and student achievement orientation were congruent. Other studies (Dowaliby and Schumer, 1973; Peterson, 1979) have produced similar results.

The empirical support for person-environment interactions, however, is limited (Bracht, 1970; Glass, 1970; Cronbach and Snow, 1977); furthermore, many conceptual, methodological, and practical obstacles still inhibit interaction research and subsequent translation of findings into practice (Gehlbach, 1979).[2] Nonetheless, the concept of person-environment interaction is becoming increasingly important to educators and psychologists, because it suggests what many persons have intuited all along; that is, no single educational environment is capable of meeting the needs of all individuals.

---

[2] Bracht's (1970) scorecard on person-environment interaction research is perhaps unnecessarily pessimistic. He counted only those studies that yielded what researchers refer to as "disordinal interactions." When ordinal interactions are counted, the empirical support for person-environment interaction research is considerably stronger.

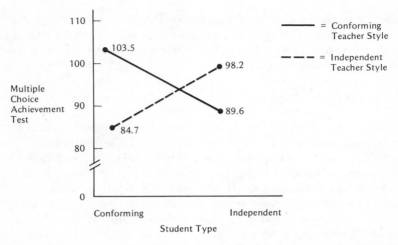

FIGURE 1–3. Means for Independent and Conforming Students Taught by Independent and Conforming Teachers. Data from Domino (1971).

Environments × Tasks

Much less is known about the relationship of educational environments (E) to activities or tasks (T). We believe much as Berliner and Cahen (1973) did in their review of trait-treatment interaction and learning when they wrote:

> We had hoped to incorporate the concept of "task" into our discussion, thus focusing on the interactions between traits, treatments, and tasks (TTTI). We believe . . . that a thorough understanding of the psychological processes in a specific learning task is prerequisite to the development of theory on the interaction between traits and treatments . . . The analysis of educational or psychological tasks, however, is in its infancy and, therefore, is presently inadequate as a guide for the development of such theory.

There are obvious reasons that knowledge about the relationship between environments and tasks is limited. Tasks are often conceptualized as parts of the environment, both in theory and practice. That is, the activities in which learners engage (learning tasks), whether overt or tangible (writing, mixing chemicals, jumping rope) or intangible (empathizing, analyzing, or evaluating), are often characterized not as separate, distinct variables but as components of the larger, more inclusive educational environment. In addition, the tendency to lump tasks and environments together has severely limited knowledge of the nature or attributes of tasks or how tasks compare to each other. The problems of categorizing tasks and differentiating tasks from environments, then, are fundamental issues that must be addressed in any effort to understand the complexity of human behavior.

Many logical and educationally significant activities, however, can guide teacher educators in their attention to the dimension of task. As will be discussed in Chapter 2, such activities may be derived from a variety of sources. For example, teachers suggest that being able to motivate children and to control inappropriate student behavior are important tasks to be accomplished in their work. Students suggest, among other things, that teachers must be able to listen to their concerns and to provide learning experiences that are interesting and challenging. Researchers, professional educators, parents, and others suggest still additional tasks to be accomplished by teachers.

An environment created by a teacher educator for a teacher might be expected to vary not only according to the teacher's needs but according to the nature of the task. For instance, it is reasonable to suspect that there is something different about planning a mathematics lesson, as opposed to teaching a social studies lesson; such differences in tasks may necessitate a change in the educational environment created for a teacher by a teacher educator. Admittedly, raising the notion of teacher tasks as separate or in some way different from educational environments may be premature in light of what is known from research about tasks. But perhaps by at least acknowledging another dimension in the relationship between teacher and teacher educator, it will be possible to begin unraveling some of the complexities of teaching behavior.

Environments × Persons × Tasks

Adding the dimension of task (T) to Lewin's formula suggests that as teacher educators work to promote the growth of teachers, it may be useful to consider what researchers refer to as higher-order interactions, or interactions of more than two variables. Cronbach and Snow (1977) and others have stated that first-order interactions (aptitude × treatments, or persons × environments) may be a much too simple or limited model to explain what occurs in teaching and learning. As noted earlier, person × environment models of behavior propose that different persons function differently in different environments. In contrast, a person × environment × task model implies that as different persons in different environments engage in different tasks, they may be expected to function differently.

It should be apparent to the researcher as well as the practitioner that comprehending the idea of first-order interactions (person × environment) can be either very complex or so simple as to appear to be ordinary common sense (Hunt and Sullivan, 1974). But as Cronbach (1975) has noted, when higher-order interactions are considered, the result may be analogous to entering a hall of mirrors—coming face-to-face with infinity. It is true that an environment × person × task model may not seem a simple way of conceptualizing, investigating, or practicing teacher education. What it can mean for teacher educators is that educational environments may need to be adapted not only to teachers' needs but to the demands of the tasks in which teachers engage. Using the previous analogy of the decathlon, this would mean that training must take into account the capabilities of the athlete and the particular events in which the athlete must compete.

The Characteristics of Teacher Development

Teacher development, as a way of thinking about and practicing teacher education, is based on the $B = (f)$ P, E, T conceptual scheme and the characteristics of a matching model suggested by Hunt (1975). It is concerned necessarily with the tasks and behaviors of teaching and learning, but never in isolation from the people who function as teachers. Therefore, we see it as *personalized* in the sense that the environments created by teacher educators must be congruent with teachers' needs and abilities. It is not sufficient to consider only teacher characteristics; teacher development is also *interactive* in that persons, behaviors, tasks, and environments are assumed to be interdependent. They must therefore be accommodated systematically when teacher development processes and procedures are designed, practiced, or investigated.

Teacher development is also intended to be *contemporaneous* in the sense that it must enable teacher educators to be attuned to the immediate conditions of teaching and learning. For instance, teacher educators may need to know how to support teachers who are concerned about involving students in an afternoon's discussion on the legislative process or managing a morning's reading group so as to increase student attention without appearing dictatorial. That teachers are faced with such concerns on a day-to-day, moment-to-moment basis is no surprise. The very best preplanning will not guarantee desired results or save teachers from a certain amount of worry about the work of teaching. If teacher educators expect to help teachers, they must address the immediate realities of each individual teacher.

Teacher development must also be *developmental*. That is, it must be concerned with the growth of a teacher over time. It may be that the teacher who starts in September is not the same person who finishes in June.[3] In the course of teaching and learning each day, a teacher changes, but not always in a positive direction. If the teacher educator were to attend only to the present, ignoring the teacher's history over the course of the year (or years), the prospects for teacher growth would be greatly diminished. For this reason, teacher development should encourage people to view changes in teacher behavior as points on a continuum rather than as isolated events. In clinical teacher development activities (that is, the kind of classroom interac-

---

[3] See Ryan, K., K. Newman, G. Mager, J. Applegate, T. Lasley, R. Flora, and J. Johnston, *Biting the apple: Accounts of first-year teachers.* New York: Longman, Inc., 1980. This book illustrates vividly how teachers' needs and abilities can change over the course of one academic year.

tions between teacher educator and teacher described in Chapter 7), separate episodes are viewed in a context of those occurring in both the past and future. Each encounter of teacher and teacher educator, therefore, is an increment that builds on previous episodes and projects to future episodes to move a teacher through a planned sequence or cycle of activities toward greater proficiency in personal and instructional skills.

Teacher development is intended to be *reciprocal*, not one-way. Just as teachers are affected by environments created for them by teacher educators, the latter are affected in turn by teachers. Being aware of and attempting to respond to differences in needs and abilities among teachers will stretch teacher educators to more complex ways of thinking and acting. The greater the number and developmental range of teachers whom teacher educators encounter, the more likely they will be to extend their own repertoire of behaviors.

Finally, teacher development must lend itself to *practical* use. Teacher educators who are not teachers need to temper their thinking and their action with a sense of what is important to students and teachers. With a little effort, many teacher educators should be able to remember what it was like both to be a student and a teacher. Being aware of the needs of teachers and students is especially important if teacher educators are to identify with their clients and concentrate on real concerns. It is only when teacher development is viewed as practical and useful that it will become a positive force for enrichment of life in the classroom.

Implications for Research and Practice

Viewing teacher education pluralistically, or as a process of working differently with different persons, could have several important implications that extend beyond typical teacher educational activities. Ties between theory and practice might be strengthened by supplying paradigms for research and practice. These would allow for investigation of individual differences and of teaching and learning and lend practical direction to application of field-based teacher development activities. Figuratively, the modern college- or university-based teacher educator is expected to have one foot on campus and one in the field. He or she must encourage and conduct research over an extended period of time but not neglect the immediate demand to apply knowledge and skills in the conduct of ongoing programs. Now that in-service teachers are playing a larger part in their own education, they, too, must assume responsibility for research and development. In-service teachers, like college and university people, must be charged with building knowledge as well as using it.

In teacher development, there may be opportunities to ask new research questions designed to investigate not which approach to teacher education is best but which approach is best with which person and for what objectives. As teacher educators formulate and explore such questions, they might extend their own knowledge about teacher education and, at the same time, provide a positive, credible model of instruction. Teacher educators who model respect and concern for differences among personal needs and abilities can be expected to nurture the same attitudes in teachers.

Thinking about and treating teachers as individuals at the pre-service level is always critical, but particularly so in a tight job market. Today each prospective teacher needs to be stronger than ever in order to enter the profession. It is obvious that college and university teacher education programs owe each individual the best opportunities for learning—not only to enhance prospects for employability but also to ensure that those students who get teaching positions are able to sustain vitality in the profession over the long term. At present teachers live in a disposable economy: the thoughtless consumer can buy them cheaply and quickly wear them out. If college and university enrollment trends continue and fewer new teachers aspire to the profession, the supply of strong candidates will inevitably decrease (Weaver, 1978). A conscious effort must be made to conserve and strengthen the talents of young teachers for the future.

The possibilities for usefully applying teacher development at the in-service level may be most promising of all. It is not unlikely that teacher development might be integrated into everyday practice by teachers to move one another forward in their professional development. In-service in this context takes on a new connotation—teachers supporting teachers on site in their regular classroom activities rather than through the familiar workshops and courses offered by outside consultants. Teachers now share greater responsibility for their own in-service growth and often their own evaluation. Recent federal legislation (Federal Register, 1977) establishing teacher centers attests to this:

> The new teacher centers program seems to reflect shifting emphases in three aspects of teacher education: (a) toward greater attention to additional training for teachers who are already in the service, (b) toward recognition of the schools themselves as a major focus and locale of teacher training, and (c) toward giving the schools—and particularly the classroom teachers in these schools—major responsibility for determining the kinds of training and other experiences needed by teachers.

These new teacher centers address many of the same problems that other teacher educators have struggled with over the years. If teachers function as teacher educators concerned with the strengths and limitations of one another as individuals, they might succeed in meeting their own needs for teaching effectiveness and job satisfaction.

At least in principle, the basic idea of adapting instruction to different persons for different objectives is valued by most teachers, regardless of their areas of specialization. Although teachers may not be familiar with the particular terminology, they will have some understanding of the elements involved in tailoring instruction to fit different people. More than anyone else, in-service teachers should appreciate the possibilities of treating each other as unique.

Supporting the development of each teacher's abilities and self-worth is especially important today, if only because criticism of teachers has become such a popular diversion. Public pressure to develop students who have higher SAT scores, record-breaking runs in the 100-yard dash, and the moral awareness of adults inevitably takes its toll on even the strongest and most creative of teachers. Such pressures may drive many talented teachers to other professions where they may feel more appreciated and undoubtedly will make more money.

For those who stay in teaching, such pressures exhibit a clear and present danger to their creative spirits. In their research on teacher survival Mark and Anderson (1978) point out that teachers are remaining in their jobs longer today than in the past. Decreasing teacher attrition creates increasing economic burdens on school districts because more experienced teachers receive higher salaries. But the problem is more than financial. As teachers grow older on the job they may, in some cases, grow weary. In the coming years, teacher educators—professors, principals, supervisors, curriculum developers, and teachers—will face a challenge of finding new ways to protect and nurture the creative spirit in each and every teacher.

SUMMARY

This chapter has emphasized that supporting the initial preparation as well as the continual development of teachers should be approached from a pluralistic perspective. Past models of teacher education have exemplified various philosophies and methods, but none has proven universally applicable. Teacher education should tailor its approach to individual teachers to meet their immediate needs and to enhance possibilities for long-term growth. Teacher educators must design environments that accommodate the unique needs and abilities of teachers who undertake various teaching tasks. The results of investigating, designing, and practicing a pluralistic approach to teacher development might be measured not only in terms of more effective teaching and learning but also in the satisfaction of teachers as complete individuals.

⤜ 2 ⤛

Teacher Tasks and Behaviors

T HE goal of teacher development is to support the growth of classroom teachers in their performance of various tasks. The more tasks teachers can accomplish, the better persons and professionals they are likely to become. As emphasized in Chapter 1, this task-oriented approach to teacher development must be tempered by a concern for the teacher as a person and as a student of the teaching craft. We view teacher performance or behavior therefore not only in terms of a teacher's ability to perform particular classroom instructional tasks but also in terms of a teacher's personal growth. Teachers must be encouraged to become more knowledgeable, more complex, more sensitive individuals. To say that all teachers can and should expand their instructional skills and grow as persons, of course, does not suggest that they are either inept clinicians or lack developmental skills. Instead, growth in both of these respects implies a stretching of one's capabilities and ideas and a filling-out of one's professional identity.

The intent of this chapter is threefold: (1) to discuss our conceptions of teacher tasks and behaviors so as to formulate teacher developmental objectives; (2) to give direction to these objectives by discussing specific examples of teacher tasks and behaviors considered important by professional educators, students, and the general public; and (3) to offer recommendations for setting priorities for developmental objectives to determine which teacher tasks and behaviors are most appropriate in a given situation.

Teacher Tasks

Tasks are the myriad activities, duties, or obligations teachers face in the performance of their roles. As any classroom teacher can attest, there are many tasks, either self-imposed or dictated by others, that must be accomplished. First, teachers perform a variety of instructional activities. Even before undertaking teaching, they must organize and manage students. Then, during the course of their teaching, they may be required to perform a variety of tasks—from calling up computer programs to reading poems. Finally, they must be able to communicate the results of instruction to others. Teachers as persons also face a multitude of personal tasks. They must sustain enthusiasm for their work; they must build their knowledge to maintain or increase their pride as academicians; and they must enrich their reasoning abilities, develop strong interpersonal relationships, and fulfill their needs for belonging, if they are to do the same for their students.

These tasks, both personal and instructional, may be categorized generally in terms of simple or complex activities that demand varying degrees of the teacher's time and energy (Figure 2–1).

The first category includes simple personal tasks that require the teacher to perform only a few behaviors in a short period of time. A simple personal task might be one intended to increase one's technical knowledge about teaching a concept related to human sexuality, for instance. In order to accomplish this task the teacher might read some articles, consult a physician, or view a film on human sexuality. Such behaviors could serve to enhance the teacher's

FOCUS

		Personal Needs	Instructional Needs
D E M A N D	Simple	Example: To increase one's technical knowledge about human sexuality.	Example: To teach a child how to make the letter "A".
	Complex	Example: To improve one's attitude toward students.	Example: To involve students in a unit on human rights.

FIGURE 2–1. Teacher Tasks.

technical knowledge about human sexuality and thus prepare him or her to deal with the concept in the classroom. A simple personal task, then, concentrates more on the characteristics of the teacher (here, knowledge of a concept) than on the technical skills of teaching.

The second category includes simple instructional tasks. These require the teacher to perform only a few behaviors, but the teacher is usually more concerned with developing his or her methods and techniques of instruction than with altering a personal quality or aptitude. A simple instructional task might be one intended to teach a child how to make the letter A. With a typical child this could demand that a teacher provide paper and pencil and spend a few moments writing examples and giving feedback on the child's performance.

The third category includes complex personal tasks. These require teachers to demonstrate numerous behaviors directed toward their own personal development. A complex personal task might describe the effort to improve one's attitude toward students. This could require a teacher to interact with young people outside the school setting, participate in a series of encounter sessions, or visit children and parents in their homes. Complex personal tasks place a high demand on a teacher's time and energy.

The fourth category includes complex instructional tasks. Like complex personal tasks, these require the teacher to demonstrate a variety of behaviors. In contrast, however, they are directed toward a teacher's development of instructional methods and techniques. Involving twenty-five students in an inquiry unit on human rights might be characterized as a complex instructional task. The teacher might use a film to present the concept of equality under the law. Along with the film, background information might be necessary to illustrate how, when, and where human rights are protected or violated. A guest speaker might also be invited to discuss the responsibilities associated with the exercise of particular rights, and assignments could be devised for independent student work. A complex instructional task, then, can be considered a composite of more simple, intermediate tasks, which together create a conceptually single demand.

This categorization of teacher tasks is admittedly artificial; it represents only one possible view of the kinds of activities teachers are expected to accomplish. Furthermore, the categories can overlap; that is, as teachers undertake instructional tasks, they may build their knowledge or heighten their own motivation. Conversely, as teachers develop their own personal capabilities they are probably improving their instructional skills. In the absence of any validated taxonomy or scheme of teacher tasks, however, this categorization may be useful when thinking about the role of teacher in terms of what that person must do, and how such varying activities may influence teacher behavior.

Teacher Behaviors

Teacher behaviors may be thought of as observable indications of a teacher's ability to perform tasks. As previous examples have shown, tasks can in some instances dictate a narrow range of behaviors teachers may need to demonstrate. But not all teachers can or should be expected to behave the same way in all situations. Because tasks vary, just as do teacher abilities, the behaviors teachers exhibit may be different from situation to situation.

Some teacher education programs specify various levels of behavior that teachers must perform in order to demonstrate competence. Such levels of teacher behavior, when viewed as general guidelines for appraising a teacher's personal and instructional growth, may provide useful direction to teachers and teacher educators. In general, teacher behaviors might be characterized as progressing from simple awareness of the demands and implications of a task to performing the same task in different ways. New teachers (or experienced teachers undertaking new and unfamiliar tasks) might do the following:

1. Demonstrate awareness of the demands and implications of the task (for example, mock up a unit on human rights by outlining goals, learner objectives, and materials to be used).
2. Demonstrate awareness of one's own ability to perform a task (for example, appraise his or her own experience teaching about human rights by comparing a mock-up to a commercially prepared unit in terms of strategies used, materials drawn upon, and methods employed for evaluating student learning).
3. Demonstrate awareness of alternative ways of performing the task (visit other classrooms to see how different teachers ask questions that promote student discussion, read a book on various approaches to teaching social studies, or work through a set of protocols designed to increase student participation in the classroom).
4. Practice alternative ways to perform the task (complete a situation designed to teach human rights by using a legal model, teach a series of lessons on human rights using a lecture approach, or assign a group to investigate the topic).

This progression or sequence of teacher behaviors is not an empirically validated description of the way teachers behave to increase their abilities. Instead, it is a guideline that suggests the development of the teacher as teacher and the teacher as person may be viewed as a process of undertaking more tasks and behaving in various ways in order to accomplish them. The following sections present more specific directions for the identification of particular teacher behaviors and suggestions about how teacher educators may appraise them.

Using Tasks and Behaviors to Establish Behavioral Objectives

If teacher tasks can be categorized and teacher behaviors outlined, it might be possible to determine behavioral objectives for teachers, or objectives that specify certain kinds of teacher behavior in advance of performance. Although it may be possible to specify levels of teacher behavior directed toward the accomplishment of some tasks, it would not in all cases be desirable.

To illustrate the difficulty of equating teacher tasks and behaviors with behavioral objectives, we draw upon Eisner's (1967a, 1967b) notions of "instructional objectives" and "expressive objectives" for children. He describes instructional objectives as those that specify particular outcomes in advance. For example, instructional objectives may be designed for student acquisition of skill and knowledge in arithmetic or foreign language vocabulary. In contrast, expressive objectives do not lend themselves to precise specification of outcomes. They may describe the kinds of experience learners are to have but not exactly what the outcomes will be. Objectives designed to stimulate creativity in student acting or writing, for instance, might be considered expressive in nature.

Similarly, some teacher tasks might specify desired levels of teacher behavior in advance but others might not. Learning how to write a lesson plan, for example, is a simple and predictable instructional task. It involves forecasting goals, procedures, materials, and methods for evaluation. Even the development of a school curriculum in mathematics, which is a more complex instructional task, possesses a fairly well-defined set of behavioral expectations for teachers, including the scope and sequence of learner objectives, lesson construction, and unit organization. Either simple or complex personal tasks designed to develop teacher motivation or to lower anxiety, however, are not readily amenable to specification of teacher behaviors in advance. If teacher educators were to establish strict behavioral indicators of accomplishment for these tasks, personal growth would likely be reduced to the measure of one's ability to conform to a vapid checklist of competency requirements. Such a course of action would obviously work against a rich definition of personal development.

Tasks and Behaviors as Determinants of Developmental Objectives

Because the goal of teacher development is to help teachers accomplish various tasks, developmental objectives depend on these tasks for their form and function. As Figure 2–2 illustrates, developmental objectives for teachers may be characterized, therefore, in terms similar to those used to describe teacher tasks.

The larger, more inclusive goal of promoting teacher growth toward the ac-

FOCUS

		Teacher as Person	Teacher as Instructor
D			
E	Simple	To exhibit behaviors directed toward the accomplishment of simple personal tasks.	To exhibit behaviors directed toward the accomplishment of simple instructional tasks.
M			
A			
N	Complex	To exhibit behaviors directed toward the accomplishment of complex personal tasks.	To exhibit behaviors directed toward the accomplishment of complex instructional tasks.
D			

FIGURE 2–2. Teacher Developmental Objectives.

complishment of tasks may be divided into four categories relating to teacher developmental objectives. One pair of objectives is intended to encourage the accomplishment of fairly simple, short-term teacher tasks that are both personal and instructional. These objectives are simple in that they require relatively small amounts of time and resources. The other pair of teacher developmental objectives is intended to encourage the accomplishment of more complex, long-term teacher tasks that may be either personal or instructional. These are complex in the sense that their achievement depends on the expenditure of greater amounts of time and resources.

The Effectiveness of Teacher Development

As will be discussed in greater detail in Chapter 6, the effectiveness of teacher development, or the accomplishment of objectives, can be determined in a number of ways. One way is to examine teacher behavior directly. To illustrate, a teacher educator might help a teacher build knowledge about a concept by providing opportunity to discuss this concept or to role play a lesson on the concept with another adult. The teacher's behavior, then, could indicate almost immediately whether or not the developer had met his or her own objectives; that is, the teacher would behave in a way that indicated an increase, decrease, or little change in knowledge.

Another important test of teacher development occurs when teacher tasks are assessed in terms of student growth. In this respect, Gage (1978) is quite correct when he states that the study and practice of supporting teacher effectiveness cannot be divorced from student learning. Ultimately, the worth of teacher development must be measured at least in part in terms of teachers' effects on students.

Finally, as we will discuss later, assessing one's own behaviors as a teacher educator offers yet another indication of the effectiveness of teacher development. But for now, the important thing to keep in mind is that the process of meeting teacher developmental objectives, like the process of accomplishing teacher tasks, can and should be subject to appraisal.

Identifying Appropriate Teacher Tasks and Behaviors

Establishing worthwhile teacher developmental objectives depends on identifying appropriate teacher tasks and behaviors. The teacher educator, then, must answer a number of difficult questions. Why is a particular task worth undertaking? What makes another task trivial? What sorts of behaviors can or cannot be specified in advance as reasonable representations of successful task accomplishment? What teacher behaviors are inconsequential or even dysfunctional? Answers to such questions must be sought if teacher educators are to encourage teachers to spend their precious time and resources in ways that will benefit their students and themselves.

Identifying appropriate teacher tasks and behaviors is at the very least challenging, but not impossible. On the surface, determining teacher tasks and behaviors that are educationally and practically significant would appear to be a simple matter. For answers, one might look to state departments of education, colleges and universities, or the public schools. These institutions provide some direction, but they do not provide all the answers. The challenge, of course, arises largely because *appropriate* is a relative term. What some people view as important for teachers to accomplish in one situation others may regard as inconsequential or ludicrous in another. To return to our earlier task examples, for instance, helping just one youngster learn to make the letter A may be at least as urgent, if not more so, than facilitating an investigation of human rights for twenty-five students. Encouraging twenty-five young social scientists to practice making the letter A, however, could be rather devastating to their attitudes and performances.

The appropriateness or significance of many teacher tasks and behaviors is determined as much by subjective opinion as by theoretical evidence, empirical support, or some higher social good. One good way for teacher educators to distinguish significant tasks and behaviors is to examine the sources from which they emanate.

Let us turn now to various sources of information for deriving teacher tasks and behaviors, illustrated in Figure 2–3. Among these are ideas, feelings, and concerns expressed by teachers, by students, by other professional educators, by researchers, and by various public sectors. It should soon become apparent that tasks and behaviors deemed important can be either reasonably simple or incredibly complex. We try to infer from various sources the kinds of activities they believe teachers must accomplish. In so doing, our intent is to encourage teacher educators to be aware of various needs and expectations so that they may formulate their own objectives in line with the needs of their constituents.

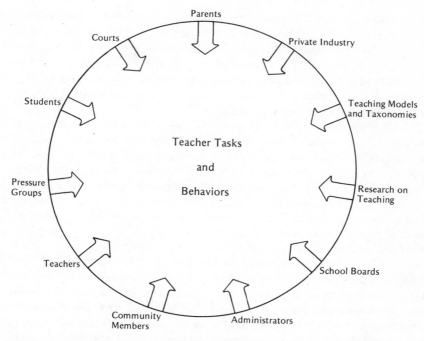

FIGURE 2–3.   Some Sources Contributing to Teacher Tasks and Behaviors.

Teachers as a Source

The claim that teachers know, perhaps better than anyone else, how and in what directions they should grow will come as no surprise. But teachers are often among the last persons to be consulted about teacher growth. As this section indicates, teachers have some strong opinions about what they need to do in order to be complete and fully functioning persons and professionals. Yet, teacher opinion as a source of teacher tasks and behaviors can be effectively obscured by a number of other competing sources.

Teachers' concerns are represented most visibly by their professional organizations. There are virtually hundreds of national, state, and regional teachers' associations, as well as thousands of locals. The two major national teachers' organizations, however, are the National Education Association (NEA) and the American Federation of Teachers (AFT). In 1979 NEA claimed some 1.7 million members and AFT had more than a half million members. As the leading national organizations, NEA and AFT work to bring teachers' professional concerns before the public.

Each year at its annual meeting, the NEA representative assembly refines the association's goals by reviewing "continuing resolutions" and acting upon "current resolutions." These resolutions reflect what association members believe to be their major concerns. In 1979 there were sixty-seven continuing resolutions, or permanent statements of philosophy and goals, dealing with issues such as national educational priorities, teacher salaries, and equal rights for women. In addition, the ninety-seven current resolutions drawn up reflected members' immediate concerns.

Recent resolutions indicate that one of the most pressing concerns of the NEA is that of teacher stress. Willard McGuire, the president-elect of the NEA in 1979, has stated that literally thousands of teachers are leaving the profession as victims of "teacher burn-out." According to an Associated Press release, McGuire said that "the problems stem from teachers not knowing how to cope with violence and vandalism, disruptive students, inadequate salaries, demanding parents . . . and a multitude of other problems." It would appear from McGuire's analysis that many teachers know only too well what their problems are but feel powerless to resolve them.

The AFT, as the NEA, is concerned with the well-being of teachers and the quality of education for children. The AFT, too, has tried to alleviate teacher concerns related to salary, tenure, and retirement, and to upgrade the conditions of teaching and learning. In 1979 the AFT had formulated some ninety resolutions on education issues related to the needs of teachers. At the 1979 national conference in San Francisco, members reinforced earlier proposals to reduce class size in proportion to declines in student enrollment. They also emphasized the need for the support of teachers' efforts to provide early childhood education and make lifelong learning a reality.

The AFT and the NEA draw attention not only to the rather broad or complex tasks deemed important by teachers, but to the more specific responsibilities teachers have to students and to the profession. NEA's Code of Ethics, adopted in 1975, demonstrates what teachers believe they should and should not do if their commitments to students and to the profession are to be honored.

Principle I—Commitment to the Student

The educator strives to help each student realize his or her potential as a worthy and effective member of society. The educator therefore works to stimulate the spirit of inquiry, the acquisition of knowledge and understanding, and the thoughtful formulation of worthy goals.

In fulfillment of the obligation to the student the educator

1. Shall not unreasonably restrain the student from independent action in the pursuit of learning.
2. Shall not unreasonably deny the student access to varying points of view.
3. Shall not deliberately suppress or distort subject matter relevant to the student's progress.

4. Shall make reasonable effort to protect the student from conditions harmful to learning or to health and safety.
5. Shall not intentionally expose the student to embarrassment or disparagement.
6. Shall not on the basis of race, color, creed, sex, national origin, marital status, political or religious beliefs, family, social or cultural background, or sexual orientation, unfairly:
    a. Exclude any student from participation in any program;
    b. Deny benefits to any student;
    c. Grant any advantage to any student.
7. Shall not use professional relationships with students for private advantage.
8. Shall not disclose information about students obtained in the course of professional service, unless disclosure serves a compelling professional purpose or is required by law.

Principle II—Commitment to the Profession

The education profession is vested by the public with a trust and responsibility requiring the highest ideals of professional service.

In the belief that the quality of the services of the education profession directly influences the nation and its citizens, the educator shall exert every effort to raise professional standards, to promote a climate that encourages the exercise of professional judgment, to achieve conditions which attract persons worthy of the trust to careers in education, and to assist in preventing the practice of the profession by unqualified persons.

In fulfillment of the obligation to the profession, the educator

1. Shall not in an application for a professional position deliberately make a false statement or fail to disclose a material fact related to competency and qualifications.
2. Shall not misrepresent his/her professional qualifications.
3. Shall not assist entry into the profession of a person known to be unqualified in respect to character, education, or other relevant attributes.
4. Shall not knowingly make a false statement concerning the qualifications of a candidate for a professional position.
5. Shall not assist a noneducator in the unauthorized practice of teaching.
6. Shall not disclose information about colleagues obtained in the course of professional service unless disclosure serves a compelling professional purpose or is required by law.
7. Shall not knowingly make false or malicious statements about a colleague.
8. Shall not accept any gratuity, gift, or favor that might impair or appear to influence professional decisions or actions.

Beyond concerns expressed by teachers' organizations, modern teacher-authors such as Silberman, Holt, Kozol, and others paint vivid pictures of the tasks they find abhorrent or totally incapable of being performed, as well as the objectives they believe teachers should strive to achieve. Herndon's (1968) account of teaching seventh- and eighth-grade ghetto students is a good example of what it means to undertake the tasks of teaching "deprived" children. The very specific advice that Herndon, as a new teacher, got from his colleagues points this out dramatically:

> The advice was of two kinds. The first kind was useful enough and was about methods and equipment you could use to do certain things—sets of flash cards, how to group students, controlled readers, recorders, easily corrected tests, good films—but after a short time I was already using most of these. My problem was not what to use but how to get the kids to respond in such a way that they learned something. That brought up the other kind of advice, which was also the most common and which was useless to me. This advice was a conglomeration of dodges, tricks, gimmicks to get the kids to do what they were spozed (sic) to do, that is, whatever the teacher had in mind for them to do. . . . Everyone agreed that our students were on the average a couple of years below grade level, everyone agreed that was because they were "deprived" kids, but no one agreed that simply because nothing was going on the way they were doing it, they ought to try something else.

But when encouraged or even just left alone to try "something else," at least some teachers turn to themselves to find what is important in teaching and learning. Herndon put it this way:

> Whatever I read during this time, the fall of the year, seemed to lead me into some idea for the classroom and I would come charging in with the idea, usually half-baked, to try it out on them [seventh-grade students]. They would respond as enthusiastically as they could, sometimes while utterly confused, often just humoring me awhile and passing out subtle hints for me to come to my senses. But with them the pressure was always off—I was free and easy. In effect, they allowed me to teach myself.

Surveys of teacher attitudes and concerns often reveal where they need encouragement most. In an analysis of the attitudes of more than 2,000 teachers toward the profession, Ream (1977) points out that elementary and secondary teachers believe the factors that hinder them most are negative student attitude and discipline, incompetent administration, and heavy work loads. Teachers also suggested, not surprisingly, that they render better service when they are confident with their subject matter and able to work together with their colleagues. From a teacher's point of view, as Ream implies, there are many important personal and professional tasks to be accomplished: to improve student attitudes, to decrease the need for discipline, to obtain knowledge of the subject matter, and to cooperate with one's own colleagues.

In another survey of more than 300 pre-service teachers, in-service teachers, and paraprofessionals from nine metropolitan school districts, respondents expressed a need for support to accomplish a variety of instructional tasks (McNergney, 1978). More than 75 percent of the student teachers questioned wanted skill training for effective discipline techniques, and the same proportion wanted help in diagnosing basic learning difficulties. In-service teachers asked for support to individualize their instruction (60 percent) and ways to involve pupils in self-evaluation (55 percent). Other instructional personnel expressed concerns about identifying pupil attitudes and values that related to learning problems (63 percent). But the major concern of a vast majority of respondents in this survey was that of being able to motivate pupils to learn (teachers, 67 percent; student teachers, 73 percent; other instructional personnel, 72 percent).

Yet it may be as important to find out what and how teachers think as it is to attend to what they say. Research on teacher thinking, therefore, may lend direction to what teachers view as important in teaching and learning. According to Clark and Yinger (1979):

> A relatively new approach to the study of teaching assumes that what teachers do is affected by what they think. This approach, which emphasizes the processing of cognitive information, is concerned with teachers' judgment, decision making, and planning. The study of the thinking processes of teachers—how they gather, organize, interpret, and evaluate information—is expected to lead to understandings of the uniquely human processes that guide and determine their behavior.

Hunt suggests examining teachers' own concepts of student characteristics, teaching environments, and learning behaviors in order to determine what they think is important. One study designed to investigate such implicit theories found that teachers think about students, teaching, and learning in quite different ways (McNergney, Bents, and Burcalow, 1979). For example, some teachers characterized students in terms of their friendliness; others thought of students in terms of their cooperativeness. Some teachers regarded teaching as developing honesty and respect for others; some teachers characterized it as helping students to develop new ideas and discover new relationships. Student learning was described alternately as developing one's self-image and expressing satisfaction about one's success.

Translating how a teacher thinks about teaching and learning into an objective for growth might seem complicated, but in practice it could be straightforward. For instance, teachers who think of student learning only in terms of developing self-concept might be encouraged to expand their notions of acceptable learning outcomes to include learning as developing independence and acquiring factual knowledge. Such an enriched definition of learning is important because as research on thinking or cognitive functioning suggests, teachers who view their world in complex terms are better equipped to meet student needs than teachers who do not. The teacher educator who is aware of not only what teachers say but what they think, therefore, should be better able to help teachers grow toward richer personal definitions of their work.

Teachers also reveal the tasks and behaviors they believe to be important by their choice of personal and professional development activities. Investigating how teachers choose to invest their time and energy in teacher centers, then, is another good way to identify teacher tasks. Schmeider and Yarger (1974) describe teacher centers as places that help teachers grow by offering resources that meet teachers' needs. Such centers allow participants to share successes, to utilize a wide range of education resources, and to receive training directly related to their most pressing teaching problems.

From an examination of the history and practice of teacher centers, Joyce and Weil (1973) derived three general types of teacher center objectives, or activities teachers believe are important for their own growth. Informal objectives provide opportunities for teachers to improve themselves on their own terms, or to follow their own personal interests and to expand their own abilities. Corporate objectives serve school needs by helping teachers acquire the competencies required to implement new curricula or to improve existing ones. Competency-based objectives are directed toward increasing teachers' skills along predetermined lines or in response to diagnoses of peers or supervisors. Admittedly, because financial resources in many teacher centers are not controlled directly by teachers, center goals and objectives cannot be said to reflect only their interests and needs. Yet, in the vast majority of cases, their governance is structured to represent teacher interests. Joyce and Weil's general types of objectives, therefore, are useful illustrations of the activities teachers deem important.

A look at one teacher center program that is designed to support teacher growth illustrates what participants choose to do when given the opportunity. This program, called the University of Minnesota Project Motivate, consisted of forty-three mini-projects designed by elementary school teachers to stimulate pupil interest in the basics as well as in such areas as photography, the performing arts, gerontology, and economics. These projects represent examples of teachers helping students, but in subtle ways they also reflect opportunities for teachers to improve themselves on their own terms. In one project, Bill Stanley, a sixth-grade teacher, designed a unit to study the stock market—something he was interested in and thought his students would find interesting as well. He organized a project to allow his class to consult brokers, to purchase odd-lot stocks, and to form its own corporation. In another project, Patricia Heimbaugh Tschohl, a second-grade teacher, developed a set of activities that reflected her own interests as well as the needs of her pupils. The students and teacher studied life in another country by exchanging letters, tapes, and slides with a class of children taught by the teacher's friend in Prestwick, Scotland. Other teachers and students in this teacher center worked with artists in residence, produced animated films, wrote poetry under the guidance of local poets, and visited elderly care facilities. From this program alone, it is fairly obvious that many teachers know what tasks are important for themselves as well as their pupils.

Deriving Teacher Tasks and Behaviors from Teachers

Teachers express a variety of opinions about what they must be allowed to accomplish and how they can be supported if they and their students are to grow. They have a strong personal need to be recognized as professionals, and they want to keep their commitments to students and to themselves. As professionals, they want a greater voice in determining who enters the field, what credentials are to be required, and how fellow members are to be disciplined (Fiske, 1979). Teachers want to know their subject matter well and be able to share it effectively with students; they want to be able to determine the needs and abilities of students and to adapt their own instruction accordingly. Teachers are deeply concerned about the quality of life in schools. That is, they want to eliminate the physical and mental abuse that is present in the system and to replace it with conditions that will realize the possibilities of teaching and learning.

As teacher educators try to establish appropriate objectives for teacher growth, they must first be aware of the needs expressed and implied by teachers. Even though other sources of evidence may dictate other tasks, their accomplishment may not be feasible or desirable until teachers' needs are met. As we discuss at length in Chapter 4, understanding teachers in terms of what they know, what they know how to do, how they feel, and how they think is prerequisite to setting appropriate objectives for their growth.

Students as a Source

Students provide another source of information on the value of particular teacher tasks and behaviors. To some people, however, the suggestion that students can play even a minor part in determining what teachers should do and how they should perform their teaching activities is heretical. It conjures irritating visions of teachers having to cater to the desires of the immature who could not possibly know what teachers need to do. Others believe as a matter of faith that students should not merely play a part but should take the lead in formulating the role of the teacher. To them, teaching without substantial student direction and participation is no more than administrative maintenance. For the majority, whose opinions range somewhere between these two poles, seeking student reaction to teaching is a matter of common sense. To ask students, or educational consumers, about effective and ineffective teaching is not merely a courtesy or even an obligation; it is a recognition that students occupy a unique position vis-à-vis teachers. Although students' opinions may not be totally uniform or unbiased, they are based on strong but sensitive first-hand impressions of the realities and possibilities of teaching.

The most frequently used method of soliciting student reactions to teachers and schools is the survey. Student ratings of instruction provided by teachers, particularly at the post-secondary level, have provided information on teaching behavior for some time (McNeil and Popham, 1973). Soliciting the reactions of public school students to teaching methods through survey ratings, though not an unknown practice, appears to be less common. Generally, teacher educators will not be able to draw upon existing student ratings of instruction for direction. They must instead look to other survey information on student attitudes and opinions in order to extrapolate the kinds of teacher tasks and behaviors students consider important.

A survey conducted jointly by George Gallup and the Charles Kettering Foundation (Elam, 1978) provides insight into the attitudes of teen-agers in general and toward teachers and schools in particular. In telephone interviews with a national sample of more than 1,000 culturally diverse young people, researchers discovered that the youngsters rated their local public schools higher than adults did. More than 55 percent of the respondents gave schools grades of A or B. About 40 percent said they enjoyed going to school "very much," 50 percent had mixed feelings, and only 10 percent expressed displeasure. A slightly earlier survey, however, revealed that only 36 percent of the general population rated schools this highly. But if teen-agers' opinions of school in general are favorable, in this survey teachers fared even better. More than 66 percent of the sample gave teachers grades of A or B. As the opinion takers point out, perhaps the most surprising result of the study is that about 50 percent of the young respondents complained that they do not have to work hard enough on their studies, either in school or at home. It appears, according to the researchers, that young people are asking for more work, not less.

The Minnesota School Affect Assessment (MSAA) gives an even more specific picture of student attitudes toward teachers and schools. MSAA solicits student feelings about academic subjects, school personnel, and peers by concentrating on their perceptions of support, constraint, motivation, and adequacy of communication within the school. In contrast to the Gallup-Kettering poll, which solicits only teen-agers' opinions, MSAA has been used to tap systematically the feelings of secondary and elementary students toward their teachers and schools.

In general, studies using MSAA reveal that the relationship between grade level and student attitude is usually negative. Responses collected over a two-year period (1971–1972) from 6,000 students in grades one through twelve in a suburban and semirural district are a particularly good example. The importance of learning mathematics and science, for instance, was rated as high throughout the elementary grades but began to decline in junior high school. The importance of learning English and learning about people also declined but was reversed in later years.

The desire to learn about music, poetry, art, and drama declines dramatically in importance as students approach the middle grades, reaching its nadir in the eighth grade and rising only slightly in the later grades (Figures 2–4 and 2–5). It would appear from these data that whatever teachers might do to encourage student appreciation for the fine arts may be thwarted by what researchers have called the "pubescent trench" for the fine arts. This trench is also evident in data from various other parts of the country. As developers of the assessment point out, the fine arts programs may contribute to this feeling in students. But it is also possible that at work is a general cultural influence that schools and teachers can do little to counteract. The implica-

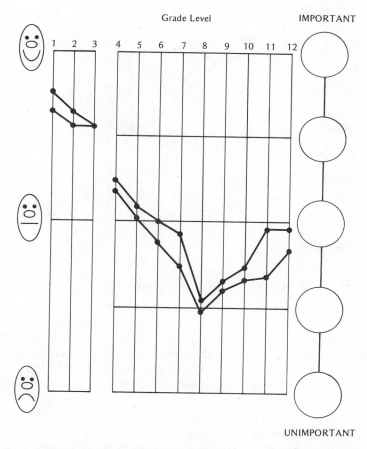

FIGURE 2–4. Learning about music and reading poems. [From Ahlgren, A., D. J. Christensen, and K. Lun. *Minnesota School Affect Assessment*. (Minneapolis, Minn.: Center for Educational Development, University of Minnesota, 1977), p. 31. Reprinted by permission.]

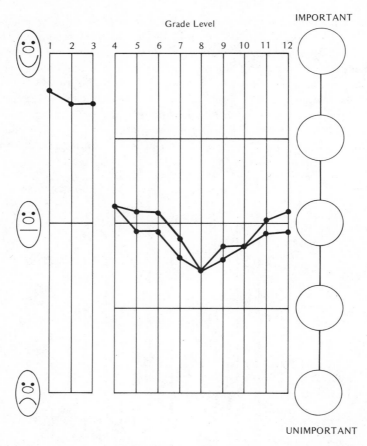

FIGURE 2–5. Looking at art and watching plays. [Ibid. Reprinted by permission.]

tions of such student attitudes for teacher behavior are not altogether clear. One possibility, of course, is that the instruction teachers provide in the fine arts is simply too little, too late. But it might also be that teachers would be well advised to capitalize on student interests in other areas during the junior high years.

Student reactions on the MSAA to teachers follow much the same downward pattern as their reactions to other facets of their education. In the early years, teachers are perceived as extremely pleasant but only modertately so in junior and senior high school. Beyond such general reactions, however, students seem to be offering more specific suggestions to teachers (Figures 2–6 to 2–8).

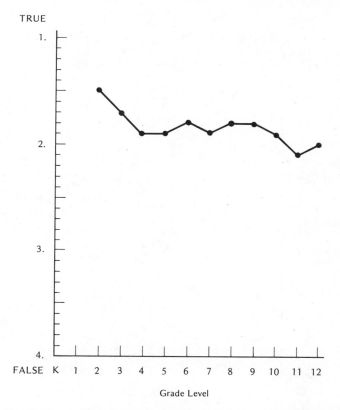

FIGURE 2-6. "I like to learn by working together with other students." This line shows that students, regardless of their age, like to work together. [From Ahlgren, A. and D. J. Christensen. *Minnesota School Affect Assessment of Independent School District 196, Rosemount, Minnesota.* (Minneapolis, Minn.: Center for Educational Development, University of Minnesota, 1972), p. 123. Reprinted by permission.]

The appeal of using the survey questionnaire technique to sample student attitudes and values is in its methodological convenience, efficiency, and cost effectiveness. Because of their economy and ease of interpretation, survey results lend themselves readily to the identification of the kinds of activities teachers should be concentrating on. But as anthropologists and ethnographers have pointed out, reducing student attitudes to various group statistics and charts inevitably masks individual feelings. The most frequently chosen successful alternative to survey questionnaires appears to be the open-ended, face-to-face interview. Researchers who have used open-ended interview techniques with students argue quite persuasively that what may be lost in terms of the generalizability of such results is offset by a real insight into

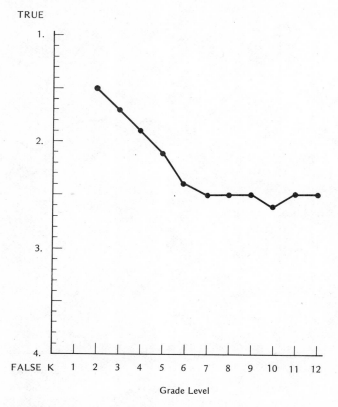

FIGURE 2–7. "My teachers care about my feelings." This line indicates a dramatic decline over time in students' perceptions of teachers' capacities to care about student feelings. From about junior high school on, students would agree only moderately that teachers care about their feelings. [Ibid., p. 113. Reprinted by permission.]

human needs and aspirations. Such interviews with students, therefore, provide additional directions for the identification of objectives for teacher growth.

Konopka (1976), for example, paints a striking picture of female adolescent attitudes among 1,000 young women from a variety of backgrounds across the country. Supplementing her interviews were group discussions with these teen-agers and written material, such as diaries, poetry, and stories, which students voluntarily gave to the interviewers. Konopka's work is interesting for two reasons. Even though she interviews young women only, her results suggest what teachers may need to do in order to help all young people grow. Also, and perhaps more important, her work suggests how crucial it is for

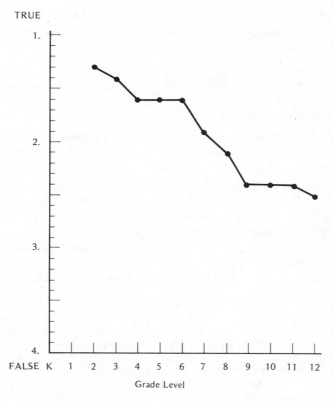

FIGURE 2–8. "I like teachers to tell me exactly what to do in class." This line shows that younger students would agree that they like to be told exactly what to do. Not surprisingly, older students tend to react less favorably to being told what to do. [Ibid., p. 112. Reprinted by permission.]

teachers and teacher educators to allow students to say in their own words what they like and dislike about teachers and schools.

In this respect, Konopka points out that the young women she interviewed had many positive comments to make. Nearly three fourths of the interviewees who expressed opinions about school were generally positive, whereas only about one fifth were strongly negative. Clearly, "school" (generally defined in terms of "teachers") was a very large and important part of these young persons' lives.

According to Konopka, the most important positive aspect of school is its social function. Simply stated, school offers a place for students to meet and be with their friends. She suggests that schools have underestimated the importance of this social function for shaping the attitudes of students toward other people and toward their own learning. A white, suburban sixteen-year-old put it this way:

> The main thing I like about it is going and whooping around with my friends. I get good grades and I study hard but the main thing that really makes me get up in the morning and want to shoot out there is that I know my friends are there. The fun part is social, and the learning part is a must.

In schools where students could choose their own subjects, Konopka found among her interviewees a positive relationship with teachers and no expression of boredom.

> Well, let's see, about school—I really like it. I enjoy it. I know that I'm learning something. I find it enjoyable. It gives me a chance to take whatever courses I want to take, and the school I go to is pretty liberal—I take what I want, and that's the most important thing. (Age 16, Oriental, urban.)

> I feel free at school for one thing. The classes I have, a lot of them are discussion classes and I feel that I can say what I want. And if other people disagree or don't like it, I can say, "That's too bad." (Age 16, white, urban.)

However, Konopka emphasizes that students did not want teachers to give them total freedom. Many discussed discipline in favorable terms. But to them, discipline meant at least in part that a teacher was fair and could keep students interested in a subject. A white, suburban fourteen-year-old said:

> I like about school the informality, I guess. You call the teachers by their first names and all that. I have been used to that cause I've been going to schools like that since the sixth grade. The reason I like this school is because of the people, including teachers . . .

But she described the teacher she did not like in these terms:

> Doesn't control her classes at all. She knows it but she can't control the kids. Otherwise she would be a really good teacher. Well, the kids gotta respect the teacher. I suppose you got to like them first if you're gonna respect them. You can't respect somebody without liking them. You have got to remember that they know more than you do. They are just trying to teach you.

The teachers who appeared to be most successful in these students' eyes were those who were able to relate to and respect students. They were understanding, warm, and humorous on occasion. These teachers were characterized as authority figures who knew their material and kept order in the classroom without being ogres. Some of the students who enjoyed good rapport with their teachers explained it this way:

> Well, he's young and he laughs and he smiles and he's easy to get along with and he remembers how it feels to be a kid, and he can understand many of our feelings about school, and about teachers and about writing papers. He's easy to talk to. (Age 16, white, urban.)

When a teacher sort of devotes himself to the students, you know, and tries to do everything to help you understand what he is trying to explain to you. That's what I like best about a teacher who tries to do—some teachers, they just say and explain it once and if you don't understand it, that's just your tough luck, and I have had several teachers like that. (Age 15, American Indian, small town.)

They were a lot of fun to be with, they make you laugh and talk about things that you like to talk about. They were old, older people. (Age 18, Eskimo, rural.)

In the context of this last student's culture, the word *old* had positive connotations. To her, the ideal teacher was an older and respected friend, but also a person who could teach.

Overall, Konopka found that most of the adolescents she interviewed liked school, but most adjudicated delinquents (about one third of the sample) did not. Most students viewed school and their teachers positively in terms of the opportunities afforded for peer social contact, for learning, and for having contact with understanding adults. Others expressed negative and, in some cases, quite hostile attitudes toward teachers and schools when there were poor opportunities for social contact, when racism and other forms of discrimination were present, when there was little choice of subjects, and when teachers exhibited a lack of concern or a propensity for racism or harsh disciplinary measures.

When negative conditions exist, student feelings of frustration and anger can erupt in violence. As the National Institute of Education (1978) reports, "A firm, fair, and consistent system for running a school seems to be a key in reducing violence. Where rules are known, and where they are firmly and fairly enforced, less violence occurs. . . . However, a hostile and authoritarian attitude on the part of the teachers toward the students can result in more vandalism." At least in some instances, then, it would seem that student hostility, vandalism, and violence, although unjustifiable, are expressions of what they believe to be wrong with schools.

As we pointed out earlier of teachers, what and how students *think* may be as important as what they reveal explicitly. Hunt (1971), Hunt and Sullivan (1974), and others have used the phrase *student pull* to describe how students "tell" teachers what is important to them. This refers to the subtle things students do that "pull" teachers to behave in certain ways. This notion is illustrated in a study by Rathbone (1970). He found that students who thought in conceptually complex ways, and thus had lower needs for structure, influenced the kinds of statements teachers made and the kinds of questions they asked. In his study, teachers encouraged students to theorize and to think for themselves nearly twice as much when they were matched with conceptually complex students. In terms of the present discussion, these and similar findings raise interesting implications for teacher development. The results suggest that it may be useful for teachers to understand how students communicate their needs in subtle or indirect ways. But perhaps even more important, teachers need to be aware that teaching and learning are reciprocal processes—that is, teachers affect the way students behave, but students just as certainly should be expected to affect the way teachers behave.

Many young people have important things to say about teachers, but they are rarely heard. The teacher educator who relies on only the typical research results of student opinion and attitudes to formulate objectives for teacher growth risks overlooking those young people who are chronically truant or have dropped out of school. Sewall, Sherman and Lee (1979) estimate that a minimum of two million students, including a rising number at the elementary level, regularly cut school without an excuse. They report that

> the problem is most severe in big-city school systems. In Boston high schools, the truancy rate has doubled to 25 per cent since 1974. It runs about 15 per cent in St. Louis and Philadelphia. In some Los Angeles and New York City high schools, more than half the classroom desks are empty on a given day.

But what might teachers and teacher educators learn from these young people? The research of Yankolovich (1974) on school dropouts suggests, for instance, that teachers must be able to tolerate sometimes unconventional norms and life-styles. Teachers who go out of their way to be sensitive to radical ideas and opinions might just help keep some young people in school longer. Reporting on American Indian youth, White (1979) points to alienation, boredom, and dissatisfaction with curriculum as major reasons for dropping out. If students' needs are to be considered when helping teachers grow, then it would seem crucial for teacher educators also to be aware of the feelings and attitudes of those young people who have given up.

Deriving Tasks and Behaviors from Students

Students strongly hold some attitudes about what and how teachers should perform. It seems that in contrast to what many people think, a substantial proportion of students like their schools and their teachers. They are willing to work hard and to accept—even welcome—reasonable discipline. Although junior high school appears to be a difficult time for students, particularly in certain subject areas, student attitudes toward schools and teachers pick up somewhat in high school. It is difficult, of course, to tell how much of the change in student attitudes stems from a student's own maturation and changing world view or to the quality of instruction he or she receives in later years. But the evidence indicates that teachers can either encourage or inhibit student learning and attitudes by their treatment of students. The choices teachers do or do not provide, the ways they allow or disallow student-student and student-teacher interaction, and whether or not teachers seem to care about students as persons (at least from students' points of view) will affect student achievement and attitude.

Student attitudes toward teachers and teaching, just like the attitudes of other groups, are most likely modified by the students' own values. When considering students as sources for direction on teacher tasks and behaviors, therefore, the teacher educator would be well advised to consider the needs and attitudes of students most directly involved rather than relying too heavily on national or regional samples of opinion.

Research on Teaching as a Source

Another important source of information on the tasks teachers should undertake and how they might be expected to perform is knowledge derived from scientific investigation. In the main, it is the scientist's concern for explaining the way things *are*, as opposed to the way things are *supposed to be*, that sets research apart from other sources of knowledge. The complexities of teaching and learning, and their interrelationship, however, make asking the right research questions, let alone finding answers, an almost overwhelming undertaking. Research on teaching—a relatively young science marked by various growing pains—has therefore only begun to provide substantive direction to the teacher educator.

Research on teaching, according to Mitzel (1960) and Dunkin and Biddle (1974), has investigated four types of variables in order to understand and thus encourage effective teaching (Figure 2–9). These variables form a general sequence of instructional events. First come *presage* variables, or those characteristics that teachers carry with them to the classroom—characteristics such as age, sex, training experiences, and various personality traits such as motivation or intelligence. Existing side by side with presage variables in the sequence are *context* variables. These are the givens or conditions to which teachers must adapt. Context variables include pupil characteristics such as age, sex, social class, or abilities as well as characteristics of the school and community in which teaching and learning are embedded. *Process* variables are human transactions that occur in the classroom during the course of teaching and learning; they may include all observable behaviors of teachers and pupils directly related to teaching-learning activities as well as other seemingly unrelated observable behaviors of teachers and pupils. *Product* variables, the final category in the sequence, are outcomes of teaching as measured in terms of immediate pupil growth or long-term pupil effects. Learning to read, write, calculate, or acquire job skills and mature into an adult have been used by researchers as product measures.

Researchers have investigated different combinations of these variables to enlarge the scientific knowledge on teaching and learning. Many studies have been concerned with the relationship of teacher characteristics (presage variables) to teacher behaviors (process variables). They have investigated rela-

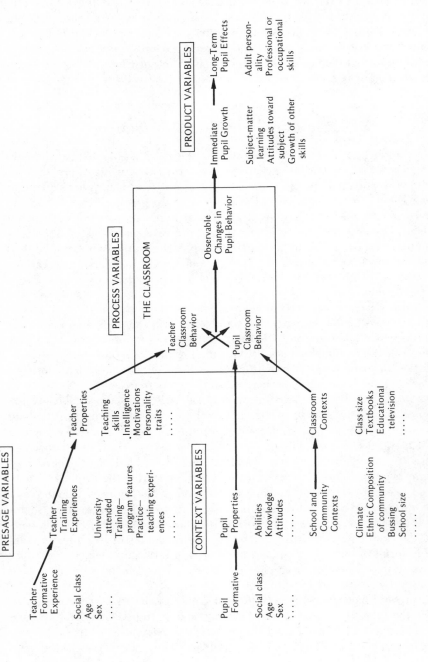

FIGURE 2–9. A model for the study of classroom teaching. [From Dunkin, M. J. and B. J. Biddle. *The Study of Teaching.* (New York: Holt, Rinehart and Winston, Inc., 1974), p. 38. Reprinted by permission.]

PRESAGE VARIABLES

Teacher Formative Experience

Social class
Age
Sex
. . . . .

Teacher Training Experiences

University attended
Training—program features
Practice—teaching experiences
. . . . .

Teacher Properties

Teaching skills
Intelligence
Motivations
Personality traits
. . . . .

PROCESS VARIABLES

THE CLASSROOM

Teacher Classroom Behavior

Pupil Classroom Behavior

Observable Changes in Pupil Behavior

PRODUCT VARIABLES

Immediate Pupil Growth

Subject-matter learning
Attitudes toward subject
Growth of other skills

Long-Term Pupil Effects

Adult personality
Professional or occupational skills

CONTEXT VARIABLES

Pupil Formative

Social class
Age
Sex
. . . . .

Pupil Properties

Abilities
Knowledge
Attitudes
. . . . .

School and Community Contexts

Climate
Ethnic Composition of community
Bussing
School size
. . . . .

Classroom Contexts

Class size
Textbooks
Educational television
. . . . .

tionships between such variables as teacher motivation or anxiety and the amount of praise or criticism teachers give. Many other studies have concentrated on the relationship of contextual variables to teacher behavior (context-process). They have investigated, among other things, whether teachers of low socioeconomic students behave differently from teachers of high socioeconomic students. Few studies have attempted to link any more than two of these variables at one time. Presumably, this limitation in the scope of research explains in part why its results have not been more revealing.

Medley (1972) places the origin of research on teacher effectiveness, a presage-product variety, in the publication of a study by Kratz (1896) entitled, "Characteristics of the Best Teachers as Recognized by Children." This study, as well as other examples of early research, was governed almost totally by student perceptions of "good" and "bad" teachers. Later research along this line consisted largely of collation of lists of characteristics of "good" teachers as "recognized" by students or "experts"—that is, supervisors or professors. The results of such investigations consisted of a potpourri of conflicting opinion. As Dunkin and Biddle (1974) point out, the bankruptcy of this early research can be attributed to failure to actually observe teaching-learning activities, theoretical impoverishment, use of inadequate criteria for teacher effectiveness, and lack of concern for the context in which teaching and learning occurred.

Surprisingly, it was not until the late 1950s and early 1960s that researchers made substantial progress toward remedying some of the problems of early research, primarily by concentrating on process-product relationships. Flanders (1960), with his "verbal interaction analysis" of classroom events, threw open the door to research on teacher behavior in the classroom. His work was followed closely by many others who were interested in the study of the relationship of teacher behavior to student outcomes. Rosenshine and Furst's (1971) often quoted review of process-product research illustrates the state of knowledge at that time. They reviewed some fifty, mostly correlational, studies and derived what they believed were the eleven teacher behaviors that related most strongly and consistently with pupil outcomes. The first five teacher processes on Rosenshine and Furst's list were the strongest; the next six were characterized as promising. These variables are as follows:

1. *Clarity* of presentation, including the teacher's ability to organize.
2. *Variability* as defined in terms of the types of materials, tests, and teaching devices a teacher uses, as well as the variability of discourse.
3. *Enthusiasm* as defined in terms of teacher movement, voice inflection, and the like.
4. *Task-orientation*, or the businesslike, achievement-oriented behaviors of teachers.
5. *Student opportunity to learn;* that is, teachers' behaviors directed toward covering material in class on which students are later tested.

6. *Use of student ideas and general indirectness* as defined in terms of teachers' acknowledgement of student ideas, expansion of student ideas, or use of praise.
7. *Criticism*, or disapproval, rejection, giving directions, or justifying authority (negatively related to student outcomes).
8. *Use of structuring comments*, including such teacher behaviors as providing overviews and indications of transitions within lessons.
9. *Types of questions* teachers ask as defined in terms of lower and higher cognitive levels (convergent-divergent) as well as classifications of questions according to what, where, why, and how.
10. *Probing*, or teacher responses to student answers that encourage student elaboration.
11. *Level of difficulty of instruction*, including teacher behaviors that indicate the material students are to cover is challenging and high standards of performance are important.

With the Rosenshine and Furst review of process-product studies, it appeared that research on teaching had begun to provide objective information about what teachers do that relates or contributes to student learning. It was generally thought that such information would lead to programs of teacher education based on objective evidence rather than on personal or theoretical opinion. As critics point out, however, even the studies cited by Rosenshine and Furst were marked by serious problems and made the prescription of teacher training objectives based on such evidence risky (Heath and Nielson, 1974).

But as limited as process-product research may be, it remains one of the best types of evidence available on the value of particular teacher tasks and behaviors. The results of such studies are beginning to define teacher effectiveness in terms of what teachers actually do and how such behaviors relate to student learning and satisfaction. Evidence derived from such investigation, therefore, should enable teacher educators to help teachers function in ways that can be expected to support student growth.

Gage's recent analysis (1978) of process-product studies that have been discounted as weak or inconclusive suggests that existing evidence is stronger than many have believed. He examined several independent studies of the teacher process-student outcome relationship. From this research procedure he identified four clusters of studies that are highly significant in that the relationship of particular teacher behaviors and student outcomes in all likelihood did not occur by chance. The first cluster consisted of nineteen studies of the relationship of teacher indirectness and student achievement. *Teacher indirectness* was defined in terms of the teacher's acceptance of students' ideas and feelings, ability to give praise and support, and willingness to provide a good emotional climate. The second cluster included five studies of the relationship of teacher praise and student attitudes. *Teacher praise* was defined in terms of teacher encouragement, use of humor to release tension (but not at the expense of others), and attention to the students' ideas, exemplified by such statements as "um hm?" or "go on." The third cluster included eight studies of teacher acceptance of pupil ideas as related to pupil achievement. *Acceptance* was defined in such terms as clarifying, building, and developing ideas suggested by students. The fourth cluster consisted of seventeen studies of the relationship of teacher criticism or disapproval and student achievement. *Criticism and disapproval* were defined largely in terms of teacher statements intended to change student behavior from nonacceptable to acceptable, reprimanding a student, or justifying authority. In this cluster the relationship was negative—that is, where criticism and disapproval occurred, student achievement was low. Such findings suggest that existing process-product research provides substantive knowledge from which researchers and practitioners can project useful objectives for teacher growth.

From evidence on teacher behavior and pupil achievement in reading and mathematics in the early grades, Gage presents other directions for the identification of teacher tasks and behaviors that, although especially important in the third grade, may be important in other grades as well. These directions are summarized in the following statements:

1. Teachers should have a system of rules that allow pupils to attend to their personal and procedural needs without having to check with the teacher.
2. A teacher should move around the room frequently, monitoring pupils' seatwork, and communicating an awareness of their pupil's behavior while also attending to academic needs.
3. When pupils work independently, teachers should insure that the assignments are interesting and worthwhile, yet still easy enough to be completed by each third grader without teacher direction.
4. Teachers should keep to a minimum such activities as giving directions and organizing the class for instruction. Teachers can do this by writing the daily schedule on the board, insuring that pupils know where to go, and what to do.
5. In selecting pupils to respond to questions, teachers should call on a child by name before asking the question as a means of insuring that all pupils are given an equal number of opportunities to answer questions.
6. With less academically oriented pupils, teachers should always aim at getting the child to give some kind of response to a question. Rephrasing, giving cues, or asking a new question can be useful techniques for bringing forth some answer from a previously silent pupil or one who says 'I don't know' or answers incorrectly.
7. During reading-group instruction, teachers should give a maximal amount of brief feedback and provide fast-paced activities of the "drill" type.

Medley (1977) presents one of the most comprehensive reviews of the process-product research to date. Although his methods are too complex and his conclusions too numerous to detail here, we highlight some of his findings and encourage the reader to examine his work. Medley's results, like those of Gage and Rosenshine and Furst, are based largely on correlational rather than experimental studies; thus the relationships cited do not prove that teacher behaviors actually *cause* particular student outcomes. Instead, they indicate only that a relationship exists. In addition, the studies to which Medley refers consist entirely of pupil performance on reading and mathematics achievement tests in the primary grades. They exclude short-term measures of performance, measures of performance in other subject matter areas at other grade levels, and measures of learning not available from achievement-type tests. Nonetheless, his results have striking implications for practice.

First, Medley's findings suggest that competent teachers behave differently with different types of students. For example, the most effective teachers of low socioeconomic pupils spend less class time discussing matters unrelated to lesson content.[1] Those teachers engage their pupils in more lesson-related activities than do less effective teachers. Whether or not this teacher behavior related to pupil attitudes toward school is unclear, but in other respects, such as in the organization of the classroom, teacher behavior seems to have an effect on student attitudes. For instance, when teachers of low socioeconomic students permit more independent work, the students appear to like school better but learn less. When teachers use small, unsupervised groups in the classroom, students seem neither to like school nor learn much. On the other hand, when teachers permit the least amount of individual or small group work, students show the greatest gains in achievement but also a more mixed set of attitudes. It also appears that independent seatwork does not do much to improve the self-image of low socioeconomic pupils.

The quality of instruction, or the kinds of questions teachers ask and the ways they respond to students, also seems to be important. According to Medley, the most effective teachers of low socioeconomic pupils keep interaction at a low level of complexity and pupil initiative. Instead of asking pupils to analyze, synthesize, or evaluate, they concentrate on getting answers to narrow questions. Those who encourage pupils to think, question, and discuss seem to be less effective in teaching them to read or to do arithmetic. Effective teachers with high socioeconomic groups either tend to anticipate which students will answer questions or call on ready volunteers, but the more effective teachers in low socioeconomic classes generally ask questions and call on students who do not volunteer a response. In sum, although the methods used by these more effective teachers of low socioeconomic students seem to

[1] Medley's references to socioeconomic status are derived from the work of Brophy and Evertson. Brophy (1977) has stressed that since SES was used as a substitute variable for ability, achievement level, and motivation, it should therefore not be overemphasized, leading to still further stereotyping according to SES.

elicit better performance, their pupils' attitudes toward school appear to be low.

Classroom management styles of more effective and less effective teachers also vary. According to Medley, "the effective teacher maintains an environment that is supportive and, if not always quiet, free from disruptive pupil behavior. She or he maintains this environment with little apparent effort or expression of negative affect." But as Koehler (1977) points out, this statement is somewhat deceptive for it is possible that the more "effective" teachers may simply have fewer behavioral problem students in their classrooms.

Overall, Medley's work strongly suggests that those who would support teachers must be aware of teachers' needs to learn different strategies for dealing with different pupils, at least in the early grades. It also appears to be very much in line with an effective teaching pattern that Rosenshine and Meyers (1978) have labeled "direct instruction"—teaching that carefully allocates time, prescribes setting, monitors student progress, provides feedback, and reinforces pupil responses. Medley's results, of course, do not yield absolute laws of "effective" and "ineffective" teaching behavior, but they do help to separate "more effective" from "less effective" teaching behavior when achievement test score gains are the measure of success.

The more researchers learn about relationships between teacher performance and accompanying pupil results, the richer and more complex teacher and learning appear to be. Soar (1977), for example, suggests that certain teacher behaviors and student behaviors exhibit curvilinear relationships. In other words, some teacher behaviors may be effective only up to a certain point; beyond this, they may be detrimental to student achievement. He also found that effective teaching may depend on *what* is taught as well as *who* is taught. In his work, a less structured teaching approach was found to be more useful for teaching abstractions, whereas higher structure worked better in teaching concrete kinds of knowledge. As research grows, then, so does the number of caveats—what works with some students and for some objectives is inappropriate for other students and other objectives.

It seems that Gage's (1979) notion of teaching as a "practical" art with a scientific basis has considerable merit. He states this as follows:

> Scientific method can contribute relationships between variables taken two at a time and even, in the form of interactions, three or perhaps four or more at a time. Beyond, say, four, the usefulness of what science can give the teacher begins to weaken, because teachers cannot apply, at least not without help and not on the run, the more complex interactions. At this point, the teacher as artist must step in and make clinical, or artistic judgments about the best ways to teach. In short, the scientific base for the art of teaching will consist of two-variable relationships and lower-order interactions. The higher-order interactions between four and more variables must be handled by the teacher as artist.

Is such a limited scientific basis of knowledge, we might ask, even worth having? According to Gage, and as reason dictates, the answer is clearly yes. But as Dewey (1929) suggests, the ultimate value of scientific findings may not be realized in terms of "laws" that can be translated directly into practice. Instead, research may be most important for the potential it holds for making teachers more observant, flexible, and responsive to student needs.

Deriving Tasks and Behaviors from Research on Teaching

Research suggests that encouraging the growth of teachers and students is apparently a matter of considering many human variables in a variety of contexts. A few fairly simple relationships between teaching and learning are relatively strong, stable, and generalizable—that is, they explain variation in student achievement as measured by achievement tests and hold up across time and across varying student types or objectives of instruction. But even the teacher behavior of keeping students "on-task" may have adverse effects on some students' attitudes toward school. Further, time on task may not be as important in such areas as those dealing with creative expression, where relatively unexplored, nonempirical qualities such as insight or creative energy might make a difference in student outcomes.

Beyond the findings of particular studies, research on teaching offers other directions to the teacher educator. For example, examining low-inference teacher and student behaviors, or behaviors that can readily be seen and counted, is useful because results are concrete and specific. High-inference measures, or measures that call for observers to make judgments, however, may also provide helpful kinds of information for teachers. They yield a wealth of description that may suggest as yet unexplored but potentially important areas of classroom behavior. In addition, teacher educators would be well advised to be aware of smaller, task-specific samples of teacher and student behavior as opposed to relying on standardized achievement test scores for indications of teacher effectiveness. The day-to-day transactions in the classroom bear heavily on the more long-term results of student achievement and satisfaction, not to mention the attitudes and performances of teachers.

Teaching Models and Taxonomies as a Source

Various educational theories also provide important directions for the practice of teaching. Historically, education has been allied with philosophic ideas or systems whose ends are to ensure personal happiness and the welfare of society. From the teachings of Socrates, Plato, and Aristotle down to the present day, teachers have learned from systematic organizations of ideas how, both directly and indirectly, to express and interpret their own behaviors and thus to make contact with different students in a variety of ways. In recent times, various models of teaching or interpretive frameworks of pedagogy (Polyani, 1958) have been instrumental in guiding both teaching and learning. According to Nuthall and Snook (1973), a model of teaching is a "general and influential point of view." It is a philosophical approach that describes the way teaching can be conceptualized for purposes of research and practice.

Perhaps better than anyone else, Joyce and Weil (1980) illustrate the range of teaching models and the potential diversity of teacher tasks and behaviors. They reviewed more than eighty approaches that create "environments for learning" or teaching models from such areas as education, psychology, and sociology. From their original list, they selected twenty-two models that met the criteria of being "communicable" and "rationalized." This reduced list, in turn, was organized into four families or models with similar orientation. These families or groups, although similar in some ways, are recognizably different from each other in the requirements they place on teachers.

One family of models Joyce and Weil term *social interaction* is concerned with relationships a person establishes with others and with society. Many of these models were developed to improve democratic methods and to prepare students to function effectively in society. Another family, consisting of *information-processing* models, emphasizes the ways in which learners react to environmental stimuli, organize information, generate concepts, solve problems, and manipulate symbols. Some of these models emphasize teaching behaviors directed toward enhancing learner creativity, and others concentrate on the development of learner intellectual ability. A third, or *personal sources*, family is concerned with personal and emotional development. The distinctive feature of this family is its focus on the development of the individual as a source of educational ideas. The last family, *behavioral models*, is oriented toward the manipulation of the environment to shape individual behavior. This family builds upon the research and methodology of behavior theory. These four related families, identified and categorized by Joyce and Weil, are designed to accomplish a variety of educational goals (Table 2–1).

Depending on who is to be taught and what is to be learned, teacher tasks and behaviors may vary considerably across models of teaching. In some models, a teacher must manipulate time and materials, give feedback, and structure support in ways that will lead to the direct and immediate learning of specific information. Here the instructional effects on some students can be quite obvious. In other models, the teacher's main tasks are to organize time, materials, feedback, and support to create a climate that fosters student exploration and self-expression over an extended period of time. The value of these particular models lies primarily in the subtle nurturant effects they have on students. The importance of models of teaching as sources for teacher tasks and behaviors, then, will be more important in some situations than in others.

Formal programs of teacher education have supported teachers in their per-

TABLE 2–1
Models of Teaching Classified by Family and Mission*

Model	Major Theorist	Family Orientation	Applicable Mission or Goals
Inductive Thinking	Hilda Taba	Information processing	Designed primarily for development of inductive
Inquiry Training	Richard Suchman	Information processing	mental processes and academic reasoning or theory building, but these capacities are useful for personal and social goals as well.
Scientific Inquiry	Joseph J. Schwab (also much of the Curriculum Reform movement of the 1960s)	Information processing	Designed to teach the research system of a discipline, but also expected to have effects in other domains (sociological methods may be taught in order to increase social understanding and social problem-solving).
Concept Attainment	Jerome Bruner	Information processing	Designed primarily to develop inductive reasoning, but also for concept development and analysis.
Cognitive Growth	Jean Piaget Irving Sigel Edmund Sullivan Lawrence Kohlberg	Information processing	Designed to increase general intellectual development, especially logical reasoning, but can be applied to social and moral development as well
Advance Organizer	David Ausubel	Information processing	Designed to increase the efficiency of information-processing capacities to absorb and relate bodies of knowledge.
Memory	Harry Lorayne Jerry Lucas	Information processing	Designed to increase capacity to memorize.
Nondirective Teaching	Carl Rogers	Personal	Emphasis on building the capacity for personal development in terms of self-awareness, understanding, autonomy, and self-concept.
Awareness Training	Fritz Perls William Schutz	Personal	Increasing one's capacity for self-exploration and self-awareness. Much emphasis on development of interpersonal

Model	Major Theorist	Family Orientation	Applicable Mission or Goals
			awareness and understanding, as well as body and sensory awareness.
Synectics	William Gordon	Personal	Personal development of creativity and creative problem-solving.
Conceptual Systems	David Hunt	Personal	Designed to increase personal complexity and flexibility.
Classroom Meeting	William Glasser	Personal	Development of self-understanding and responsibility to oneself and one's social group.
Group Investigation	Herbert Thelen John Dewey	Social interaction	Development of skills for participation in democratic social process through combined emphasis on interpersonal (group) skills and academic inquiry skills. Aspects of personal development are important outgrowths of this model.
Social Inquiry	Byron Massialas Benjamin Cox	Social interaction	Social problem solving, primarily through academic inquiry and logical reasoning.
Laboratory Method	National Training Laboratory (NTL) Bethel, Maine	Social interaction	Development of interpersonal and group skills and, through this, personal awareness and flexibility.
Jurisprudential	Donald Oliver James P. Shaver	Social interaction	Designed primarily to teach the jurisprudential frame of reference as a way of thinking about and resolving social issues.
Role Playing	Fannie Shaftel George Shaftel	Social interaction	Designed to induce students to inquire into personal and social values, with their own behavior and values becoming the source of their inquiry.
Social Simulation	Sarene Boocock Harold Guetzkow	Social interaction	Designed to help students experience various social processes and realities and to examine their own reactions to them, also to

TABLE 2-1 (continued)

Model	Major Theorist	Family Orientation	Applicable Mission or Goals
			acquire concepts and decision-making skills.
Contingency Management	B. F. Skinner	Behavioral	Facts, concepts, skills
Self-Control	B. F. Skinner	Behavioral	Social behavior/skills
Relaxation	Rimm & Masters, Wolpe	Behavioral	Personal goals (reduction of stress, anxiety)
Stress Reduction	Rimm & Masters, Wolpe	Behavioral	Substitution of relaxation for anxiety in social situation
Assertiveness Training	Wolpe, Lazarus, Salter	Behavioral	Direct, spontaneous expression of feelings in social situation
Desensitization	Wolpe	Behavioral	
Direct Training	Gagne Smith and Smith	Behavioral	Pattern of behavior, skills

* Adapted from Joyce and Weil, *Models of Teaching*, 2nd ed. (Englewood Cliffs, N.J.: Prentice-Hall, 1980), pp. 10–13. (Reprinted by permission).

formance of tasks according to one or another of the various conceptions of teaching models. This is perhaps best exemplified by performance- or competency-based teacher education (P/CBTE) programs. Trial projects funded by the U.S. Office of Education in 1968 encouraged teachers to become "managers of instruction," "innovators of change," and "human relations specialists." Although somewhat limited in their success, P/CBTE programs imply that teachers can change by adopting behaviors allied with particular teaching models (Gage and Winne, 1975). Peck and Tucker (1973) concluded that research on teacher education demonstrates that a systems approach (such as that of P/CBTE), coupled with an opportunity for direct involvement in what is to be learned, produces teachers and pupils who are better self-initiated.

Taxonomies of teaching-learning behaviors provide teacher educators with another valuable source of teacher tasks and behaviors. Taxonomies, not unlike models of teaching, are based on collections of judgments, observations, theories, and research. One important difference, however, is that taxonomies are ordered according to a single underlying principle or concept. Most familiar, of course, are the cognitive and affective classification schemes of educational objectives developed in the 1950s and 1960s by Bloom and Krathwohl and their colleagues. These taxonomies have guided researchers and teachers not only in setting expectations for student behavior but also in its subsequent assessment. As the following tables illustrate, taxonomies also allow us to extrapolate general teacher tasks and behaviors.

TABLE 2–2
Cognitive Domain of Educational Objectives*

Level	Learner Objectives	Teacher Tasks
1.00 Knowledge	To define, distinguish, acquire, identify, recall, or recognize various forms of information.	To present and/or elicit facts, conventions, categories in ways that enable learners to demonstrate knowledge.
2.00 Comprehension	To translate, transform, give in own words, illustrate, prepare, read, represent, change, rephrase, or restate various forms of information.	To present and/or elicit definitions, words, phrases, relationships, principles in ways that enable learners to demonstrate comprehension.
3.0 Application	To apply, generalize, relate, choose, develop, organize, use, transfer, restructure, or classify various forms of information.	To present and/or elicit principles, laws, conclusions, effects in ways that enable learners to apply what they have learned.
4.00 Analysis	To distinguish, detect, identify, classify, discriminate, recognize, categorize, or deduce various forms of information.	To present and/or elicit elements, hypotheses, assumptions, statements of intent or fact in ways that encourage learners to critically analyze information.
5.00 Synthesis	To write, tell, relate, produce, originate, modify, or document various forms of information.	To present and/or elicit structures, patterns, designs, relationships in ways that encourage learners to form new structures of knowledge.
6.00 Evaluation	To judge, argue, validate, assess, appraise various forms of information.	To present and/or elicit from learners different qualitative judgments.

* Adapted from Metfessel, Michael, and Kirsner (1969, pp. 228–229).

The cognitive domain (Bloom, Englehart, Furst, Hill, and Krathwohl, 1956) is organized into six major areas of increasing cognitive activity (Table 2–2). It specifies what students must be able to accomplish regardless of the particular subject matter and suggests how teachers may support their learning.

Much like the cognitive domain, the taxonomy of affective educational objectives (Krathwohl, Bloom, and Masia, 1964) is conceptualized as a hierarchically ordered system of inner growth. The steps in this classification scheme represent a person's development through awareness and assimilation of various attitudes, principles, and codes of conduct. As Table 2–3 indicates, the affective domain of educational objectives also implies direction for the identification of teacher tasks and behaviors.

A taxonomy of psychomotor objectives also implies directions for the practice of teaching. This classification scheme indicates the progression of a child's development from gross to fine motor activities and from nonverbal to

TABLE 2–3
Affective Domain of Educational Objectives

Level	Learner Objectives	Teacher Tasks
1.0 Receiving	To become aware of and able to differentiate various sounds, sights, events, shapes, sizes, and models.	To afford opportunities for learners to experience, accept, or reject new and different ideas, feelings, works, compositions, systems, or principles.
2.0 Responding	To comply with, approve, or practice various directions, policies, games, or dramatic works.	To afford opportunities for learners to tailor their own conceptually unique value schemes.
3.0 Valuing	To increase proficiency in, assist, support, or appreciate various musical and artistic productions, projects, or viewpoints. To deny, protest, or debate various deceptions, irrelevancies, or irrationalities.	
4.0 Organization	To discuss, theorize, abstract, compare, balance, organize, define, or formulate various parameters, codes, standards, goals, systems, or limits.	
5.0 Characterization by value or value complex	To revise, complete, or require various plans, behaviors, methods, or efforts. To be highly rated by others for humanitarianism, ethics, integrity, or maturity. To avoid, manage, resolve, or resist extravagance, excess, conflict, or exorbitancy.	

* Adapted from Metfessel, Michael and Kinsner (1969, pp. 230–231).

verbal communication behaviors. As Table 2–4 illustrates, teachers who attempt to enhance psychomotor development in learners must be able to engage in a variety of tasks.

As will be shown in Chapter 3, there are many other kinds of conceptual schemes that give direction to teaching. Some of these concentrate on the relationships between students and teachers; others focus more narrowly on the teacher's substantive verbal behaviors. Although each scheme in its own way may lend direction to the teacher educator, no single model of teaching

TABLE 2–4
Psychomotor Domain of Educational Objectives

Level	Learner Objectives	Teacher Tasks
1.00 Gross body movements	To enhance strength, speed, and agility in the upper and lower limbs.	To provide opportunities for learners to participate in such activities as running, jumping, or swimming.
2.00 Finely coordinated	To coordinate sight and hearing with various body movements (hand-eye-foot coordination).	To provide opportunities for learners to participate in such activities as buttoning a shirt, typing, playing the piano, and "driving" a car.
3.00 Nonverbal communication	To communicate without use of the spoken word, (i.e., to use facial expressions, gestures, and other bodily movements).	To provide opportunities for learners to participate in such nonverbal activities as showing anger or fright, giving directions, or dramatizing the catching of a fish.
4.00 Speech behaviors	To produce verbal sounds, to form and project words, and to coordinate sounds and gestures.	To provide opportunities for learners to participate in such activities as pronouncing letter sounds, reading passages aloud, projecting voices over a distance, and communicating messages by voice and gesture to another person.

* Adapted from Kibler, Barker, and Miles (1970).

or taxonomy of behaviors can accommodate the totality of tasks to be performed.

Deriving Tasks and Behaviors from Models and Taxonomies

Educators have defined a variety of ways by which teaching and learning can be planned, executed, and assessed. Many models of teaching and taxonomies of learner objectives suggest directly the sorts of tasks teachers must undertake and how they are to be accomplished if children are to benefit. Others, however, only imply what teachers must do to facilitate student growth. When the directions for teaching that conceptual schemes provide are specific, the identification of tasks and behaviors, of course, is easy. Didactic models, for example, would have the teacher organize and present information to students deductively. Inductive models, on the other hand, might emphasize the need for teachers to solicit information from students and draw conclusions cooperatively through discussion. But even when tasks and behaviors are only implied, models and taxonomies may suggest ways for teacher educators to encourage teachers to organize their thinking about teaching and learning—ways that may help teachers improve their practice and derive greater satisfaction from their work.

The Public as a Source

Teachers, students, professional educators, and researchers provide direction for the identification of important teacher tasks and behaviors, but a teacher's role cannot fully be prescribed in isolation from the societal context in which teaching occurs. In order to identify the tasks teachers should be expected to accomplish, one must look to various segments of the general public and examine what they believe to be important. Elected and appointed officials may emphasize, for instance, the need for teachers to create new curricula; the courts may suggest certain tasks to be accomplished if student rights are to be guaranteed; business and industry may create educational materials that require teachers to demonstrate new technical skills; and parents may demand that teachers perform activities related to the teaching of values or career skills. Identifying teacher tasks and behaviors at the exclusion of such interests not only courts political disaster but also risks overlooking other important sources of information on which to base tasks and behaviors.

As pollsters have demonstrated, the general public can be quite outspoken when it comes to public schools and teachers. For nine of the last ten years, the public has voiced its loudest complaints against what it perceives to be a lack of discipline in the schools. In 1969, a Gallup poll showed that the lack of discipline, or the inability of school officials to "keep students in line," was viewed by the public as an indication of "poor education." In 1978, 25 percent of parents with children in public schools and 24 percent of citizens with no children in schools saw lack of discipline as the biggest problem in their community. This problem was mentioned nearly twice as often as drug use, which was the second major concern.

Discipline and drug use, however, are not the only concerns of the public; Gallup contends that if school officials would talk to a representative sample of persons in their districts, they would find that public concerns about schools fall into seven categories. In 1978, this survey asked: "What, if anything, do you think the public schools in this community should be doing that they are not doing now?" The public responded with some strong recommendations, and although they varied from school district to school district, these recommendations coalesced into seven major points:

1. More strict discipline. . . . The public is bothered by the lack of respect shown to, or demanded by, teachers. They read about the chaos in

classrooms. They complain that teachers let children do anything they wish, dress any way they want, pay no attention to school rules, stay away from school whenever they feel like it.

2. **Better teachers.** By "better teachers," the public does not necessarily mean teachers who are better trained or more knowledgeable in the subjects they teach. . . . They are much more inclined to think of "good" teachers as the teachers who take a personal interest in each student, who try to understand each student and his or her problems, who encourage students in the subjects taught so that they will achieve high grades, and, finally, who inspire students to set high goals in life for themselves.

3. **Back to basics.** This movement has support throughout the nation and, of course, many school systems have already made changes to give more attention to the so-called basics. Even so, many people want greater emphasis placed upon what they often describe as the "fundamentals," meaning reading, writing, and arithmetic.

4. **More parental involvement.** A frequent suggestion is for closer teacher/parent relationships. Many complain that teachers show a poor attitude in communicating with parents. They suggest more conferences between parents and teachers. [Parents] would like to know much more about what [they] can do in the home to help children in school.

5. **Higher scholastic standards.** The public has been made aware through the media of declining test scores throughout the nation. People read about automatic promotion and about young persons who are graduated from high school but who can barely read or write. They complain that not enough homework is given to their children. Some say the school day should be longer. They say it is too easy to get good grades.

6. **More education about health hazards.** The widespread use of alcohol, drugs, marijuana, and cigarettes by young people has become an important worry to many parents. They want help from the schools. They want schools to point out the dangers of alcohol and drug abuse and smoking, and they want the schools to establish rules that will be a deterrent.

7. **More emphasis on careers.** Parents whose children do not intend to go on to college want to be sure that their children are ready to fill some kind of job after they are graduated. Even in the case of those whose children plan to enter college, parents see a need to give guidance about careers that are available, the abilities required, and the rewards offered in different occupations.

In a democratic society, the public's mood toward education is presumably reflected—although often in a slow and indirect fashion—by its elected representatives. The public elects legislators and members of the city council and school board who, in turn, formulate educational policy; then officers are elected or appointed to administer this policy. In other words, the public's will is translated into action through its elected and appointed officials. The attitudes, beliefs, and actions of these officials, therefore, offer further clues as to what the public considers important for schools and teachers to accomplish.

One of the best places to begin to explore the public's attitude toward education as expressed by its representatives is in federal legislation. Cynics—or maybe realists—would argue that federal legislation and the educational programs it generates are no more than haphazard political responses to constituent demands, and in some cases they may be right. A contrasting view, however, would suggest that many governmental programs reflect the public's "long view" of the important tasks to be accomplished by its schools and teachers.

A good example of federal legislation aimed directly at schools, teachers, and students is the Elementary and Secondary Education Act (ESEA) and its accompanying amendments. Even given the storm of conflicting values and recommendations surrounding ESEA, it is a graphic illustration of what our nation's representatives believe to be important in public school education. This single bill and its amendments are so comprehensive that to describe them here is not feasible. Books have been written on the machinations involved with passage and implementation of this major piece of legislation. The original ESEA, which was passed in 1965, was intended (particularly by way of Title I) to aid "disadvantaged children," to strengthen federal-state relationships, and to speed up desegregation in the South (Wirt and Kirst, 1972). The Education Amendments of 1978 (Public Law 95-561), or the latest version of ESEA, have grown to more than 200 pages of amendments, expansions, and extensions of the original legislation. The authorizations made by the Ninety-fifth Congress through Public Law 95-561 indicate recent congressional priorities.

Although Title I, or the act for Financial Assistance to Meet Special Education Needs of Children, has always been concerned with programs designed to meet the needs of migratory, handicapped, and neglected or delinquent children, Public Law 95-561 acknowledges the need for teachers and parents to become more directly involved in planning and in carrying out relevant special education programs. The latest version of Title I points to the importance of parent-teacher cooperation and involvement by reinforcing the need for basic skills development, or competence in reading, mathematics, and effective written and oral communication. But Title II, or the Basic Skills Improvement Program, in particular emphasizes basic skills by encouraging, among other things, the development and dissemination of materials to be used by parents and children in their homes. Title IV–C echoes the concern for basic skills by authorizing funding for such things as summer school programs designed to keep "disadvantaged" youth from falling behind.

Beyond the marked emphasis on basic skills, the Ninety-fifth Congress, through Title III of ESEA, seems to be saying that schools and teachers must concentrate on a variety of additional public concerns. For example, funding has been authorized and appropriated for such programs as metric education, arts in education, consumer education, law-related education, bilingual education, women's educational equity, gifted and talented education, and education of ethnic heritage. Ultimately, classroom teachers, then, are expected to undertake the tasks of teaching the metric system, preparing students to be informed consumers, enlightening students about the needs, abilities, and rights of women, and meeting a host of other demands.

Another major piece of federal education legislation, The Education for All Handicapped Children Act (Public Law 94-142), implies yet another set of tasks for the nation's public schools and teachers. The strength of congressional commitment to providing opportunities for the handicapped is expressed not only by the overwhelming vote of support for Public Law 94-142 (404 to 7 in the House of Representatives and 87 to 7 in the Senate), but by the amount of funds appropriated for its implementation ($804 million for 1979–1980 and $875 million for 1980–1981). The act calls for the education of handicapped students to occur in the "least restrictive environment," which is usually identified as the regular classroom. In other words, this law calls for "exceptional" students to be brought into the "mainstream" of public education by being taught side by side with "typical" students in classrooms throughout the land. Consequently, classroom teachers in all grades must now provide programs, plans, and instructional activities that are tailored to the individual capabilities of all students. Corrigan (1978) asserts that Public Law 94-142 demands a number of reforms in public education if the concept of least restrictive environment is to become a reality. Many of these needed reforms will undoubtedly fall upon teachers to implement—reforms such as developing "a continuous progress-reporting system with diagnostic profiles describing each student's human variability, exceptionality, and intellectual-personal growth."

By way of rules for certification or licensure, state governments also suggest where and how teachers should appropriate their energies. In most states the laws governing teacher certification are administered by departments of education. These in turn rely on colleges and universities to elaborate the skills, knowledge, and attitudes people must have if they are to enter and remain in the teaching profession. In short, certification is dependent upon graduating from a state-approved program of teacher education. Many colleges and universities (estimated at 41 percent by NEA in 1974) follow the requirements set by the National Council for Accreditation of Teacher Education (NCATE) for direction in their program course requirements, arrangements for student teaching, and other criteria for teaching standards. Although the requirements of these particular programs differ considerably from state to state and from institution to institution, students in general must successfully complete general education courses, professional education courses, and subject-matter specializations. It has been estimated that 80 percent of the nation's new teachers graduate each year from these NCATE-approved programs (Stinett, 1974), and it may therefore be assumed that these teachers have demonstrated the ability to accomplish the tasks considered important by state governments.

In addition, the courts have specified both directly or by implication what teachers should and should not do in the classroom. In *Brown* v. *Board of Education*, 1954, the Supreme Court injected itself dramatically into school politics and consequently into the lives of teachers and students. Since the Brown case, teachers have been called upon to meet the demands of school integration by developing and implementing programs aimed at reducing prejudice and discrimination as well as enhancing communication and understanding among races. In other cases, the courts have influenced teachers' activities with respect to the handling of flag salutes, student protests, corporal punishment, prayer in the classroom, and scheduling for religious education classes.

If there is any segment of society that should be expected to represent the public's wishes about teaching and learning, it is the local school board. The school board is charged directly with the responsibility for formulating local policy. Modern boards of education frequently mirror mainstream public sentiment toward teachers and teaching in how they spend the public's money and in how they conduct the ongoing business of the schools. Whether fighting for or against particular issues such as teacher tenure, revised curricula, or teachers' rights of sexual preference, boards of education often reflect the public's demands for what is to be accomplished in public education.

However, as Ziegler, Tucker, and Wilson (1977) discovered in a fairly intensive study of three boards of education in metropolitan areas across the country, board members' expectations can differ widely. These researchers point out that in two of the three districts studied, a single topic dominated the discussion at meetings. In Barwig Park, 30 percent of the discussion time focused on students; in Grahamdale, 43 percent dealt with district operations; and in Leeville, no single topic took precedence. In all three districts, general operations received greater-than-average attention, and students, curriculum, student services, and teachers were particularly important in two of the three districts. One might infer from board discussions in Barwig Park, for instance, that the teachers responsibilities in building student values or enhancing student performance were of particular interest to this community. But different inferences might be drawn from the activities of school boards in other districts. These study results are shown in Table 2–5.

Ziegler and colleagues (1977) and other researchers have suggested what school boards believe to be important, but it is the superintendent who represents the active public interest. The superintendent, therefore, is another important official public source of teacher tasks and behaviors. The superinpositions, and makes policy recommendations. The influence he or she exerts

TABLE 2–5
Distribution of Topics Discussed at School Board Meetings, in Percentages*

Topic Categories	District		
	Barwig Park	Grahamdale	Leeville
Curriculum (general education programs; basic skills; vocational education; bilingual education; sex education; topical education)	19	9	3
Student services (athletics; guidance, counseling; special extra programs; programs for special studies; transportation; food, health services; safety programs)	11	6	14
Parents (parental responsibilities; parent-teacher conferences; parental participation in decision making; relations with teachers)	4	0	2
Teachers (teacher values; teacher performance; teacher-staff unions; teacher support staff)	5	11	15
Administrators (principals; staff administrators; consultants; superintendent; administrative reports, research; administrative professional activities)	6	4	15
Local schools (alternative schools; community schools; other innovative schools, methods)	0	4	4
Students (student values; student performance; student misbehavior; student records; enrollment, attendance)	30	6	5
School Board (school board evaluation; appointment, election of board members; board behavior)	2	6	5
Finance (appropriations, revenues; bond issues)	7	7	11
Discrimination (equality; busing; affirmative action)	0	0	1
Other government (activities of federal government, state government, county government, municipal government; other educational institutions)	5	4	4
District operation (maintenance; facilities; materials	12	43	15

* From Ziegler, A., H. J. Tucker and L. A. Wilson. Communication and decision making in American public education: A longitudinal and comparative study. In *The politics of education*. J. D. Scribner, (Ed.). The Seventy-sixth yearbook of the National Society for the Study of Education (Chicago: University of Chicago Press, 1977), p. 233 (Reprinted by permission).

over such personnel decisions as hiring, promoting, assigning, and granting tenure often indicates the order of educational priorities within a district. Although superintendents are often characterized as being squeezed by increasing federal regulations from above and teacher organizations from below, their values, particularly as they affect curriculum, or what is to be taught and learned, can be very influential.

Accrediting agencies also reflect public school administrators' opinions about teacher tasks and behaviors. For example, the North Central Association, the largest regional accrediting agency in the country, is made up primarily of school administrators. Its Commission on Schools, the official body charged with generating and refining the standards for accreditation, is composed of 400 members, all of whom are either building principals, central office staff, or professors of educational administration. In 1978–1979, the commission suggested in general terms how teachers should appropriate their energies. These policies and standards for the accreditation of elementary schools identified many teacher tasks such as helping children sustain positive self-esteem, encouraging children to practice stable limits of behavior, utilizing diverse teaching strategies, and holding parent-teacher conferences. These may be taken as direct expressions of administrative opinion today.

By the time federal and state guidelines, accreditation standards, and district policies filter down to individual schools, and in turn are modified to a lesser or greater degree by administrators and community interest groups, teachers often face additional, and sometimes quite diverse, tasks that compete with each other in importance. In one metropolitan "fundamentals" school, for example, teachers have a primary responsibility to enforce a policy of strict discipline. In the case of persistent misbehavior, they are to isolate a child either within or outside the classroom, telephone parents or guardians, detain misbehaving children, administer corporal punishment, and even suspend the offender. In addition, teachers in this school are expected to provide homework, keep hallways and classrooms quiet and orderly, issue quarterly report cards, monitor a dress code, enforce rules for riding the bus, and retain children who are not performing up to standard. In contrast, a "modified open" school in the same metropolitan area emphasizes quite different activities for teachers. In this school, teachers are expected to function as facilitators, instructors, advisors, and counselors; they organize learning experiences, clear obstacles to learning, suggest learning possibilities, and help students establish their own personal goals.

Other tasks teachers encounter arise, at least in part, as a result of pressures to respond to special interest groups. Although not typically outspoken, the National Congress of Parents and Teachers (also known as the National Parent-Teacher Association) and its local affiliates have actively educated their members in the merits and drawbacks of school testing programs, and particularly in competency-based testing. The PTA has drawn attention to the favorable potential of minimum competency testing, but it has also warned that competency testing, if misused, can have a demeaning and debilitating effect on children. Accordingly, the national PTA opposes state or nationally controlled curricula and accompanying performance criteria, believing that such standardization would suppress the individuality of students. Instead, it advocates that teachers supplement both norm-referenced and criterion-referenced tests with a variety of locally developed approaches for measuring student performance, such as interviews with students, student journals, debates, skills checklists, problem-solving exercises, and open-ended questions (Ryan, 1979). One set of tasks teachers may face as a result of public demand, then, is to develop a variety of tests, use them to assess student performance, and report the results to local administrators and school boards. Other special interests, of course, advocate political or social causes that require teachers to perform quite different kinds of activities. For instance, the League of Women Voters works to promote "political responsibility" in students as among other citizens, and the National Association for the Advancement of Colored People has long directed its efforts toward racial cooperation. These, of course, are only two of the many special-interest groups nationally that affect teacher tasks and behaviors in the schools.

Business and industry may also substantially influence teacher activities through the development of educational materials and new types of educational technology. Control Data Corporation's Programmed Logic for Automated Teaching Operations (PLATO) is a computerized system of instruction that can place unfamiliar demands on teachers. Capable of both computer-assisted and computer-managed instruction, this system allows students to learn directly by computer and can monitor student progress or prescribe new areas of study. For teachers to help students obtain such computer instruction, however, teachers must know the rudimentary details of the system, become aware of the computer programs available and how to access them, know how to use the evaluation capabilities of the system, or perform simple programming. The ability to use such computer programs and systems, however, requires not only a demonstration of some technical skills but also a knowledge of how to incorporate isolated units of content into more comprehensive instructional plans for students. Similarly, Westinghouse Learning Corporation's Program for Learning in Accordance with Needs (PLAN) places other kinds of demands on teachers. This computer-managed instructional system requires teachers to guide students in planning individualized curricula. With this system, modules or teaching-learning units in language arts, social studies, science, or mathematics can be selected to coincide with a student's aptitudes and preferences. Once particular modules are selected, the teacher helps the student select various alternatives to meet his or her personal objectives. Whereas some students might be encouraged to learn from textbooks or filmstrips, others might be directed toward programmed instruction or lectures. PLATO and PLAN represent only two of the many examples of commercial products that demand special teacher skills for proper implementation.

Deriving Tasks and Behaviors from Public Sources

The public places an incredible number of diverse demands on schools and teachers. Citizens press for strict discipline in the classroom, attention to the basics, improved communication with parents, and development of a curriculum that is responsive to student and community needs. Through legislation and governmental programs, the federal government stresses the importance of meeting the needs of all children—handicapped, gifted, members of ethnic minorities, and the so-called typical child. School boards and their agents emphasize the need for teachers to monitor student performance, boost academic achievement, provide vocational and sex education, and involve parents and students in decisions about curriculum. The courts, too, mandate—or in some cases proscribe—teacher activities in order to guarantee that rights of students are protected. Business and industry shape the behaviors of teachers by the kinds of educational programs and materials they produce.

As a number of Gallup polls indicate, the general public expects teachers to exhibit favorable personal qualities as well as instructional skills. In the collective mind of the public, teachers must be understanding, encouraging, and inspirational if they are to succeed. At the same time, many of the personal and instructional demands placed on teachers by various public sources are neither simple nor uniform from one locale to another. Identification of the most important teacher tasks and behaviors, then, calls for attention to national and regional concerns plus an awareness of the needs of different communities.

Selecting Appropriate Teacher Tasks and Behaviors

At the outset of this chapter we described the goal of teacher development as helping classroom teachers in their performance of various tasks directed toward both personal and instructional ends. Yet no single theory or method holds a corner on knowledge about which teacher tasks and concomitant behaviors are most important.

A common method of identifying appropriate teacher tasks and behaviors is one of responding to social pressure. As crises arise, teachers are compelled to act in ways that alleviate the severity of existing conditions. The Supreme Court rules that schools must be desegregated, and teachers respond with programs designed to accommodate a racial mix of students. The Congress mandates mainstreaming, and teachers develop new materials and techniques to teach exceptional children in their own classrooms. Neighborhood gang violence intrudes on the lives of students, forcing teachers to better understand and to cope with student fear. In these and similar instances, the most imperative tasks and behaviors are determined largely by events outside the control of the teacher or the teacher educator.

Another method of identifying significant teacher tasks and behaviors is to examine one's convictions. Advocates of a particular philosophy, such as the "open-school" or "fundamental" education, might rely on what they believe to be right or what has worked for them in the past to identify the activities in which teachers should engage.

Closely associated with the process of selecting tasks and behaviors based on personal conviction is the method of relying on expert opinion. Here, the most important tasks and behaviors are determined by consulting authorities who seem to be best capable of ensuring the right decisions. What do professors say? What do public school administrators believe to be important? What books are best to rely on? Even though these and similar methods of setting objectives for teacher growth are, to a certain extent, useful in their own ways, each quite obviously has its limits.

Establishing appropriate objectives for teacher growth is not a simple matter of responding to crises, examining one's own convictions, or examining the convictions of experts. Instead, it is a matter of weighing several critical pieces of information. One must decide whether or not particular tasks can and should be undertaken, based on the needs and abilities of the person who is a teacher (P), evidence about the importance of the task (T), the behaviors that can be performed (B), and the potential for the environment to provide support (E). The following three questions and corresponding recommendations suggest how teacher educators might proceed to identify appropriate tasks and behaviors.

QUESTION 1: What evidence shows that this particular task is important for this particular teacher?

RECOMMENDATION 1: Tasks (T) must be congruent with the needs and abilities of the person (P) who functions as teacher.

A hypothetical situation will serve to illustrate this principle. Eve, a beginning teacher in an inner-city school, is reduced to tears every evening in anticipation of the coming day. Over the past month, her fifth-grade class has grown increasingly unmanageable. Two boys in particular have instigated trouble to the point that other children not only react to their disturbance, but initiate disturbances on their own. Yesterday, the principal came to Eve's room and told her that a mother had called to find out "just exactly what was going on" in her daughter's classroom. Apparently her daughter had been feigning illness to avoid going to school. Acting on the advice of another, more experienced teacher, Eve tried to crack down on the whole class, but with minimal success. She now feels that she is being harsh and overbearing, exhibiting behaviors that she detested in her own teachers. Although her student teaching was judged a resounding success and the first four months of the year were rewarding, she is beginning to have doubts about herself and her career as a teacher. She believes that she desperately needs help keeping students interested and involved in school.

Eve's needs could, of course, revolve around her own personal feelings of inadequacy. That is, she may not be comfortable or able to manage students constructively until she develops better feelings about herself as a person and as a professional. But in this instance, it is not unrealistic to suspect that Eve's self-concept is inextricably bound up in her ability to keep student work involvement high and deviant behavior low. On the surface, the evidence from a variety of sources is quite strong that Eve's most urgent and important need is to undertake the rather complex instructional task of keeping students actively involved in learning while reducing inappropriate student behavior.

QUESTION 2: How might this teacher, undertaking this task, be expected to perform?

RECOMMENDATION 2: Expected teacher behaviors (B) must be congruent with the demands of the task (T) and the capabilities of the person (P) who functions as teacher.

Extending the example, the teacher educator must infer to what degree Eve can be expected to keep students actively engaged in learning and simultaneously reduce deviant behavior. Given Eve's lack of experience and present state of mind, it would not be reasonable to expect her to demonstrate a variety of behaviors indicative of "the effective classroom manager." She could not, for example, be expected to step in the classroom the next day and accomplish the task in all of the following ways: (1) stop the inappropriate behaviors of offending students in a timely fashion; (2) suggest alternative behaviors or describe desirable behaviors to students; (3) concurrently praise students for what they do well (Borg, 1974); or (4) reduce her possible tendencies to leave topics dangling, to cut students off in mid-sentence, or to overdwell on inappropriate behavior (Kounin, 1970). It might be reasonable, however, for Eve to begin to grow toward effectiveness in classroom management by becoming *aware* of her own management behaviors and a few alternative ways to keep students involved. Once she understands her own problems and some possible solutions, she might be ready to try one or two new techniques. In other words, the most appropriate behaviors to expect from Eve, at least initially, would be those that fit simple intermediate tasks of classroom management, as well as those that fit her own present capabilities.

QUESTION 3: How might this teacher, undertaking this task be supported to perform the necessary behaviors?

RECOMMENDATION 3: The characteristics of the person (P) who serves as teacher, the task (T), and the anticipated teacher behaviors (B) must be congruent with the capabilities of teacher educators to provide supportive environments (E).

This third and final recommendation would mean that the environment created by the teacher educator must fit Eve's needs, the demands of the task, and the behaviors Eve may demonstrate. *Fitting the environment to the teacher* means that the teacher educator must examine his or her own abilities to respond to this inexperienced, troubled teacher, as well as to the possibilities for drawing upon outside resources. *Fitting the environment to the task* means that the teacher educator must examine the potential resources or the environmental support system, specifically as this relates to classroom management. For example, the teacher educator might reexamine his or her own knowledge of contingency management or behavior modification, think about other teachers who have had similar problems and would be willing to help, or explore the available training materials on classroom management. *Fitting the environment to the behaviors* means that the teacher educator must be aware of various levels of behavior that may be considered appropriate indicators of growth and help the teacher demonstrate these behaviors.

As this extended example illustrates, the most appropriate teacher tasks are determined not only by evidence that the task is important but also by the context in which the task is placed. There may, of course, be teacher tasks and levels of behavior that could be considered minimum requirements for all teachers such as maintaining a certain degree of order in the classroom. But the appropriateness of tasks and behaviors is determined mainly by the theoretical, empirical, and practical evidence of their importance, as well as the relationship of this evidence to the needs and abilities of teachers and the possibilities for creating supportive environments.

SUMMARY

The goal of teacher development is to help teachers accomplish a variety of personal and instructional tasks. This chapter has discussed the sorts of tasks teachers might undertake and some of the behaviors they might demonstrate in order to grow both personally and professionally.

Teacher tasks and their accompanying behaviors emanate from a variety of sources. Teachers have indicated that they want to be able to cope with behavior problems, to be competent in their subject matter, and to display a variety of human and technical skills on demand. Students have indicated that they want teachers to be humane disciplinarians, to provide work that is challenging and interesting, to create opportunities for students to interact with one another, and to allow students to share in the decisions that affect their lives in school. Researchers and educational theorists point to the need for teachers to be flexible in their approach to teaching, to possess a diverse repertoire of skills and strategies for setting objectives, to devise learning activities that enhance student work involvement, to give feedback, to ask questions, and to monitor progress. The general public and its official representatives demand that teachers enforce rules, teach students how to get along with one another, provide extra support for the disadvantaged and alternatives for the gifted or career-oriented—all the while sharing decision-making power with administrators, parents, and students. It is clear that those who would teach, as well as those who support them, face a mountain of demands.

Deciding where to begin to support teacher growth is not a simple matter of responding to the loudest outcry. It involves, instead, a careful process of weighing the information about the needs and abilities of teachers, the relative importance of various tasks and behaviors, and the potential for providing support to teachers.

❧ 3 ❧

Assessing Behavior

T HE purpose of this chapter is to suggest some instruments and
methods that may be used to observe classroom teaching-learning
behaviors. Teacher behaviors are indications of teachers' abilities to
perform various tasks. Examining teacher behavior systematically in the context of the classroom, therefore, should provide overt indications of teachers'
needs and abilities as they are revealed in their work with students.

There are other reasons that systematic observation of classroom behavior is
important. It yields information that helps teachers become more aware of
their own behaviors and those of their students. The data collected enable
teachers to compare and contrast their behaviors with those of their students
and to decide what changes in teaching styles might be appropriate. Also, by
documenting classroom behaviors, teacher educators can encourage change
based on fact. Finally, teacher educators can learn much about the personal,
social, and cognitive development of teachers and students by observing how
they interact with one another. Such knowledge should enable teacher
educators to adapt the environments they create to meet the needs of
teachers.

The Nature of Observation Systems

Literally hundreds of systems might be used to observe behavior in the
classroom. They may be classified in various ways but usually have the following common characteristics: (1) a purpose or reason for observation, which
might include providing research data, evaluation data, or information to be

used for training; (2) a recording procedure that specifies when and in what units behaviors are to be recorded; (3) the person, content, or materials to be observed; and (4) methods of analyzing data.

Although many observation systems are quite comprehensive, no single system is appropriate for all situations. All possess certain limitations. A system that concentrates on verbal behaviors, for instance, ignores nonverbal behaviors. One that emphasizes social and emotional climate probably deemphasizes the importance of classroom content. To begin to address the diversity of behaviors that occur in classrooms, teacher educators need to be able to use or create a variety of observational methods that address tasks teachers are trying to accomplish.

The process of selecting or creating an appropriate system for observation (thus maximizing chances for collecting useful information) should be guided by the following criteria:

1. Observation must be valid.
2. Observation must be reliable.
3. Information obtained from observation must be usable and pertinent to the tasks to be accomplished.

Validity.   The term *validity* is defined in a variety of ways. This concept will be further discussed in Chapter 5; for now, let it suffice to say that an observation or measurement is valid when it measures what it purports to measure (Kerlinger, 1973). In order to test the validity of observation, a teacher educator might ask: Will the observation system I have chosen measure the intended teacher/student behaviors as nearly as possible? If the answer is yes, then the measurement of behaviors using the selected method of observation can be considered valid. Despite the simplicity of this definition of validity, arriving at an affirmative answer to the question can be complex. Valid observation requires selecting or creating unambiguous observational items and applying them at the appropriate time to accurately reflect the reality of classroom behavior—a demanding process amidst the complexities of classroom life.

Because drawing inaccurate conclusions from observational data can adversely affect many people, an additional check on validity is warranted. Observers might ask themselves: What kinds of conclusions do I wish to make after observation, and will the type of data I plan to collect allow me to make such conclusions? Often observers make general assertions about teaching-learning behaviors that cannot be supported by their observations or do not relate to tasks teachers are trying to accomplish.

Reliability.   To generalize or extrapolate from observations of teacher/student behaviors, teacher educators must assess classroom actions and interactions with consistency and accuracy as well as with validity. In other words, observations must exhibit a high degree of *reliability* before worthwhile judgments can be made about teaching-learning performances. Reliability demands that observations meet at least two—and possibly three—conditions. First, the observation instrument must be internally consistent (that is, constructed of similar items of unambiguous quality to allow accurate interpretation). Second, the observer must be consistent in his or her own perceptions of behavior. Third, in special instances, consistency must be maintained between or among two or more observers.

Usability. Another requirement of an observation system is that it be useful. If the observation instruments selected by the teacher educator are valid and reliable but do not yield information upon which persons can base decisions, then a great deal of time and energy is likely to be wasted resulting in the creation of ill will. Concerning the usability of instrumentation for evaluation, Popham (1975) states:

> In addition to the more esoteric considerations associated with classical measurement operations, a number of practical issues can be considered under the general heading of "usability." Evaluators must be sensitive to the ease with which the tests can be administered. How long will they take to administer? How readily can the tests be scored? How readily can test results be interpreted? How expensive are the tests? Are there equivalent forms available for pretesting, posttesting, and so forth?

Selected Observation Systems

Observation systems can be both high-inference and low-inference. The first requires observers to infer or make judgments about what they see and hear; the second more precisely defines the behaviors to be observed and the procedures for collecting data, thus reducing the need for observers to make judgments. Neither type of system is necessarily better than the other. It is well to consider, however, that observers who make many qualitative or quantitative judgments about teaching-learning behaviors obviously run the risk of jeopardizing the validity and reliability of their findings. The more inferences one makes, the greater the chances for inaccuracy and inconsistency. On the other hand, observational methods that allow for at least some observer judgments may yield a richness of results that low-inference systems cannot.

For a number of reasons, we have chosen to exclude from our discussion of observation systems a type of high-inference measure known as rating scales.[1]

---

[1] Our comments on rating scales are based largely on a discussion in R. M. Brandt, *Studying behavior in natural settings* (New York: Holt, Rinehart and Winston, 1972), pp. 118–128.

In brief, the ambiguity of many behaviors makes it difficult to assess them accurately. For example, what may appear as "teacher acceptance" to one observer may seem to be "teacher tolerance" to another. Rating scales also assume that behaviors are distributed consistently across time and in different situations. In all likelihood, that is not the case. Furthermore, rating scales tend to yield information that is more subjective than in other types of observation systems; raters' biases about the kinds of behaviors they deem socially or personally acceptable may cause them to be either too lenient or too severe in their ratings. There are, of course, ways to minimize these deficiencies, but for the most part, it is advisable to rely on other types of observational systems.

We have chosen six systems that might serve as useful starting points for observation. They are systems that can be fitted to a variety of tasks in order to assess teacher behavior. With a reasonable amount of practice, these can be used to yield valid, reliable, and understandable information that is important and useful in many different situations. Teacher educators might modify the systems presented here, select others, or create new systems as needs arise.

The remainder of this chapter will treat each of the systems identified below in terms of its purpose, description, procedures for implementation, and procedures for data analysis.

1. Flanders system: An instrument that examines teacher-student verbal interaction in the classroom.
2. Galloway system: An instrument that examines nonverbal behaviors in classroom interactions.
3. Kounin system: An instrument that examines a teacher's classroom management techniques and student work involvement and misbehavior.
4. Goldhammer system: A method for collecting narrative descriptions of classroom behaviors.
5. Morine system: A method for creating an observation instrument that can be used to examine behaviors of particular interest.
6. Blumberg system: An instrument that examines the interactions of a teacher and supervisor or teacher educator in conference.[2]

Flanders Interaction Analysis Categories

Purpose. The Flanders system investigates the verbal behaviors of a teacher and students in a classroom setting in order to enhance understanding and thus improve teaching behavior (Amidon and Flanders, 1971). The Flanders system of verbal interaction analysis is probably the best known and most

---

[2] We include the Blumberg system here because of its implications for the practice of teacher development. Its utility should be more obvious in our discussion of teacher developmental environments (Chapter 6) and the clinical process of teacher development (Chapter 7).

widely used observation instrument available. Originally designed as a research instrument, it has become a popular training device for pre-service and
in-service teachers.[3]

Flanders suggests several reasons that teachers should study and understand their own verbal behaviors. He states that it is crucial for teachers to
learn as much as possible about their own methods of working with students,
for it is not until teachers understand their own methods that discrepancies
between teaching intentions and teaching performances can be reduced.
Furthermore, he suggests that studying one's own behavior is particularly
rewarding, for it is one aspect of teaching that, given proper support and
opportunity, can be changed.

Description. The Flanders system (summarized in Table 3–1) is composed of
ten categories of verbal behavior. These are divided into three major sections:
teacher talk, student talk, and silence and confusion.

The first section of the Flanders system consists of seven categories of
teacher verbal behavior that are classified as either direct or indirect. *Indirect
teacher statements* are those that give students greater opportunity to respond. They include the following teacher verbal behaviors: accepting student
feelings or emotions that may be either enjoyable or uncomfortable (category
1), praising or encouraging students with a word or phrase, or making jokes
that release tension (category 2), indicating an acceptance of students' ideas by
paraphrasing, restating, or summarizing what they have said (category 3), and
asking questions that may be either narrow or broad (category 4). In contrast
to indirect statements, *direct teacher statements* tend to restrict or minimize
student responses. They include such teacher verbal behaviors as lecturing or
giving information, facts, opinions, or ideas (category 5), giving directions or
making statements that result in student compliance (category 6), and criticizing or justifying authority (category 7) by telling students, in effect, to change
their behavior.

The second section of the Flanders system consists of two categories of
student talk. Student talk-response (category 8) refers to student responses to
questions that are narrow or convergent. This category also includes student
behaviors that indicate compliance with teacher directions. Student talk-
initiation (category 9) refers to verbal behavior that is an expression of a
student's own opinions or ideas. This type of behavior often occurs as a result
of teachers asking broad or divergent questions.

The third section of the Flanders system is composed of a single category of
silence or confusion (category 10). This category refers to classroom communi-

[3] Ned A. Flanders, *Teacher Influence, Pupil Attitudes, and Achievement.* University of Minnesota, Minneapolis, Minnesota, November 30, 1960. Final report, cooperative research project,
number 397.

TABLE 3–1
Summary of Flanders Interaction Analysis Categories †

Teacher Talk	Indirect Influence	1.	*Accepts feeling
		2.	*Praises or encourages
		3.	*Accepts or uses ideas of students
		4.	*Asks questions
	Direct Influence	5.	*Lecturing
		6.	*Giving directions
		7.	*Criticizing or justifying authority
Student Talk		8.	*Student talk — response
		9.	*Student talk — initiation
		10.	*Silence or confusion

* No scale is implied by these numbers; each number merely designates a particular kind of communication event. To write these numbers down during observation is to enumerate, not to judge a position on a scale.

† Adapted from N. A. Flanders, *Analyzing teacher behavior* (Reading, Mass.: Addison-Wesley, 1970).

cation that is garbled, to periods of silence, or to periods when the observer cannot determine who is talking.

Procedures for Implementation. The Flanders system can be used to examine teacher-student verbal behaviors in any classroom setting, regardless of student age or class content. In order to acquire information that is valid, reliable, and useful, an observer must do three things. First, he or she must be able to recognize and consistently record verbal behaviors as they occur. This requires that each of the ten categories be committed to memory and called up on demand. Second, behaviors must be coded in the sequence in which they occur. For example, if a teacher gives a direction and a student responds, then a 6 must be recorded, followed immediately by an 8. Third, behaviors must be sampled to yield a reliable representation of what actually occurs in the classroom. Flanders suggests recording a category number every 2.5 to 3.5 seconds during a selected period of time within a lesson.

The first and most important requirement is that an observer be accurate in fitting category numbers to verbal behaviors. As the following transcript of classroom dialogue and corresponding category numbers illustrate, the variability of classroom discourse can make observation quite demanding.

TEACHER: "Would one of you tell us about your book review?" (4)
FIRST STUDENT: "I reviewed *All the President's Men*." (8)
TEACHER: "What did you like about the book?" (4)
FIRST STUDENT: "It was a fascinating account of Watergate written by the reporters who uncovered the scandal." (9)
TEACHER: "It sounds as though you really felt the book was exciting." (1)
TEACHER: "We should all read this book." (5)
SECOND STUDENT: "I didn't like it." (9)
TEACHER: "Wait to speak until I call on you." (7)

Through practice, an observer can develop the skill to categorize various teacher-student behaviors consistently. Flanders suggests using a set of ground rules, some of which follow.

1. When uncertain about placing a statement in one of two categories, choose a category on the scale that is farthest from category 5.
2. If the teacher's behavior is either consistently direct or consistently indirect, avoid shifting from one classification to the other unless such a shift is clearly indicated by the teacher.
3. Record such teacher statements as "Uh hum," "yes," "yeah," "all right," and "okay" as a 2 (encouragement) when they occur between two 9 statements by the student.
4. Record an 8 when several students respond to a narrow question in unison.

In addition to coding teacher-student behaviors accurately and consistently, observers must record these behaviors in sequence as they occur. This may be done in one of two ways. Flanders, Werner, Elder, Newman, and Lai (1974) have recommended using a timeline (Figure 3–1) designed to facilitate coding in sequence and interpreting final results. Row numbers refer to the interaction analysis categories, with the most frequently encountered categories grouped in the middle. Each column represents a three-second interval. The observer places a check mark or number in the appropriate cell from left to right across the time line to coincide with the observed behavior. Although the time-line is a useful device, it involves memorizing the categories in a prescribed order—a requirement which may detract from its utility.

A second method of preserving the sequence of behaviors and, at the same time, facilitating the interpretation of final results may be even more useful.

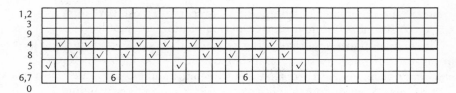

FIGURE 3–1. Time line for Coding Flanders Categories. [Adapted from Flanders, and others. *A minicourse on interaction analysis* (San Francisco, Calif.: Far West Laboratory for Educational Research and Development, 1974), p. 17.]

In his earlier writings, Flanders recommended drawing vertical lines on a sheet of horizontally lined paper and recording category numbers in columns instead of in rows (Figure 3–2). Twenty codings in a column equal one minute of coded observation. This method, as opposed to the timeline, demands neither learning the categories in a prescribed order nor possessing a special form for observation.

The final requirement for using the Flanders system is that observers must obtain representative samples of teacher-student verbal behaviors. Flanders suggests recording a category number about every three seconds, whether or not there is any change in behavior. If a teacher lectures continually for about thirty seconds, for example, the observer would record ten fives. Before an observer starts to code, Flanders recommends that he or she spend five to ten minutes in orientation to the classroom. Once coding has begun, it must stop when a change in activity makes coding inappropriate (for example, when silent reading takes place). No exact amount of time is required for observation; some observers, who are experienced in the use of the system, believe that ten minutes during the middle of a lesson is more than enough time to get a good idea of what typically occurs in a particular classroom.

Once a teacher educator memorizes the categories and practices them on transcripts of dialogue and live examples, use of the system becomes fairly automatic. Flanders estimates that after six to ten hours of practice, an observer can make appropriate judgment easily and consistently.

Procedures for Data Analysis. Organizing and interpreting data obtained from the Flanders system can be simple or elaborate, depending on one's needs. Flanders suggests organizing recorded observations in a matrix of ten rows by ten columns, numbered to correspond with the categories of the system. Overlapping pairs of observations are entered in the appropriate cells of the matrix; then, row, column, and cell totals are analyzed in various ways to study particular patterns of behavior. This method is revealing, especially for research, but it is cumbersome when used to translate results into practice.

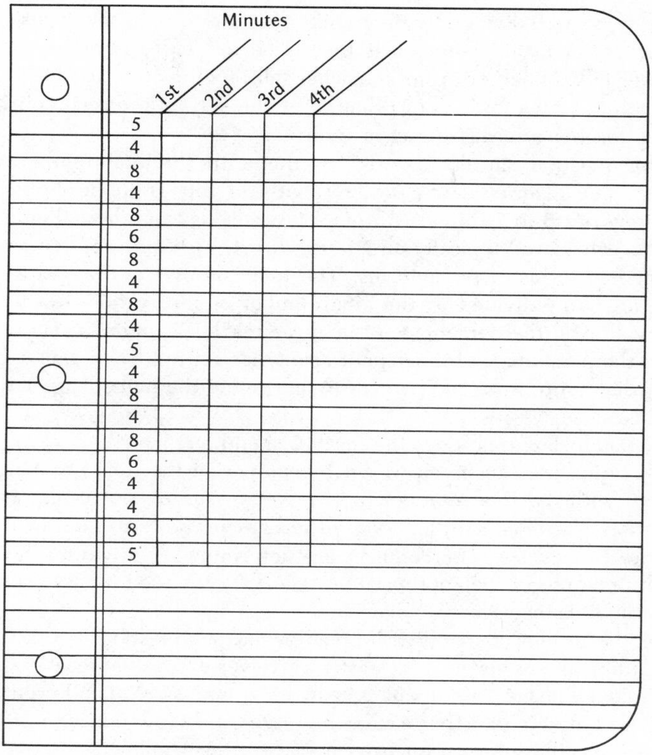

FIGURE 3–2. Coding Flanders Categories on Ruled Paper.

There is usually not enough time to perform these operations and then explain the results to teachers.

Instead of using a matrix, teacher educators might prefer to organize and interpret data obtained from the system by posing various questions that relate to the tasks teachers are trying to accomplish. The following questions are adapted from Amidon and Flanders (1971) and represent possible directions for data organization and analysis:

    1. What is the relationship of teacher talk to student talk?

        This can be answered by comparing the total number of observations of categories 8 and 9 with the total number of observations of categories 1 to 7. In order to determine what percentage of time the teacher talks, one would add the number of observed categories 1, 2, 3, 4, 5, 6, and 7 and divide that number by the total number of observations in categories 1 to 9. The percentage of student talk equals the number of observations in categories 8 and 9 divided by the number of observations of categories 1 to 9. There is no magic percentage that indicates an appropriate amount of teacher talk. Whether or not a teacher talks too much or too little depends on both the situation and on what he or she is trying to accomplish.

2. Is the teacher typically direct or indirect?

This question can be answered by comparing the total number of observations of categories 1 to 4 (indirect) with the total number of observations of categories 5 to 7 (direct). If one total exceeds the other, then a teacher can be considered typically direct or indirect. This question can also be examined in terms of percentages. The total number of observations of categories 1 to 4 divided by the total number of observations of categories 1 to 7 will yield the percentage of time the teacher is indirect. Having calculated the percentage of time spent using indirect influence, one would subtract that figure from 100 percent to determine the percentage of direct influence.

3. How much class time does the teacher spend lecturing?

This question can be answered by comparing the total number in category 5 with the total number of observations in all categories. This same question can, of course, be asked of teacher praise, criticism, or direction-giving. In each case, percentages are determined by dividing the number of observations of the appropriate category by the total number of observations in all categories.

4. Does the teacher generally ask broad or narrow questions?

Finding an answer to this question involves examining teacher questions (4) in relationship to student responses (8 and 9). A 4 followed by an 8 usually indicates that the teacher has asked a narrow question or one that solicits specific information from a student. A 4 followed by a 9, on the other hand, would indicate that the teacher has asked a broad question or one that calls for students to use higher levels of thinking in order to answer. A preponderance of fours followed by eights would indicate a tendency toward narrow questions. A greater number of fours followed by nines would mean that the teacher generally uses broad or divergent questions.

5. How does the teacher typically communicate subject matter?

This question can be answered in several ways. One can examine the number of fives, or instances of lecturing. The percentage of time spent lecturing can be calculated as noted previously. Further, when fives appear in a long, uninterrupted sequence, that is an indication of extended lecturing, or one-way communication. It is also possible to determine the opportunities teachers provide for student participation by examining the data for particular pairs of behaviors that indicate how the teacher transmits subject matter, for example, 5–4 (lecture-question), 4–8 (question-student response), 4–9 (question-student initiation), 8–4 (student response-question), and 9–4 (student initiation-question).

Analyzing data obtained from the Flanders systems, as described here, has one distinct disadvantage: the element of sequence is lost. The analysis reveals, for example, how much time a teacher spends praising and criticizing, but it does not reveal *when* these behaviors occur. In order to overcome this deficiency and yet avoid tabulating data in matrix form, the teacher educator might refer to the raw data collected. By scanning the originally coded categories, it is possible to determine not only what behaviors have been demonstrated but when particular behaviors occurred.

Comments. Flanders has enriched his initial ten categories by encouraging observers to use subscripts when coding. An interesting and potentially valuable teaching concept that may be noted in a subscript is that of *because-extension statements* (Flanders, Werner, Elder, Newman, and Lai, 1974). *A because-extension statement is an explanation that accompanies a particular teacher statement.* For instance, if a teacher were to say, "Read Chapter Two *because* it suggests why Rommel lost North Africa," the statement would be categorized as 6_B (giving directions with a because-extension). The because-extension also applies to a teacher's use of praise (2_B) or criticism (7_B). That is, if a teacher explains *why* he or she is praising or criticizing, then a *B* subscript may be coded. Research and practice suggest that when students understand why they are supposed to comply with directions, why they are being praised, and why they are being criticized, the positive impact of such teacher statements is enhanced.

Galloway System

Purpose. The Galloway system investigates the nonverbal behaviors of teacher and students in the classroom to understand more fully how people communicate without words and thus how teaching behavior may be improved. According to Galloway (1968), nonverbal cues operate as a part of a silent language that influences teacher-student understandings and interactions. Although other systems of nonverbal behavior analysis are used for research and training, this appears to be one of the most popular.

As Galloway suggests, it is important that teachers study and understand their own nonverbal behaviors.[4] By their gestures, body movements, or facial expressions, he points out, teachers can either inhibit or encourage student participation in the classroom. He also points out that students use teachers' nonverbal behaviors to check the fidelity or authenticity of their verbal statements. The teacher who is unaware of the impact of his or her own nonverbal cues on students, therefore, runs the risk of transmitting conflicting or confusing messages.

[4] Charles Galloway, "An exploratory study of observational procedures for determining teacher nonverbal communication." Unpublished doctoral dissertation, University of Florida, Gainesville, 1962, University Microfilms Number 6206529.

TABLE 3–2
Summary of Categories for the Galloway System in Relationship to
Flanders Interaction Analysis Categories*

Verbal Categories (Flanders)	Nonverbal Categories (Galloway)
1. Accepts student feeling	(None)
2. Praises or encourages	Congruent-Incongruent
3. Accepts or uses ideas of students	Implement-Perfunctory
4. Asks questions	Personal-Impersonal
5. Lectures	Responsive-Unresponsive
6. Gives directions	Involve-Dismiss
7. Criticizes or justifies authority	Firm-Harsh
8. Student Talk-Response	Receptive-Inattentive
9. Student Talk-Initiation	Receptive-Inattentive
10. Silence or Confusion	Comfort-Distress

* Adapted from R. L. French and C. M. Galloway, A description of teacher behavior, verbal and nonverbal (ERIC document ED028 134, 1968), p. 6.

Description. The Galloway system, adapted from his original dissertation research and summarized in Table 3–2, is composed of nine categories of nonverbal communicative behavior. These correspond generally to the ten categories of verbal behavior developed by Flanders. Galloway's categories, however, refer mainly to *teacher* nonverbal behavior. Only the final category may refer to teacher or student behaviors. Each category in the Galloway system represents a continuum of behaviors ranging from encouraging to restricting interaction in the classroom.

According to French and Galloway (1968), the nonverbal and verbal behaviors associated with Flanders's category 1 (accepts students' feelings) are so closely related that distinguishing nonverbal from verbal behaviors is extremely difficult. The first of Flanders's categories, therefore, does not have a nonverbal equivalent in the Galloway system. The first Galloway category (congruent-incongruent) corresponds to the Flanders's category 2 (praises or encourages). When teachers praise or encourage verbally, their nonverbal cues indicate the degree to which the praise or encouragement is genuine (congruent with verbals) or insincere (incongruent with verbals). Galloway's second category (implement-perfunctory) corresponds to Flanders's third category (accepts and uses ideas of students). When teachers verbally accept students' ideas, their own nonverbal cues will indicate whether that acceptance means merely acknowledgement (perfunctory behavior) or if they really find the idea useful (implementing behavior). Galloway's third category (personal-impersonal) corresponds to Flanders's fourth category (asks questions). When teachers ask questions in a personal manner, they convey a sense of warmth, nearness, or proximity. When they ask questions in an impersonal manner, they avoid face-to-face confrontation or intimate physical expression and thus convey a sense of distance or detachment. The fourth category (responsive-unresponsive) corresponds to Flanders's fifth category (lectures). When a teacher changes the pace and direction of his or her own talk because students appear bored or inattentive, this is responsive behavior. Teacher talk that does not take student nonverbal cues into consideration is unresponsive.

The fifth category (involve-dismiss) is associated with Flanders's sixth category (gives directions). When a teacher gives directions for learning or maintenance tasks and seeks student clarification, such behavior is involvement. If, however, the teacher communicates in a nonverbal way that directions are intended to control student activity, this behavior is considered as dismissing. Galloway's sixth category (firm-harsh) corresponds to Flanders's seventh category (criticizes or justifies authority). As one might suspect, harsh but unspoken teacher behaviors can be hostile, severe, and aggressive. Firm teacher nonverbal behaviors associated with criticism are characterized as crisp, clean, and intended to clarify expectations. Galloway's seventh and eighth categories (receptive-inattentive) are associated with Flanders's eighth and ninth categories (student talk-response and student talk-initiation). The teacher who is nonverbally receptive to student talk listens, makes eye contact with students, and changes facial expressions. But the teacher who is inattentive to student talk may neither listen nor make eye contact and may perhaps move about the room as a student speaks. Galloway's last category (comfort-distress) corresponds to Flanders's silence or confusion category. Moments of comfortable silence or confusion are those in which people work, reflect, or think. Periods of distressing silence or confusion, on the other hand, are those moments of embarrassment, tension, or disorientation.

Procedures for Implementation. The Galloway system is designed to allow the observer to use the categories, time intervals, and ground rules of the Flanders system. In fact, it is designed to be applied at the same time one uses the Flanders system. The Galloway system, like Flanders's, can be applied to any classroom setting regardless of class content. In order to record nonverbal behavior while using the Flanders system, the observer marks a slash (encouraging) or dash (restricting) to the right of the recorded Flanders tallies. The observer circles a category number when teacher behavior is solely nonverbal. If, however (as often happens), a teacher's nonverbal cues are neither encouraging nor restricting but pro forma (expressions, actions, or voice intonations that convey no communicative significance), the Flanders category stands as is.

The following transcript of classroom dialogue, which was used earlier in the Flanders section, illustrates how the Galloway categories can be used in conjunction with Flanders.

TEACHER: "Would one of you tell us about your book review?" (4/, teacher moves away from desk and toward class.)

FIRST STUDENT: "I reviewed *All the President's Men.*" (8/, teacher smiles and moves toward student.)

TEACHER: "What did you like about the book?" (4/, teacher continues to smile.)

FIRST STUDENT: "It was a fascinating account of Watergate written by reporters who uncovered the scandal." (9/, teacher sits in chair next to student and raises brow.)

TEACHER: "It sounds as though you really felt the book was exciting." (1, no Galloway category recorded here.)

TEACHER: "We should all read this book." (5/, teacher responds by turning to the whole class.)

SECOND STUDENT: "I didn't like it." (9-, teacher turns abruptly to face second student.)

TEACHER: "Wait to speak until I call on you." (7-, teacher frowns.)

TEACHER: (⑦, glares at student but says nothing.)

To reiterate, each Galloway category of nonverbal behavior is conceptualized in terms of a continuum that moves from encouraging to restricting behavior. These categories are useful, therefore, to better understand the nonverbal cues that may encourage or restrict student participation. Out of the seemingly limitless range of possible nonverbal cues that a teacher might signal, Galloway (1962) suggests looking to facial expressions, actions, and vocal language (voice quality) as indicators of a teacher's intent to encourage or restrict students (Table 3–3).

Data Analysis. Organizing and interpreting data obtained from the Galloway system may follow the methods used with the Flanders Interaction Analysis Categories. French and Galloway have also suggested using a matrix of ten rows by ten columns but suggest adding a third dimension of nonverbal behavior. This method of analysis seems to be much too elaborate for practical purposes. It also suggests a certain degree of precision, both in the observation and in the analysis of nonverbal behaviors, that is unlikely to be achieved under ordinary circumstances.

Instead, teacher educators might more usefully organize and interpret data from the Galloway system by asking and answering questions that relate directly to tasks teachers must accomplish. The following questions represent some possible directions for the organization and analysis of data on nonverbal behaviors.

1. What is the relationship of a teacher's encouraging nonverbal behavior to his or her restricting nonverbal behavior?

    The relationship of encouraging to restricting nonverbal cues can be obtained by dividing the total number of encouraging (/) observations by the grand total of encouraging (/) and restricting (-) observations. This fraction or decimal can be converted to a percentage for ease of interpretation.

TABLE 3–3
Encouraging and Restricting Teacher Nonverbal Behaviors*

Encouraging (/)	*Restricting (−)*
Teacher's facial expression connotes enjoyment or satisfaction.	Teacher avoids eye contact, thus communicating inattention, disinterest, or unwillingness to listen.
Teacher's facial expression implies understanding or acceptance of a student's need or problem.	Teacher's facial expression implies that he or she is unenthusiastic, condescending, impatient, unsympathetic.
Teacher maintains eye contact and indicates patience, attention, and willingness to listen.	Teacher scowls, frowns, sneers.
Teacher moves toward students.	Teacher slouches or stands with a don't care attitude or with an attitude that he or she is engrossed in own work or thought.
Teacher pats student on back.	
Teacher uses gesture that indicates student is on the right track.	Teacher uses gestures to indicate that students stop, e.g. hand up, waving, anger.
Teacher stands or sits in a way that suggests alertness or readiness to respond to student.	Teacher pokes, slaps, grabs student.
Teacher's voice intonation or inflection suggests approval or support.	Teacher uses vocal utterance to indicate that students are to stop talking or one that interrupts, e.g. "shhh," "ugh."
Teacher utters approval or suggests that student go on, e.g. "um-hm."	Teacher's voice intonation or inflection connotes antagonism, irritability, depreciation, or discouragement.
Teacher displays understanding, compassion, supportiveness by laughing.	

* Adapted from C. M. Galloway, An exploratory study of observational procedures for determining teacher nonverbal communication. (Doctoral dissertation, University of Florida, 1962).

2. How much time does a teacher spend using encouraging (or restricting) nonverbal cues in the classroom?

An estimate of time so spent can be calculated by dividing the total number of encouraging or restricting observations by the total number of encouraging, restricting, and pro forma observations. This figure, too, can be converted to a percentage.

3. Are a teacher's questions usually accompanied by nonverbal cues that encourage or restrict student communication?

This question might be answered by comparing the number of fours with slash and the number of fours with dash. The same question can, of course, be asked of teacher directions, teacher praise, or teacher reaction to student talk.

As noted in the discussion of Flanders's methods of data analysis, bypassing the matrix in favor of asking and answering questions risks destroying the notion of sequence of behaviors. One can determine *what,* but not *when,* a teacher exhibits certain behaviors. Here, too, we suggest that a teacher educator remedy the situation by looking to the original data to determine when nonverbal behaviors occur. For example, by studying the slashes and dashes, one might find an early pattern of encouragement followed by a let-down later in a lesson.

Comments. Recording and analyzing nonverbal behaviors must be done cautiously. Nonverbal behaviors can be quite ambiguous and thus subject to a variety of interpretations. Attaching meaning to a facial expression, gesture, or particular voice intonation also requires the observer to make value judgments. An observer's assumptions and inferences might well be checked by examining a videotape of a teacher's behavior. A taped segment of activity would allow the observer and the observed together to examine nonverbal cues after the fact and thus reduce the ambiguity of some behaviors. Cogan (1973) suggests that analyses of nonverbal behavior on tape or film follow these steps:

1. Review film without sound. Review and check nonverbal patterns.
2. Review the film in shorter takes. Record impressions for each take.
3. Review the entire film with sound. Record general impressions about students' learnings, students' behaviors, and the teacher's behavior.
4. For closer analysis or micro-scanning, some researchers use a time-motion analyzer, which permits the viewer to examine the sound film frame by frame. This is especially useful in identifying complex and rapid nonverbal behavior that is otherwise not apprehended by the analyst. Such sophistication should perhaps be avoided by the naive observer. Clinical supervisors might be well advised to stick to simple behavior and gross analysis at present.

Teachers, of course, communicate nonverbally without even being present in the classroom. The way they arrange furniture, decorate bulletin boards, organize desks, and so forth may imply a propensity for either encouraging or restricting student participation. Inferences that are drawn from these kinds of nonverbal behaviors, as well as the nonverbal cues signaled by teachers during the course of instruction, must be made cautiously, however. Just because desks are arranged in rows or in a circle does not automatically mean the teacher is restricting or encouraging student participation.

The Kounin System

Purpose. The purpose of the Kounin system is to investigate a teacher's classroom management and discipline techniques.[5] It is concerned with the relationship between teacher management behaviors, pupil work involvement, and pupil deviancy or misbehavior in the classroom. Kounin's research has focused on the behaviors of teachers and pupils in a variety of situations, from kindergarten through college. The system presented here is derived from

[5] Jacob Kounin, *Discipline and group management in classrooms.* (New York: Holt, Rinehart and Winston, 1970).

Kounin's (1970) videotape analysis of seventy-nine urban and suburban elementary classrooms. Although designed for purposes of research, the system has been adapted for training (see Borg, 1974).

Description. The Kounin system, summarized in Table 3–4, is composed of two sections—a pupil observation schedule and a teacher observation schedule. The first examines pupil work involvement and deviancy. Pupil work involvement, which consists of three categories, is defined as the amount of time pupils spend engaged in assigned academic work. The first category is labeled *definitely in.* A pupil who is definitely in the assigned work

TABLE 3–4
Kounin Categories for Observing Classroom Management and Discipline*

Categories of Pupil Behavior	

I. Work Involvement
  A. Definitely in
  B. Probably in
  C. Definitely out
	II. Deviancy
	  A. No misbehavior
	  B. Mild misbehavior
	  C. Serious misbehavior

Categories of Teacher Management Behavior	

I. Desist Techniques
  A. "With-it-ness"
    1. Target
    2. Timing
  B. Overlapping
    1. None
    2. Some
 	
II. Movement Management
  A. Smoothness-Jerkiness
    1. Stimulus-bounded
    2. Thrust
    3. Dangle
    4. Truncation
    5. Flip-flop
  B. Momentum
    1. Overdwelling
    2. Fragmentation
	III. Group Focus
	  A. Alerting
	    1. Create suspense
	    2. Pick reciter randomly
	    3. Mass unison response
	    4. Alert nonperformers to possibility of being called on
	    5. Present new or novel material
	    6. Ignore group in favor of reciter
	    7. Prepick reciter before asking question
	    8. Predetermine sequence of reciters
	  B. Accountability
	    1. Ask students to hold up props
	    2. Actively attend to mass unison response
	    3. Bring in others
	    4. Ask for raised hands and require performance
	    5. Circulate and check products of nonreciters
	    6. Require student to demonstrate and check performance

* From Kounin, J. S. *Discipline and group management in classrooms.* (New York: Holt, Rinehart and Winston, 1970).

exhibits such behaviors as writing in a workbook, performing or volunteering to recite, reading, or visually attending. The second category is referred to as *probably in*. A pupil who is probably in the assigned work demonstrates involvement by looking at the props or having materials before him or her as though thinking or listening, but does not show clear signs of being definitely involved. The third category of work involvement is labeled *definitely out*. A pupil who is definitely out of the assigned work shows no indications, either through action or posture, of being involved in the assigned work.

Pupil deviancy, which is also divided into three categories, is defined as intentional misbehavior directed against a teacher, another child, or some classroom convention. The first category is labeled *no misbehaving*. A pupil who is engaging in no misbehavior is not purposefully acting out against another child, the teacher, or in defiance of a classroom convention. In the second category, *mild misbehavior*, a pupil may exhibit behavior of which most teachers would disapprove under the circumstances (whispering to neighbors during seatwork, making faces at a camera, or reading a comic book). The third category of pupil deviancy, *serious misbehavior*, describes a pupil who demonstrates highly aggressive or violent behavior that interferes with others, damages property, harms himself or herself or others, or violates an important school code.

The teacher observation schedule, the second section of the Kounin system, examines teacher behaviors related to stopping misbehavior, making transitions from one activity to another, and utilizing techniques that keep the group involved. The teacher observation schedule, therefore, is divided into three separate parts referred to as *desist techniques, movement management,* and *group focus*. Desist techniques include "with-it-ness" and overlapping. The "with-it-ness" category is defined as the teacher's ability to communicate to pupils by action that he or she "knows what's going on"—or, as Kounin puts it, "has eyes in the back of her head." A teacher who is "with it" stops the misbehaving pupil and does so in a timely fashion, that is, in a way that is on target and in time. If, however, a teacher stops the wrong pupil or a minor offender while allowing more serious misbehavior to go unchecked (off-target), and the deviant behavior spreads or increases in seriousness (untimely), then the teacher is not "with it." The overlapping category is defined as the teacher's ability to handle more than one matter at a time. Although overlapping is listed as a category of desist techniques, overlapping may occur during events other than those related to misbehavior. For example, a teacher may be listening to one pupil read and be interrupted by another pupil with a question or comment. If the teacher attends to both pupils, he or she would be said to exhibit "some overlapping." If, when faced with two or more issues, a teacher were immersed in the initial ongoing activity, or dropped the initial activity totally to attend to an intruding activity, then, he or she would be said to exhibit no overlapping behavior.

The second part of the teacher observation schedule, referred to as movement management, also contains two categories: smoothness-jerkiness and momentum. The smoothness-jerkiness category is defined as the teacher's behaviors that interfere with the smooth flow of academic activities. This category is broken into five subcategories.

1. Stimulus-bounded. In order to be stimulus-bounded, a teacher must be engaged with a group of children and then distracted by a fairly unobtrusive event external to the ongoing activity, becoming totally immersed in that external event. Kounin uses the analogy of an iron filing being pulled to a magnet to describe the kind of behavior exhibited by a teacher who is stimulus-bounded.

2. Thrust. A teacher who bursts in on the pupil's activites with an order, statement, or question in such a way as to indicate that his or her own interest or desire is the only determinant of the interjection is said to demonstrate thrust. That is, the teacher shows no signs of being aware of a child's or a group's readiness to receive his or her order.

3. Dangle. A teacher who begins, or has been engaged in, some activity and then leaves it hanging in midair only to return to it much later is said to demonstrate dangle.

4. Truncation. Here the teacher stops an activity abruptly and never resumes it.

5. Flip-flop. A teacher who terminates one activity, starts another, and then initiates a return to the previously terminated activity is said to have demonstrated a flip-flop.

Momentum, the second major category of movement management, refers to the pace of instruction and has two subcategories.

1. Overdwelling. A teacher who engages in extended action or talk that is clearly beyond what is necessary for most pupils' understanding is said to overdwell. Overdwelling may take various forms ("preaching" or "nagging" about misbehavior, overemphasizing the use of such props as pencils, books, crayons, or giving too many directions or lengthy explanations).

2. Fragmentation. A teacher who demonstrates fragmentation impedes or slows down the momentum of the class by breaking an activity into subparts when it could be performed as a single unit and thus creates periods in which pupils have nothing to do. For example, a teacher who calls members of a reading group up to the table, one by one, when he or she might call the whole group at once, demonstrates fragmentation.

The third part of the teacher observation schedule is referred to as group focus, which includes two categories: alerting and accountability. The alerting category is defined in terms of the techniques teachers use to involve nonreciting children in a recitation task. Generally, anything the teacher does overtly to help students other than those reciting become attentive and involved is considered to be alerting behavior. In his research, Kounin notes the following five positive alerting cues (which enhance the involvement of nonreciters in a recitation task).

1. Any method used to create suspense before calling on a child to recite: pausing and looking around to "bring children in" before selecting a reciter; saying, "Let's see now, who can . . ." before calling on a reciter.
2. Keeping children in suspense in regard to who will be called on next; picking reciters randomly so that no child knows whether he will be called on next or not.
3. Teacher calls on different children frequently or maintains group focus: intersperses mass unison responses; says, "Let's put our thinking caps on; this might fool you," asks group for show of hands before selecting a reciter.
4. Teacher alerts nonperformers that they might be called on in connection with what a reciter is doing: They may be called on if reciter makes a mistake; presignals children that they will be asked about recitation content in the immediate future.
5. Teacher presents new, novel, or alluring material into a recitation (a high attention value prop or issue).

The accountability category is defined in terms of the techniques a teacher uses to hold students responsible for their task performances during recitation sessions. In general, a teacher exhibits accountability cues by requiring students to produce or demonstrate work that is being done in the current setting and monitors these demonstrations. It should be noted that accountability and "with-it-ness" are very similar concepts. "With-it-ness" refers to communicated knowledgeability about behavior and misbehavior. Accountability, however, refers to communicated knowledgeability about students' task performances during specific recitation sessions. Kounin presents the following kinds of teacher behaviors as examples of accountability cues.

1. Teacher asks children to hold up their props, exposing performances or answers in such a manner as to be readily visible to the teacher.
2. Teacher requires children to recite in unison while the teacher shows signs of actively attending to the recitation.
3. Teacher brings other children into the performance of a child reciting. (Teacher says, "Jimmy, you watch Johnny do that problem and then tell me what he did right or wrong.")
4. Teacher asks for the raised hands of children who are prepared to demonstrate a performance and requires some of them to demonstrate.
5. Teacher circulates and checks products of nonreciters during a child's performance.
6. Teacher requires a child to demonstrate and checks his performance.

Kounin presents one other concept that bears noting—that of *satiation*. He discusses satiation in terms of the potential of the classroom environment to reduce or satiate student interest in particular learning activities. In Kounin's research, the concept of satiation was applied to seatwork activities, as opposed to recitation work. Video tapes were studied to determine the degree to which repetition and variety of activities affected student behavior as students worked alone at their desks. The results of these studies indicated that when a variety of seatwork activities was provided for first- and second-grade children, students were more involved and less deviant. In contrast, variety of seatwork activities for third- and fifth-grade children was related negatively to their work involvement and disruptive behavior. As Kounin suggests, program planning to reduce satiation is an important management task for teachers, but planning may need to be done differently for younger children than for older.

Because of the difficulty of assessing satiation without video tape recording equipment, this category is not included on the observation schedules. The important point to remember, however, is that the appropriateness of different management techniques can depend on the students in question and whether a teacher is dealing with recitation (where group focus and movement management are relevant) or with seatwork (where avoiding satiation is most relevant).

Procedures for Implementation.   The Kounin system can be applied in a variety of classroom settings, regardless of student age or class content, and is a useful tool in the analysis of management tasks. In order to observe both teacher and pupil behavior simultaneously, however, one must make a video or audio tape of a classroom episode and apply the observation schedules to the tape. Because it is not always feasible to tape classroom behavior, it is suggested that the system might be applied to live classroom episodes by observing teacher and pupils independently.

Applying the pupil observation schedule involves observing pupils at regular intervals and coding their behaviors according to work involvement and deviancy. Kounin has suggested constructing a schematic diagram of the classroom prior to coding so as to draw representative samples of pupil behavior. The map divides the classroom into quadrants representing major areas of pupil activity, as shown in Figure 3–3. Once the schematic is constructed, the observer randomly identifies one boy (B) and one girl (G) in each quadrant to be observed. The selected pupils are then observed and coded by quadrant for ten-second intervals over a number of minutes. For example, an observer looks at B_1 and G_1 and codes how each of these pupils spends the majority of his and her time during the ten-second interval. At the end of the interval, the observer looks to B_2 and G_2 and so on. Table 3–5 illustrates how coded pupil behavior might appear.

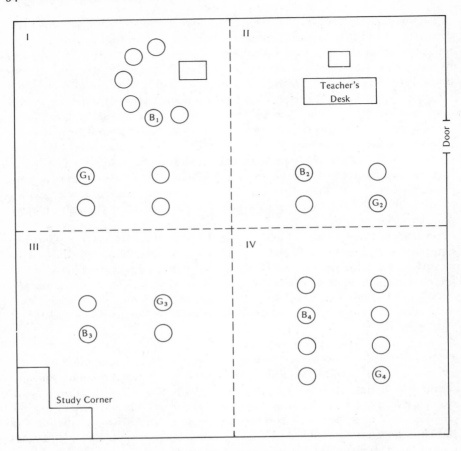

FIGURE 3–3. An Example of a Schematic Diagram of a Classroom.

The teacher observation schedule is applied by following a somewhat different set of procedures. Particular teacher behaviors are noted only when they appear, not at regular, pre-established points in time. Table 3–6 illustrates how coded teacher behavior might appear.

It is virtually impossible for one person to observe teacher and pupil behaviors simultaneously without the aid of tape recording equipment. An observer might, therefore, spend some time observing pupils to establish a base line of pupil work involvement and deviancy, and then turn his or her attention to teacher behaviors. The major disadvantages of this approach are that conclusions drawn about connections between pupil and teacher behaviors are more speculative because they are based on different time samples and, of course,

TABLE 3-5
An Example of Coded Pupil Behavior Using Kounin System

	B$_1$	G$_1$	B$_2$	G$_2$	B$_3$	G$_3$	B$_4$	G$_4$
	+N	√N						
			+N	√N				
					−M	−M		
							+N	+N
	+N	√N						
1 minute			+N	√N				
					−M	−M		
							+N	+N
	√N	√N						
			+N	√N				
					√N	−M		
2 minutes							+N	+N

Work Involvement: + = Definitely in
√ = Probably in
− = Definitely out

Deviancy: N = No misbehavior
M = Mild misbehavior
S = Serious misbehavior

there is no taped record that can be replayed to check the accuracy of one's observations. With practice, however, an observer's accuracy and consistency will increase.

Data Analysis. Organizing and interpreting data obtained from the Kounin system, just as with the systems presented earlier, can be accomplished in several ways. Scores for individual pupils on work involvement can be calculated by comparing the number of intervals coded as "definitely in" to the number of intervals observed. The scores on individual students can then be averaged to arrive at a score for classroom work involvement. In order to obtain a measure of the rate of pupil deviancy, Kounin suggests calculating the percentage of ten-second intervals in which no misbehavior occurred. Thus, the deviancy rate is stated in a positive way (freedom from deviancy).

Analysis of teacher behavior coded by the Kounin system might be ac-

TABLE 3–6
An Example of Coded Teacher Behavior Using Kounin System

I. Desist Techniques																

A. With-it-ness

Target: + + − −
Timing: + − + −

(+ = on target or in time; − = off target or too late)

B. Overlapping (Also scored during child intrusions or "bring-ins.")

None: √ √
Some: √ √

(√ indicates demonstrated behavior)

II. Movement Management

A. Smoothness-Jerkiness

Stimulus-Bounded: √ √
Thrust: √ √ √ √
Dangle: √
Truncation:
Flip-Flop: √

(√ indicates demonstrated behavior)

B. Momentum

Overdwelling: √ √ √
Fragmentation: √

(√ indicates demonstrated behavior)

III. Group Focus

A. Alerting: hands up(+), mass response(+), random call ons(+), ignore group (−).

B. Accountability: hold up props, circulate/check, hold up props

complished by scanning the behavior coding sheet and calculating totals by category. The two categories under desist techniques ("with-it-ness" and overlapping) have the potential of conveying "successful" classroom management; that is, plus marks (+) for target and timing and checks (√) for some overlapping are positive behaviors. Various cues of alerting and accountability may also indicate the ability to manage a class effectively. Marks in any other categories are not viewed as indicators of "successful" classroom management.

Kounin's research suggests that "with-it-ness" is more important for a teacher to demonstrate than the ability to overlap; that is, teachers who are "with it" have pupils who typically are involved and do not misbehave. It is also more important to maintain momentum (avoid slowdowns) in recitation sessions than during periods of pupil seatwork. Smoothness (lack of jerkiness) has been found to relate positively to student work involvement and freedom from deviancy.

Comments. Kounin's research has been concerned largely with determining what teachers do that detracts from pupil work involvement and increases the likelihood of pupil deviancy. His system, therefore, draws attention to what teachers should not do as well as what they should do. Borg's (1974) protocol materials, which are designed for training teachers in the use of effective classroom management, expand on some of Kounin's ideas by suggesting other positive management techniques that might be incorporated into the teacher observation schedule. For instance, an observer might look for other desist techniques, such as suggesting alternative behaviors (SAB), or describing desirable behaviors (DDB) to misbehaving pupils, as well as concurrently praising (CP) students for the things they do well. These categories could easily be coded under "with-it-ness" by jotting the appropriate abbreviations in a box or margin. In addition, Borg's work implies that information about movement management might be enriched by noting delayed responses (DR), or responses to external stimuli that occur during natural breaks in activity (as opposed to stimulus-bounded responses). Timely interjections (T) and smooth transitions (ST) could be coded along with thrusts and flip-flops in like manner. Although there are numerous techniques for involving children and controlling misbehavior, it should be noted that many successful teachers often ignore inappropriate behavior rather than step in with a direct technique.

Goldhammer Note-Taking Procedure

Purpose. The purpose of the Goldhammer system[6] is to "capture the realities of lesson objectivity enough and comprehensively enough to enable supervisor and teacher to reconstruct the lesson as validly as possible afterwards" (Goldhammer, 1969). The Goldhammer method of note-taking is similar to other methods of observing behavior in various naturalistic settings (see Brandt, 1972). It was specifically designed, however, to be used by clinical supervisors in their work with teachers. Because Goldhammer's method does not prescribe categories of behavior, it can be used to address a variety of teacher tasks.

---

[6] R. Goldhammer, *Clinical supervision: Special methods for the supervision of teachers* (New York: Holt, Rinehart and Winston, 1969).

Goldhammer suggests several reasons why constructing a narrative of classroom events is desirable. He asserts that observation systems that use preexisting categories are limiting because they determine in advance which behaviors are important and thus may not be valid in a given situation. Further, he suggests that only in having a hypothesis-free, comprehensive written record of what has occurred can one identify patterns of behavior in the classrooms that are credible to teachers and therefore amenable to change.

Description. The Goldhammer note-taking procedure is a process and not a set of pre-established categories for observation. The procedures involve writing down what is seen and heard in the classroom as completely as possible. As Goldhammer points out, however, the observer's job is to record *perceptions,* not *inferences.*

Procedures for Implementation. The following procedures for constructing a written narrative of classroom behavior are adapted from Goldhammer (1969):

1. Record as much verbal and nonverbal behavior as possible. Speeches should be recorded verbatim.
2. Record in the margin of the page (or separate from the actual transcript of events) comments or questions about what is occurring.
3. Record nonverbal behaviors as objectively as possible; that is, try to describe what is observed without making value judgments.
4. Stand or sit in such a way as to be minimally distractive to pupils but with a different vantage point from the teachers.
5. Do not intervene in teaching and learning. If approached by students with questions, explain to them afterward that your job is to write down what is happening in the class.
6. Intervene in teaching and learning only when a prior agreement has been made with the teacher, or when a physical emergency dictates.
7. Note periodically in the margin the time of day.
8. If the pace of the lesson is too rapid to permit complete note-taking, record specific episodes in their entirety rather than incomplete episodes across time.
9. Identify individual students in your notes so that specific responses can later be tied to particular persons. This may be facilitated by using a schematic representation of the classroom and running a tally of verbal participation.

As Goldhammer notes (and as anyone who has tried to construct comprehensive narrations of classroom behavior can testify), it is often difficult to keep pace with the flow of events. To alleviate this difficulty, he suggests several strategies. Multiple observers might be used, one noting verbal behaviors and another recording nonverbal behaviors. Another technique is to use shorthand or speedwriting. The most realistic way to keep pace with the lesson is to use what Goldhammer refers to as "idiosyncratic speedwriting," or writing that omits vowels, employs homonyms and abbreviations, and uses phonetic representations. With this technique, for example, the statement "Sit down and be quiet!" might appear as "st dwn & b qt!" Goldhammer presents the following abbreviations as useful examples in recording behavior:

Don't know = dk
Rather than = rt
Question = q
Teacher = T
Pupil = P# (where # indicates
            an individual pupil)
Raise hand = ψ
No response = –
Two, too, to = 2
Four, fore, for = 4
See, sea = c
You = u
Why = y

One can, of course, develop other abbreviations and signs that are intuitively reasonable. The keys to keeping pace with a lesson are to develop a system of note-taking that is practical and to use it repeatedly.

It might seem that the most obvious way to keep pace with the lesson and also document behavior completely would be to use recording equipment. As Goldhammer points out, however, there are distinct disadvantages to using taped episodes of classroom behavior. Analyzing video or audio recordings is too time-consuming. Playing and replaying tapes in order to formulate salient patterns of behavior takes much more time than is usually available. Also, tape recordings do not offer a visual representation of the entire classroom episode at one time. With written notes, an observer is free to cut-and-paste behaviors that on the surface might appear unconnected but in fact constitute a particular pattern. When time and facilities permit, of course, audio and video recordings may be extremely useful to both teacher and teacher educator.

Data Analysis. As one might expect, the Goldhammer note-taking procedure involves a more subtle kind of organization and interpretation of data than in previously noted procedures. Rather than rely on numerical data, analysis here involves detecting *patterns of behavior* from notes recorded during observation. Goldhammer's emphasis on patterns of behavior is based on the assumptions that teaching is a kind of human behavior that is repeated over time and that the cumulative effect of these patterns on the development of students is greater than the effect of random, isolated teaching behaviors. Data analysis, therefore, is a matter of deriving collections of behaviors that occur during both teaching and learning, categorizing them, and then arranging them in a hierarchical order of importance.

The initial stage in data analysis is one of detecting patterns of behavior that are demonstrable in the data, supported by theory as being important, considered important intuitively by the observer, and relevant to tasks teachers are trying to accomplish. This is accomplished in three steps. The first is to scan the notes for easily identifiable patterns. It may be obvious, for example, that a particular lesson is marked by a good deal of teacher talk, for which a pattern of "teacher centeredness" would be noted. It is also possible that by merely scanning the data, as opposed to reading it carefully for substance, the observer might identify patterns of verbal behavior, such as the use of a particular phrase or type of question. Scanning the data for patterns, therefore, is a matter of looking for obvious visual clues to the repetitious use of particular behaviors. Once the data have been scanned for patterns, the observer concentrates on the substance or content of the notes. A careful reading of the notes will determine what is happening at certain points in the lesson. Goldhammer describes this process as one of looking for the intent of the demonstrated behavior; for instance, do certain words or phrases constitute an unjustifiable imposition of a teacher's own values or attitudes on the students? Having scanned the data and read them for substance, the observer then examines how his or her own value judgments may have affected the formulation of patterns. Although the observer's own network of values and attitudes are undoubtedly in play all along, Goldhammer states that this is the point at which such values and attitudes must be confronted explicitly.

The second step in data analysis—assigning patterns to categories—is accomplished by fitting descriptions to particular sets of patterns. According to Goldhammer, the labels assigned to patterns enable an observer to place the raw data in the context of theory so that they may be understood.

The third and final step of data analysis is to arrange patterns of behaviors in a hierarchy. This is accomplished by evaluating their relative importance in terms of three criteria: saliency, fewness, and treatability. For a pattern to be salient it must (1) appear frequently, (2) have demonstrable effects on students, (3) possess theoretical significance, (4) be important in the lesson, (5) be common among teachers, and (6) be significant for teachers. In order for a pattern to meet the criterion of fewness, or to be one of the few patterns most relevant to the teacher, Goldhammer suggests that one look to (1) its substantive value, (2) the time and energy it would require for change, or (3) its emotional loading. In terms of these kinds of characteristics, the few patterns that are most reasonable would be those that are most important. Finally, for a pattern to be generally treatable, it must be accessible to the teacher or within the teacher's latitude of acceptance and abilities.

The following observation notes (written in conventional language) illustrate the first phase of Goldhammer's system:

1. TEACHER: Now children, today we are going to learn to count up to ten.
2. TIMMY: (Raises hand for recognition.)

3. TEACHER: Not now, Timmy. All right, children, now you say the numbers after me. One, two, three.
4. CLASS: One, two, three.
5. TEACHER: Four, five, six.
6. CLASS: Four, five, six.
7. TEACHER: Seven, eight, nine.
8. CLASS: Seven, eight, nine.
9. TEACHER: Ten.
10. CLASS: Ten.
11. TEACHER: That was good, but I didn't hear everybody's voice. Let's try it again, and this time say the numbers as loud as you can. All right, let's begin. (The entire exercise is repeated.)
12. TIMMY: (Waves hand.)
13. TEACHER: Yes, Timmy?
14. TIMMY: I can count to a hundred.
15. TEACHER: That's very good. Will you lead the class this time? All right, boys and girls, now you follow Timmy. (Timmy leads the exercise again.)
16. MARCIA: I know a song with numbers.
17. TEACHER: I wonder if it's the same song I was going to teach you? You listen to my song, Marcia, and then tell me if it's the same one. Now, children, let's everybody stretch—try to touch the ceiling—and then bring your chairs in a circle around the piano. (The children congregate around the piano.)
18. TEACHER: Now, children, I will sing the song once for you. See if you know it already. Then we will all sing it together. Ready?

> *One, two, buckle my shoe.*
> *Three, four, shut the door.*
> *Five, six, pick up sticks.*
> *Seven, eight, lay them straight.*
> *Nine, ten, a big fat hen.*

19. TEACHER: All right, children, now return to your seats; it's story time. (Goldhammer, 1969. Reprinted by permission.)

The following supervisor's analysis of these notes illustrates the results of Goldhammer's system. Unrecorded thoughts are represented by italics; T = teacher, P = pupil, and C = class.

1. (T1) Beginning lacks "transition" either from immediately preceding activity or from the most recently performed work in arithmetic. *Presupposes pupils will learn what Teacher teaches: teaches implicitly, "In this place Teacher decides what is to be done (learned)," presupposes all pupils commonly share ignorance of the knowledge in question (an unlikely condition).* "We" is an obvious affectation.
2. (P2, T3) Teacher's intent takes precedence over pupil's experienced need. *Press for conformity, that is, for all pupils to behave the same; the pupils may learn, incidentally, that it is better to do what Teacher directs than to raise individual questions or to develop original ideas. Timmy, particularly,*

     may learn to avoid spontaneous behavior (if Teacher's behavior in this instance reflects a continuous pattern); if Timmy needs physical relief, his learning of whatever Teacher teaches may be sacrificed under organic stress.

3. (T3–C10) No rationale for choral repetition has been made explicit. *While some pupils may understand a means-end relationship between "learning to count to ten" and this exercise, others may feel that, in the absence of reasons, their job is to do what they are told (no matter how seemingly irrational).*

    Teacher decides on the method of learning as well as the object (topic) of learning. (The principal point in this thinking is that instead of learning to be self-initiating, spontaneous, self-directing, and the like, to whatever degree Teacher may be central in such learning, the pupils may learn opposite behaviors if the teaching they experience consistently follows the present model; instead of learning rational autonomy, the pupils are more likely to learn passive dependency. Supervisor should discover, empirically, whether such teaching is fairly general in [this classroom]. In the absence of such data, it is more logical to think of this sample as typical than as atypical.)

    Although numbers are now in natural order (*which represents yet a third sequence*), an arbitrary triplet rhythm has been imposed upon them (that is, the pupils are learning a $-'$,$-'$,$-'$ rhythm in addition to reciting number names). The teaching is still nonmathematical; *that is, the children might almost as well be reciting nonsense syllables in relation to learning about "number." Indeed, despite Teacher's expressed intention to Supervisor, the children are not being taught to count).*

4. (T11) "That was good. . . ." *Should such remarks constitute a teaching pattern, the pupils might incidentally be taught, first, that evaluation is something that Teacher does (in contrast to self-initiated evaluation) and, second, either that evaluation is essentially subjective or that Teacher's evaluation criteria are secret; in any event, they may learn to depend upon other people's unexplicit evaluations.*

    What if the children's performance was good?

    Reinforcement is global rather than specific and may, consequently, serve to establish unuseful behaviors that were being manifested during the exercise. "Goodness" seems to be determined by "loudness," or, at least, by Teacher's ability to hear. No logical rationale is provided either for a repetition of the exercise or for saying things loudly (more absence of reasons).

5. (P12–T15) "That's very good." *Another evaluation by Teacher, suggesting that "good; very good" may reflect a pattern of stereotyped rewards.*

    "Will you lead the class . . ." *Instead of being acknowledged in its own right, Timmy's offering is superseded by Teacher's lesson plan; that is, his response is used (subverted) as an occasion to advance Teacher's planned lesson. "Very good, you may empty the wastebasket" would, similarly, have been an inappropriate reward, one that ignored the inherent substantive or emotional significance of the child's response. A logically predictable in-*

*cidental learning for Timmy and for the others would be (once again)
"What counts most here is what Teacher wants; Teacher's intentions and
desires and preferences count for more than pupils'." Although Teacher
may have intended to reward Timmy by assigning him leadership, he may,
in fact, have felt more of an implicit rejection than an acceptance of his
achievement by Teacher's choice of techniques. In any event, such rewards
are external and, as such, do not teach the learner to experience satisfaction
from the learning itself.*

The exercise is performed a third time, on this occasion with no stated
reason whatsoever.

6. (P16–T17) Teacher's response to Marcia is the same as to Timmy: the
   pupil's spontaneous offering is subordinated to Teacher's plan (*My song is
   better than your song.*)
7. (T18) Mnemonics, this time a different set. Another arbitrary rhythm, this
   time duplets rather than triplets.
8. (T19) No transition either into the next activity or into the next sequence of
   "mathematics." *Rather than seeming predictable and rationally organized,
   the classroom environment is likely to seem capricious to the children: they
   neither know what is to come next at any given moment nor understand
   reasons for doing whatever does come, except, as for Hillary, "because it is
   there." Sequences of activities are more ritual than logical.*

Categories	*Patterns*
Locus of initiative	All directions come from T.
	Topic chosen by T.
	Method of "learning" chosen by T.
	All rewards and evaluative comments made by T.
Rewards	External.
	Stereotyped. (?)
	Global, undifferentiated.
	No (little) intrinsic relationship to P's responses.
Rationales (reasons)	Absent or arbitrary.
	Nonmathematical.
Organization of knowledge	Arbitrary sequences.
	Different sequences.
Methods	Rote repetition.
	Uniform for all P's.
	Individual differences do not affect the teaching.
	Superfluous rhythms and mnemonics.
Evaluation	No prior evaluation. (?)
	No explicit evaluation (by T or by P's) of today's learning.
Transitions	None.
Interaction	T-P or T-C (no P-P).

(Goldhammer, 1969. Reprinted by permission.)

Comments. In our use of Goldhammer's note-taking procedures and in teaching them to others, we have found that keeping pace with the flow of activity in a typical classroom is at the very least a demanding task. Often observers tend to lapse into recording anecdotes or particular episodes of behavior instead of recording behaviors continuously. Although anecdotes, if written well, can be objective and useful descriptions of behavior, they may be biased in the way they are selected. Our first strategy in learning to use Goldhammer's procedures, therefore, has been to extend ourselves to record as much of what is happening as possible; only after we have done that do we concentrate on anecdotal information.

There is no one best method for collecting anecdotal information. However, Brandt (1972) suggests the following set of procedures for safeguarding the value and utility of such information. Although Brandt's remarks are directed primarily to researchers, they are also instructive for practitioners of teacher development.

1. Write an anecdote as soon after viewing the incident as possible. If some time lag is necessitated by the situation, jot down a key word or two (a particular term used, for example) to aid your memory during the more complete writing.

2. Include the basic action or statements of the chief person in the episode, that is, what he did or said.

3. Include enough setting details to indicate where and when the behavior occurred, under what conditions, and who was involved. The date, time of day, specific names, and a general statement of what was going on (example: "during silent reading period;" "while the class was discussing plans for the trip to Gettysburg") or what was supposed to be going on (example: "Jim's group was supposed to be studying quietly for their spelling test.").

4. Responses or reactions of others to the chief person's behavior should also be included (example: "Jim nodded affirmatively;" "I don't think so," Tom replied). Even no response when one might well be expected should be recorded (example: . . . "Nothing else was said at the time.").

5. Use direct quotations wherever possible in order to preserve the flavor of how things were stated. If too much was said to recall it all accurately, write the major points on the conversation in indirect quotation form and identify key phrases that can be remembered accurately, setting them off with question marks.

6. Generally, anecdotes should preserve the sequence of actions and responses of the original behavior incident. In other words, there is a *beginning*, including some setting details as indicated in item 3; a *middle*, which describes but noninterpretively how the incident ended (example: "The topic changed"; "John smiled and turned away.")

7. Anecdotes should describe the major units of molar behavior (example: "Bill went to the grocery store with his mother.") in an episode with sufficient subordinate molar units (example: "Bill *ran out of the house* as his mother was warming the car up, *slamming the door* behind him, and *rode*

off to the grocery with his mother.") and molecular activity (example: "panting and waving his arms") including something about how the main action was carried out. There is always a practical limit to how much subordinate molar and molecular detail can be recorded. The particular selection of such material to record should depend, of course, on the overall purposes of the study.

8. Anecdotes should be objective, accurate, and complete as far as important details are concerned. Recording errors should tend to be of commission, which can be disregarded in the analysis, rather than omission, which can never be corrected. Good literary style, correct grammar and spelling, and even complete sentences are inconsequential. Words chosen should be precise and unambiguous, nouns and verbs primarily. Subjective terminology, exemplified by most adjectives and adverbs should be used sparingly. If it is important to note the *beautiful* car John was driving, describe more precisely instead some of the qualities that make you think so (example: "a two-toned, blue hardtop Pontiac Catalina, two-door, 1972 model, freshly washed and without a scratch").

9. If research resources are sufficient, use of a tape recorder and typist to transcribe anecdotes into written form generally increases the amount of detail that can be included over stenographic or handwritten recording. Some researchers have utilized interrogators to listen to or read anecdotes and then to ask questions of the observer regarding other details of the incidents. One promising sequence of observation and recording procedures would be as follows:

   a. Make a longhand or stenographic write-up of an incident immediately after it happens.

   b. As soon afterwards as possible, and certainly on the same day, have an interrogator read this write-up and ask questions of the observer.

   c. Have the observer describe the incident in final form into a dictaphone.

   d. Type this final description for permanent record purposes.

Comments. Ethnographic procedures of data collection similar to those suggested by Goldhammer and Brandt are yielding important qualitative information on teaching and learning. Berliner and Tikunoff (1977) report that one study revealed twenty-one generic behaviors that discriminated between more and less effective teachers in reading and mathematics at the second- and fifth-grade levels. For example, "teacher monitors learning" and "students are engaged" were consistently related to more effective teaching, whereas "teacher belittles student" was consistently associated with less effective teaching. As Berliner and Tikunoff note, the kinds of results yielded by this type of methodology, as well as the methodology itself, are worth further investigation.

Another method of obtaining qualitative information on teaching and learning is the use of activity logs. These can be kept by teachers to note starting and ending times for particular activities, content covered, and descriptions of instructional settings. One study using such logs to record allocation of time in mathematics found that they yielded information accurate enough to permit analysis of the relationship between instructional time allocated and student achievement (Fisher, Marliave, Filby, Cahen, Moore, and Berliner, 1976). Logs are not a substitute for direct observation of teaching and learning, but they may provide important supplemental data on teacher-student behavior that are pertinent to selected teacher tasks.

Morine System

Purpose. The purpose of the Morine system[7] is to examine the actions and interactions of teacher and students in a classroom setting by concentrating on the behaviors teachers find most important. The Morine system is not composed of a set of pre-established categories as are the Flanders or Galloway systems; neither is it a stenographic note-taking procedure such as Goldhammer's. Instead, it is a general scheme or framework upon which a set of categories can be constructed and rearranged to fit different situational demands. The Morine system provides a practical method of observation that teachers may apply to taped episodes of their own teaching or with each other in live settings.

Description. Although the Morine system utilizes personally constructed categories for observation, it is a *sign system,* not a category system as Medley and Mitzel (1963) use the terms. The categories used to guide observation are not coded at regular intervals of time, as they are in the Flanders system; neither are they noted only once and then forgotten. Rather, one records behavioral indicators of the categories whenever such signs appear.

Categories for observation are formulated *inductively,* much as are Goldhammer's patterns. That is, a list of possible teaching behaviors is generated. These behaviors in turn are grouped together in ways that seem logical or make sense to the observer, and finally the groups or categories are given a label that describes them.

Before constructing or applying categories of teacher-student behaviors, Morine (1973) suggests that it is useful to understand the concepts of *teaching act* and *pupil act.* A teaching act is an observable activity or behavior performed by the teacher. By the same token, a pupil act is an observable activity or behavior performed by a pupil. To illustrate, Morine (1973) provides the following examples (A and C are teaching acts. B is a pupil act. D is not observable, therefore not an act and not recorded):

    A. Ms. Rubble asks, "What is one difference between a noun and verb?"
    B. Alice raises her hand.

---

[7] Greta Morine, *Entry module: An introduction to observing classroom interaction* (San Francisco: Far West Laboratory for Educational Research and Development, 1973).

C. Ms. Rubble says, "Alice?"

D. Jerry thinks to himself, "There goes smart Alice again."

As Morine notes, teacher and pupil acts can both be described with varying degrees of specificity. Those acts or behaviors that are moderately specific are probably most useful for observations. They are neither so general as to be meaningless nor so specific as to be trivial. Morine presents the following examples of such acts or behaviors:

Very specific—pupil writes $2 + 2 = 4$ on board.
Moderately specific—pupil writes answer.
Very general—pupil responds.

A second concept one must understand before constructing or applying an observation instrument using Morine's methods is that of a *transition point* in classroom interaction. Transition points are "the points at which the principal speaker or actor changes." For instance, if the teacher asks a question and a pupil responds, the transition point lies between these two separate acts. Transition points are important because they lend direction to the identification of possible behaviors to be observed. That is, if one were first to select the transition point at which the *teacher stops talking* and the *pupil starts*

TABLE 3–7
Transition Points and Associated Behaviors*

Initiating	1. Teacher stops behavior — Pupil starts (List teacher behaviors that might occur *before* this point)
	2. Pupil stops behavior — Teacher starts (List pupil behaviors that might occur *before* this point)
	3. One pupil stops behavior — A different pupil starts (List pupil behaviors that might occur *before* this point)
Responding	4. Teacher stops behavior — Pupil starts (List pupil behaviors that might occur *after* this point)
	5. Pupil stops behavior — Teacher starts (List teacher behaviors that might occur *after* this point)
	6. One pupil stops behavior — A different pupil starts (List pupil behaviors that might occur *after* this point)

* Morine discusses only transition points numbered 1, 2, 4, and 5. If pupil-pupil interactions are of interest, however, it may be useful to consider behaviors associated with transition points 3 and 6 as well.

talking, and then speculate on the pupil behaviors that could occur just *after* that point, the list might appear as follows:

Answer a question correctly.
Ask to go to the bathroom.
Say he doesn't understand.
Ask for information.
Volunteer to give some information.

Six types of transition points can be used to generate lists of possible behaviors (Table 3–7). Although some behaviors may be unrelated to other behaviors that come before or after, these transition points help one generate both teacher and pupil behaviors that are in general either *initiating* or *responding* in nature.

As noted, once a list of possible behaviors is generated, the behaviors are then grouped and labeled. Such an organization of teacher behaviors might appear as follows:

Teacher acts or behaviors	Categories of Teacher Acts or Behaviors*
Managing Information	
Thanks a pupil.	1. *Gives information:*
Asks a question about content.	Gives factual information.
Gives factual information.	Reads aloud.
Argues with a pupil.	Gives directions.
Reads aloud.	Writes answer on board.
Gives directions.	Demonstrates a process.
States a problem to be solved.	2. *Asks questions:*
Answers a question.	Asks a question about
Writes an answer on board.	content.
Praises a pupil.	Asks a clarifying question.
Gives homework.	3. *Assigns work:*
Demonstrates a process.	States a problem to be
Asks a clarifying question.	solved.
	Gives homework.
	Assigns seatwork.
Responding	
Assigns seatwork.	4. *Responds to pupils:*
Screams at pupil.	Thanks a pupil.
	Argues with a pupil.
	Praises a pupil.
	Screams at a pupil.
	Answers a question.

* This organization could be useful for a teacher who is interested in altering his or her styles of managing information and responding to pupils.

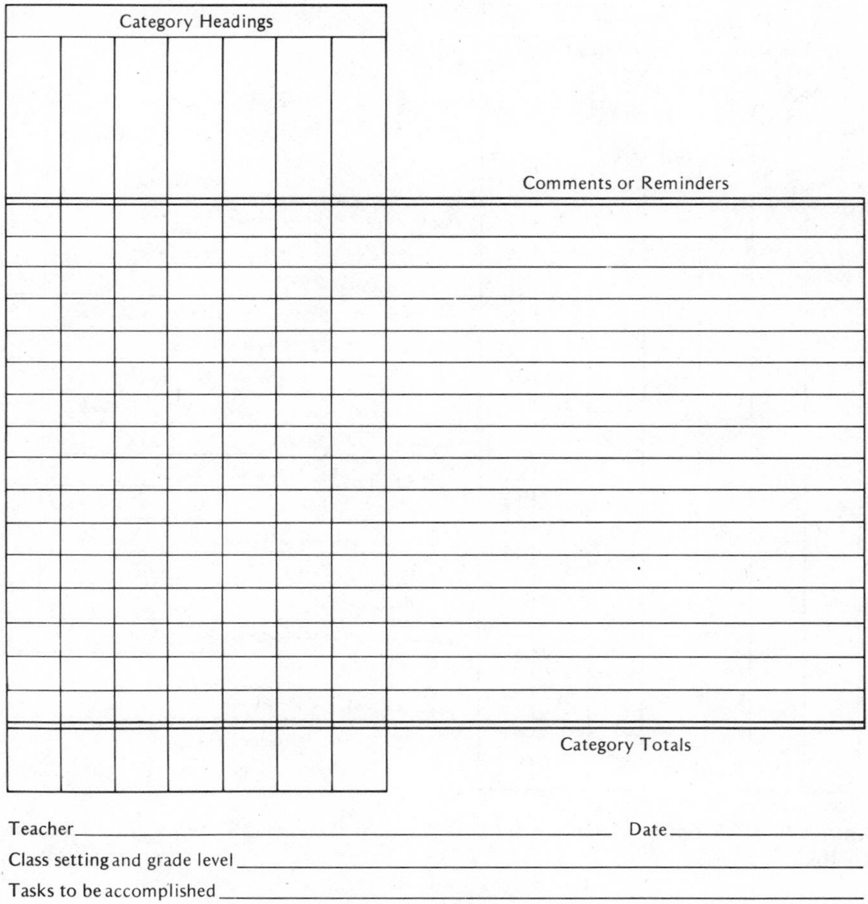

Category Headings							

Comments or Reminders

Category Totals

Teacher_____ Date_____

Class setting and grade level _____

Tasks to be accomplished _____

FIGURE 3–4. Coding Sheet. [Adapted from Morine, G. *Entry module: An introduction to observing classroom interaction* (discussion format). Bay Area Teacher Training Complex, Far West Laboratory for Educational Research and Development, 1973, p. 20.]

When behaviors have been listed, organized, and labeled, the observer places the category labels on a coding sheet (Figure 3–4). Then, one is ready to begin observation.

Procedures for Implementation. The Morine system can be used to examine teacher or pupil behaviors in any classroom setting, regardless of pupil age or class content. To apply the system, one places a check mark in the appropri-

Category Headings						
Teacher Leadership		Pupil Leadership				
Giving Teacher Directions	Giving Teacher Information	Getting Pupil Information	Getting Pupil Directions and Questions			Comments or Reminders
✓						Gave topic for discussion.
		✓				assessed what they know
						about it.
		✓				Wrote down their ideas
		✓				on chalkboard.
		✓				
	✓					corrected some misinformation.
		✓				asked what else they knew.
	✓					Added more information.
			✓			Asked what they wanted to know.
			✓			Wrote their questions on board.
			✓			asked where they could get
						answers.
			✓			Wrote suggestions on board.
✓						Gave an assignment.
						Category Totals
2	2	5	4			

FIGURE 3–5. Coding Sheet—Teacher's Personal Category System. [From Morine, G., Ibid.]

ate column when a particular behavioral indicator appears. Sequence of behaviors is preserved by moving down the coding sheet row by row. The lines provided for comments or reminders may be used for notes. These notes are often useful during later analysis of data and discussion of results.

Morine's example of a completed coding sheet (Figure 3–5) illustrates the kind of results the system provides. The sixth-grade teacher who filled this out wanted to encourage pupils to assume more leadership in a class discussion. His categories of teaching acts were "giving teacher leadership" (directions from teacher and information from teacher) and "encouraging pupil leadership" (encouraging information from pupils and encouraging directions or questions from pupils).

Data Analysis. Organizing and interpreting data obtained from the Morine system is a simple process. One totals the observations made in each category to obtain the frequency with which behaviors occurred. Examining the comments or reminders provides additional clarification of the behaviors observed. By following check marks down the coding sheet, one may get a sense of when particular behaviors were demonstrated. It is important to remember, however, that intervals between behaviors are not equal in length of time.

Comments. Because the Morine system is designed to be used by those who are knowledgeable about teaching and learning but have had little experience with observation, it is necessarily simple. Primarily because of this simplicity, the Morine system is open to several criticisms. For instance, what seem to be moderately specific behaviors to some may appear as very general or very specific to others. Thus, the information acquired by an observer may not always provide the kinds considered useful to the teacher being observed. Further, unless considerable care is taken in developing the categories, they may not be mutually exclusive. In other words, behaviors that are observed might fit under more than one category. Such a situation makes the tasks of coding and interpreting results difficult.

These faults can, of course, be rectified to a certain extent by an adept use of the system. In instructing teachers how to use Morine's techniques, we have found that once they have practiced procedures thoroughly, the problems of behavior identification and categorization are reduced considerably. Furthermore, once teachers or teacher educators are familiar with the Morine system, they begin to look for slightly more general recurring behaviors and categories that cut across situations, or those that fit a variety of teaching tasks. When this happens, we move on to the study of more formal observation systems. The Morine system is useful for teacher educators not only because it is relatively easy to use and adaptable to various situations, but because it can serve as a springboard to other types of observations.

Blumberg System

Purpose. The purpose of the Blumberg system[8] is to examine the behavioral interaction of supervisors and teachers in conference situations. Based on Flanders's and Bales's systems of interaction analysis, the Blumberg system may be used to assess one's own behavior as a teacher educator by determining (1) how help is offered to teachers, (2) the relative supportiveness or de-

---

[8] Arthur Blumberg, *Supervisors and teachers: A private cold war*, Berkeley, CA.: McCutchan Publishing Corporation, 1974.

TABLE 3–8
**Summary of Blumberg Interaction
Analysis Categories***

Supervisor Talk	1. Support-inducing communications behavior
	2. Praise
	3. Accepts or uses teacher's ideas
	4. Asks for information
	5. Giving information
	6. Asks for opinions
	7. Asks for suggestions
	8. Gives opinions
	9. Gives suggestions
	10. Criticism
Teacher Talk	11. Asks for information, opinions, or suggestions
	12. Gives information, opinions, or suggestions
	13. Positive social emotional behavior
	14. Negative social emotional behavior
	15. Silence or confusion

*Adapted from Blumberg, Arthur. "A System for Analyzing Supervisor-Teacher Interaction." In *Mirrors for behavior*, III, Anita Simon and E. Gil Boyer (Eds.). (Philadelphia: Research for Better Schools, Inc., 1970), pp. 34.1–2 to 34.1–4.

fensiveness of communication, and (3) the degree of reciprocity involved in communication, or how supervisor/teacher educator behavior affects teachers, or vice versa (Blumberg, 1974). This system has been used in both industrial and educational settings for research and training.

Description. The Blumberg system is composed of fifteen categories of verbal behavior (Table 3–8) that are divided into three major sections: supervisor behavior, teacher behavior, and silence and confusion.

The first section of the Blumberg system is composed of ten categories of supervisor talk. Category 1 includes supervisor statements that release tension, convey acceptance of feelings, and encourage teachers. Category 2 is composed of supervisor statements that attach positive value to a teacher's ideas, actions, and feelings. Category 3 is used to code supervisor statements that clarify, build on, or develop the ideas or suggestions of teachers. Category 4 includes supervisor statements that are intended to seek clarification of factual information about a problem or situation. Category 5 is the opposite of Category 4 in that it is concerned with supervisor statements that provide objective information to the teacher. Category 6 is composed of supervisor behaviors that are meant to ask the teacher to analyze or evaluate past, present, or future behaviors in the classroom or in the conference situation. Category 7 includes supervisor statements that ask the teacher to think about ways of doing things either in the classroom or in interactions with the supervisor. Category 8 is the opposite of Category 6 in that the supervisor gives information as opposed to asking for it. In a similar vein, Category 9 is the opposite of Category 7 in that the supervisor gives information about ways of doing things instead of asking a teacher for his or her ideas. Category 10 includes a supervisor's negative value judgments about the teacher that can be interpreted as defensive, aggressive, or tension-producing.

The second section of the Blumberg system is composed of four categories of teacher talk. Category 11 is comparable to Categories 4, 6, and 7 in that it includes teacher statements that request information, opinions, or suggestions from the supervisor. Category 12 is composed of teacher statements that give information, opinions, or suggestions and, therefore, is comparable to Categories 5, 8, and 9. Category 13 includes teacher statements that encourage or help build the supervisory relationship, or statements that convey agreement by choice. Category 14 is used to code teacher statements that are defensive, tension producing, or rationalizations.

The third and final section of the Blumberg system is composed of a single category of silence or confusion. Category 15 includes periods of silence or moments when the teacher and supervisor are talking at the same time so that it is impossible to discern specific behaviors. Silences occurring after either supervisor or teacher behaviors that have the effect of producing defensiveness, however, are coded as Category 10 or 14.

Procedures for Implementation. Because it deals with the verbal behaviors of supervisors and teachers, the Blumberg system can be applied to audio tapes of conference episodes. After concluding a session, a supervisor can replay the tape and code behaviors every three seconds, just as one would in using the Flanders system. As with Flanders, coding is facilitated by committing the categories to memory. As the following transcript of conference dialogue and corresponding category numbers illustrates, the Blumberg system can do the same thing for teacher educator-teacher interactions that the Flanders system does for teacher-pupil interactions.

TE: "Let's take a few moments to talk about my observation of the social studies lesson." (5)
"I was quite impressed by the way you got students to share their thoughts during the discussion period." (2)

T: "Gee, thanks. I thought it went well too." (13)

TE: "But I noticed two boys who didn't say much." (5)
"Were they the two new students you told me about?" (4)

T: "Yes, Mike and Jamie are the brothers who just entered our class last Friday. They came here from a small town in Michigan. From what their mother told me and from what I have observed so far, they are very shy. Mike has good grades from his old school, but Jamie's are pretty low." (12, 12, 12, 12)

TE: "What do you think you could do to put them at ease and get them more involved?" (7)

T: "Well, I think maybe I'll assign them each a buddy they can work with until they get better acquainted with others." (12)
"Do you think that might help?" (11)

TE: "Assign them buddies . . . h-m-m-m . . . sounds good." (3, 2)
"Maybe Bob and Luis would make good buddies." (9)

T: "Yes." (12)

TE: "I know you are pressed for time now, but could you tell me more about the simulation activity?" (1, 4)

Blumberg, too, suggests certain ground rules that enable a person to use his system reliably. By practicing one's coding behaviors and following the rules listed here, it is possible to code consistently.

1. View each act as a response to the last act of the other person or as an anticipation of the next act of the other. The point is that we are dealing with sequentially related behavior and not that which occurs in isolation. Operationally, this means that interaction is recorded from the point of view of the recipient of the behavior, not the giver. This is so because we are interested in recording the *effects* of behavior, not the intentions of the person behaving.

2. Difficulty is likely to arise in differentiating behavior in the following categories: 1 and 2, 6 and 7, 8, 9, and 10, and 13 and 14. (In the latter three categories problems arise when the person who is recording is not sure whether or not the teacher's behavior is agreement on a positive level or compliance.) In such cases the ground rule is, after replaying the sequence to understand the context, choose the lower numbered category of those that are in question. In other words, if it is in doubt whether a behavior is a 6 or a 7, choose 6.

3. If more than one category occurs during the three-second interval, then all categories used in that interval are recorded; conversely, record each change in category. If no change occurs in three seconds, repeat the previous category number.

4. The use of "Ohh-h" or "Hm" by itself is taken to be encouragement and is in category 1. When "Uh-huh" is followed by a rephrasing or use of the teacher's idea, it is in category 3.
5. Start and end the tallying with a "15"—silence. This is done for two reasons. First, it is assumed that the conference begins and ends in silence. Second, by including the "15" it is possible to insure that the total number of tallies in the rows and columns of the matrix will balance. (Blumberg, 1974.)

In the interactions between teacher educators and teachers, as in teacher-pupil interactions, it is important to be able to know not only *what* behaviors occur but *when* they occur. Putting behaviors in a sequence, therefore, is as central to the Blumberg system as it is to the Flanders system. Coding to preserve sequence can be accomplished by using ruled paper (Figure 3–6) and recording the fifteen category numbers for the appropriate behaviors. Each horizontal line denotes one three-second interval.

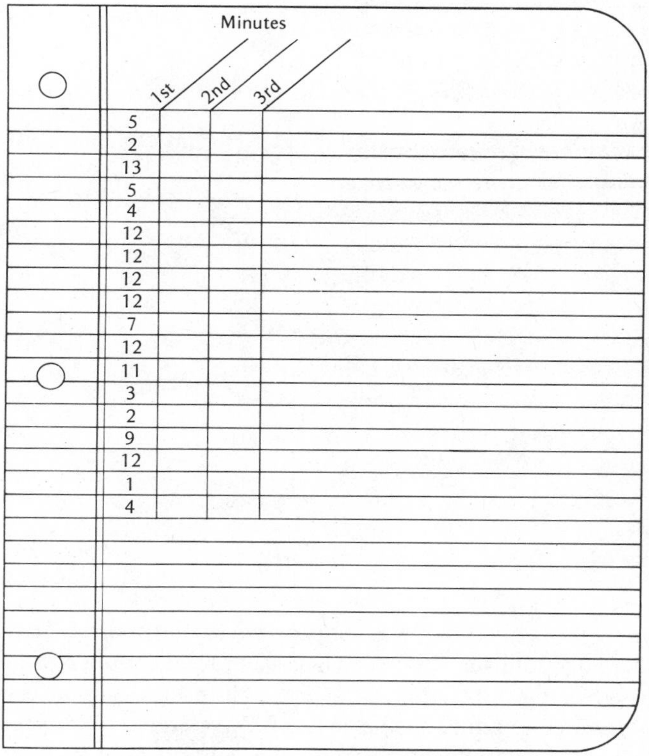

FIGURE 3–6. Coding Blumberg Categories on Ruled Paper.

Data Analysis. Whereas time for analysis of teacher-pupil interaction is often limited because of the necessity of providing immediate feedback, organizing and interpreting data from the Blumberg system on interactions between teachers and teacher educators might be done more leisurely. Thus, when time permits, Blumberg's matrix, similar to the Flanders matrix, can be a useful tool for data analysis. The heart of the Blumberg matrix is composed of fifteen rows and fifteen columns that correspond to the category numbers (Figure 3–7). The matrix also includes two extra rows for column totals and percentages and one extra column for row totals. Overlapping pairs of observations are recorded on the matrix in the appropriate cells. The sequence of paired category numbers from the transcript of dialogue presented previously is shown below and recorded on the matrix in Figure 3–7.

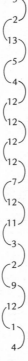

Once pairs of observations are transferred to the matrix, it is possible to calculate category totals and percentages. The total number of tallies in each row should equal the total number of tallies in each column. The grand total equals the number of tallies in the matrix. The percentages of respective column tallies can be derived by dividing the column total by the grand total. Thus, in this particular interaction (Figure 3–7), the supervisor spent 18 per-

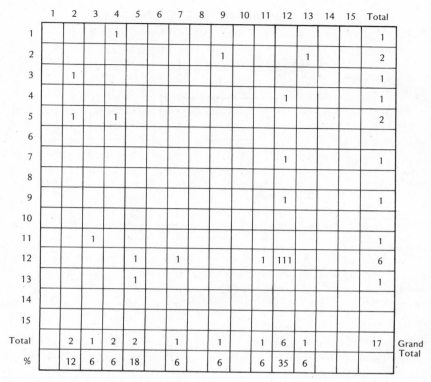

	1	2	3	4	5	6	7	8	9	10	11	12	13	14	15	Total	
1				1												1	
2									1				1			2	
3		1														1	
4												1				1	
5		1		1												2	
6																	
7												1				1	
8																	
9												1				1	
10																	
11			1													1	
12					1		1				1	111				6	
13					1											1	
14																	
15																	
Total	2	1	2	2		1		1			1	6	1			17	Grand Total
%	12	6	6	18		6		6			6	35	6				

FIGURE 3–7. Blumberg Matrix. [Adapted from Blumberg, Arthur. "A System for Analyzing Supervisor-Teacher Interaction." In *Mirrors for behavior*, III, Anita Simon and E. Gil Boyer (Eds.). (Philadelphia: Research for Better Schools, Inc., 1970), p. 34. 1–9.]

cent of the conference time giving information (Category 5). There are, of course, many questions one might ask and answer using these data. Blumberg suggests examining the *steady state cells*, or those areas in which the supervisor makes extended use of a particular kind of behavior for insight into particular conference emphases.

The steady state areas of behavior, as illustrated in Figure 3–8, can be summarized as follows: A, developing interpersonal relationships; B, using teacher ideas; C, concentrating on objective informational data; D, concentrating on evaluative opinion data; E, concentrating on method and/or control; F, controlling teacher behavior.

Other important concentrations of behavior as illustrated in Figure 3–8 can be summarized as follows: G, extended teacher talk; H, teacher reactions to supervisor behavior; I, supervisor reactions to teacher behavior; J, supervisor

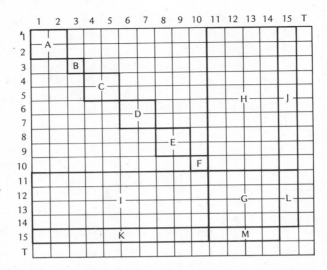

FIGURE 3–8.   Steady State Cells and Other Important Areas of Behavior. [Blumberg, Arthur. *Supervisors and teachers: A private cold war.* (Berkeley: McCutchan Publishing Corporation, 1974), p. 100. Reproduced by permission.)]

behaviors that produce silence or confusion; K, supervisor reactions to silence or confusion; L, teacher behaviors that produce silence or confusion; and M, teacher reactions to silence or confusion.

Comments.   Blumberg and Cusick (1970) studied supervisor-teacher behavior in fifty conference situations. They discovered that supervisors gave information about five times as often as they asked for it, were direct twice as much as they were indirect, and talked 45 percent of the conference time. Teachers talked 53 percent of the time, and the remaining 2 percent was taken up by silence or confusion. Supervisors spent less than 1 percent of the time asking teachers for their suggestions. From an analysis of the matrix steady state areas of behavior, they found that the extended time a supervisor spent on various behaviors ranged from 10 percent in clarifying teacher ideas to 72 percent in controlling teacher behavior—mostly through criticism. Although the subjects for this study were not selected at random and thus cannot be said to be representative, the results give at least a general clue to what one might expect to find when using the system.

Another system for observing teacher-supervisor interactions, the Multidimensional Observational System for the Analysis of Interactions in Clinical Supervision (MOSAICS), was developed by Weller (1971). MOSAICS is based on the work of Bellack and associates (1966) on teacher-student interaction. It examines teacher-supervisor interactions in terms of various pedagogical moves, for instance, structuring or making moves that direct the flow of discourse and substantive areas dealing with such matters as methods, materials, and content. MOSAICS is considerably more difficult to use than the Blumberg system, but it has the potential for providing a wealth of information on patterns of teacher-supervisor interaction. It should be useful not only for those who wish to improve supervisory relationships but also for researchers investigating conference behavior.

SUMMARY

Teacher behaviors that are effective and reasonable in one situation may be ineffective and inappropriate in another. In order to encourage teacher educators to be sensitive to such variations, this chapter has presented five systems of classroom observation that can be used to examine systematically a variety of teacher behaviors and, in some instances, accompanying student behaviors. As with teacher behaviors, those exhibited by teacher educators may be suitable in one setting but inappropriate in another. The chapter also discussed one observation system that can be used to examine the actions and interactions of teachers and teacher educators. Results derived from systematic observation and analysis of behavior can lead teacher educators to provide support that is consonant with the needs and abilities of teachers and the demands of the tasks they undertake.

Learning to use the observation systems presented in this chapter is largely a matter of practice. One might begin by coding taped examples of his or her own teaching, using different systems. Often it is useful to study with a colleague and quiz each other about the categories in various systems, discuss ground rules, and formulate new ground rules or recording procedures for personal use. In all cases, it is useful to read the articles and manuals written by the authors of these systems.

◆ 4 ◆

Teacher Characteristics

K NOWLEDGE of the characteristics of teachers is important to teacher educators for three reasons. It provides a foundation upon which teacher educators can diagnose personal needs and abilities; it offers a guide for ways to support teachers; and it helps to select teacher developmental objectives that focus on short-term or long-term personal growth. Earlier chapters suggested that not all teacher characteristics offer direction to the teacher educator. Variability along such dimensions as physical attributes, lifestyle preferences, or hobbies, although interesting and important in understanding the total person, may offer little substantive guidance for teacher educators who want to help teachers become more effective in the classroom. Teacher educators must begin to understand the needs and abilities of teachers in terms that lend direction to the practice of teacher development.

This chapter considers the characteristics of teachers as a group and then focuses on teachers as individuals. Knowledge born of practical experience, empirical investigation, and educational/psychological theory may each, in their own way, lend direction to discerning and adapting teacher education practice to teacher needs and abilities. We draw upon these sources of knowledge to recommend specific personal variables or characteristics that may be most useful to consider when working with teachers.

Teachers as a Group

Knowledge of the attributes of teachers as a group is useful if teachers are to be understood as individuals. Although teachers cannot be portrayed adequately by neatly arranged rows and columns of statistical data, extensive studies by organizations such as NEA make it possible to compile at least a limited profile of contemporary teachers across a number of important demographic dimensions. It is known, for example, that the median age of teachers is thirty-three, that they come predominantly from lower middle-class families, that they rate themselves as being moderately conservative politically, and that they have lower starting salaries than their counterparts in industry (Ream, 1977). It would not be stretching the point to say that teachers on the whole have been portrayed as second-class citizens in comparison to other professional groups. Behaviorally, teachers have been characterized as having a great need for control (Travers, 1961), preferring students who conform over those who are more independent (Feshbach, 1969), and demonstrating a susceptibility for letting their own expectations rule their behavior (Rosenthal and Jacobson, 1968).

Beyond these kinds of data, we have come to know about teachers through their public stands on controversial issues. Volatile national issues such as busing to achieve racial integration, mainstreaming exceptional children into regular classrooms, and taxpayers' revolts such as California's Proposition 13 have drawn teachers into the political arena. Reports of declining student achievement and legal suits brought against schools by graduates who charge that they were not taught basic skills have contributed further to our knowledge of teachers. From these and similar issues, we learn that teachers are growing more outspoken in their demands.

Teachers' expressions of their concerns may be reflected at least in part by the increase in number, strength, and visibility of teacher organizations. In addition to the two strong national organizations, the National Education Association and the American Federation of Teachers, numerous regional, state, and local organizations regularly speak out on behalf of teachers and thus shape perceptions of teachers' professional identities. These professional organizations have educated the public in general about teacher needs by pressing for better working conditions, higher salaries, and greater job security. But prolonged collective bargaining and teacher strikes have spurred public backlash in some areas of the country and contributed a negative component to the identity of teachers as a group.

Lortie (1975) has compiled information on teachers' motivations from an extensive review of the literature on the sociology of teachers. According to Lortie, teachers apparently do not look at teaching as a lifetime career activity. Men indicate that they hope to leave the classroom for another educational position (administration or higher education) or to work in a noneducational setting. Termination for women is predominantly related to getting married, having children, or relocating to advance a spouse's work or education. A major reason for the exodus of teachers, especially males, from the field is a lack of opportunity to improve their financial or professional status. Extrinsically generated rewards, including money and prestige, are not abundant in teaching. Salaries are low and individual ambition to earn more is hampered by the lock-step salary schedules typical of most districts, so the difference between present earnings and earning potential is usually small. Similarly, although a teacher may be given select students or certain kinds of administrative responsibilities, there is little opportunity for improvement of one's status short of leaving the classroom. Lortie argues that the more lasting rewards for many teachers are "psychic or intrinsic," meaning that they grow out of the activities on the job. For teachers, intrinsic rewards tend to be associated with their perceived impact on students. Thus, increased efforts and success with students can lead to greater job satisfaction.

Teachers as a group vary in the amount of personal resources (such as time and money) that they invest in their own professional development. For example, teachers in secondary education are likely to work longer hours than elementary teachers, and single women are likely to work longer hours than married women. Men generally spend more money than women on professional development activities such as workshops and courses, and single women spend more than married women. A closer look at the types of professional activities in which men engage would probably reveal that these activities open up opportunities for a job switch, such as moving out of the classroom and into administration. Given this tendency among men to leave the classroom, it is not surprising that satisfaction among teachers as a group seems to be higher for women and lower for men.

As members of the same professional group, teachers share similar needs, face common problems, and often voice similar demands. The need to be heard on issues ranging from broad educational policy matters to more personal and professional concerns has sometimes given teachers a militant image. Researchers state that predictable patterns of reward, frustration, and aspiration exist among teachers and that these in turn are modified by such factors as sex, level of experience, and grade level taught. A deeper probe into the makeup of teachers, however, shows that they differ in many ways, and that teacher educators must adapt their educational approaches to such differences among teachers.

The Teacher as an Individual

Determining how the individual teacher differs from general patterns of teachers is facilitated by examining various sources of knowledge about human growth and development. Three such sources of information are noted by Hunt and Sullivan (1974) as potentially useful to the educator and the psychologist: (1) informal observation and experience, (2) empirical research, and (3) educational/psychological theory. These suggest not only how people differ but also how environments may be adapted to meet special needs. Consideration of teachers as individuals must necessarily take into account how differences in people may be accommodated by environmental adaptations. No one source of information is necessarily better than another, but each contributes toward thinking about persons as individuals and adapting educational support to unique abilities and needs.

Informal Matching of Individuals and Environments

It is an axiom of our society that people's differences must be recognized and respected. This basic assumption informs not only our practical behavior but also our system of values. Barrier-free architecture, for example, was created to accommodate people with unusual physical needs; those with dissimilar tastes in food can select different restaurants; and politicians frequently use different campaign approaches with groups whom they perceive to differ with them on political issues. As is true of society in general, formal education also offers numerous practical examples of accommodation to individual differences. Teachers at all levels, from nursery school through graduate school, face the task of motivating students who differ from one another in skills, knowledge, and attitudes.

Typically, teachers have their own unstated premises about how to help different types of students learn. "I know that Johnny has problems concentrating," states a teacher, "so I praise him when he is able to stick to his math problems for fifteen minutes." Another says, "Julie isn't a leader, so I usually assign her to a group where I know one of the other students will draw her out." Or another teacher states, "Max works best when I tell him what must be done and let him decide how he will approach the task." Or, "The computer may be a useful tool, but some of my students dislike working at the terminal." Such comments reflect approaches to dealing with differences among learners that have grown out of practice.

Matching human variables and instructional treatment variables that grow out of practice in instructional settings is valuable for a variety of reasons. Through trial and error, this kind of accommodation has likely passed the tests of both utility and efficiency. Also, the degree of commitment to strategies that teachers find "do the job" is likely to run deep. Successful personal experience in using different approaches for different students may be the most compelling of all reasons for other practitioners to try similar approaches.

Informal matching of people and educational environments emerges from real situations in which all of the activities, pressures, and distractions of daily instructional interactions between teachers and students are present. In contrast to the kind of matching that is generated in artificial or experimental settings, practice-based knowledge and skill endure despite the complexity of instructional settings. It is the richness of a real setting that makes practitioner-oriented approaches particularly appealing. Teachers have the opportunity to observe individual students across many contexts over relatively long periods of time. They scrutinize numerous samples of a student's work, witness how the student relates to peers (and vice versa) and, through contact with parents or siblings, gain insight into the student's family life. Subtle cues that collectively hint at a student's abilities, needs, or interests can help the teacher create an adaptive environment. Moreover, once this environment is matched with a student, the teacher can use the student's subsequent behaviors as information to modify the environment as student needs change. This capability for refining the match over time is a major advantage for practice-based adaptations to individual differences.

Although matches generated from practice offer advantages of simplicity, high credibility with other practitioners, and a grounding in real instructional environments, these matches embody certain possible limitations. These are best illustrated by questioning various assumptions that underlie the use of such strategies:

1. *There is a causal relationship between what the teacher does and what the student learns.* As discussed in Chapter 2, research has provided some but not a great deal of conclusive evidence about relationships between what teachers do and what students learn. Thus, the belief that doing more or less of a certain activity will bring about desired changes in students may be tentative at best.

2. *The teacher is able to assess objectively the impact of his or her behavior on students.* This is similar to assumption 1, but the emphasis here is on the teacher's capacity to be objective. Teachers may believe they have met the needs of students when they have not. Teachers with a high need for student approval may, for example, sacrifice good instructional principles to ensure that they are entertaining. They may thus interpret student approval as an indicator of learning, although they have no information about what was learned.

3. *The teacher has made a careful analysis of students' characteristics and has identified critical attributes that can be attended to by his or her own teaching approaches.* Can we be certain that the teacher knows what to look for, is able to measure the characteristics of interest, and is able to perceive how these can be accommodated by instruction?

4. *The range of skills, knowledge, and strategies the teacher possesses is sufficient to allow him or her to make the most appropriate selection possible to accommodate the student.* The fallacy of this assumption may be the most obvious. Teachers have different degrees of experience, have undergone different kinds of training, and possess diverse abilities.

Some may have multiple strategies they can draw upon, whereas others may have only one or two. Thus, an individual teacher's repertoire may not contain the type of strategy needed for a particular student.

Given these assumptions, the matching of students and educational environments that is generated in practice may have some shortcomings. Teachers may diagnose student characteristics inaccurately. Teachers may be unable to deliver appropriate instruction once diagnoses have been made. And having once taught, teachers may still be unable to assess objectively the impact of their behaviors on students. In addition, informal matching often does not lead to generalizable principles of person-environment relationships. What Ms. Jones finds effective with her ninth-grade mathematics students does not allow one to make prescriptions for other students. On the basis of limited samples, one cannot judge, for example, whether these students are representative of some larger target population. Neither can one assess the replicability of the instructional approach or the reliability of student learning in these situations.

If informally matching a teacher's environment with student characteristics is both promising and limiting, then informally matching a teacher developmental environment with a teacher's characteristics may also be marked by similar strengths and weaknesses. What works well for one teacher may not be equally effective in other situations. Thus, matching that grows out of one teacher educator's experience may be highly credible to other teacher educators but will not necessarily produce expected results under different conditions. The problems of poor generalizability, faulty assumptions, and lack of objectivity may detract from informally based matching of teachers and teacher developmental environments.

Empirically Based Matching of Persons and Environments

Because empirical research may provide clues to relationships between teacher characteristics and educational environments that informal sources do not, it may lend further direction to the activities of teacher educators. The goal of empirical research is to understand relationships among the variables of a given question by using systematic procedures. Variables selected for a particular research project often emerge from theory, other research studies, practical problems, or from the hunches, interests, and curiosities of the researcher. Having once identified certain variables of interest, the researcher selects the approach or series of approaches that he or she believes to be the most appropriate for investigating the problem or question.

Much of the research addressing differences in persons and educational practices uses a *correlational* approach. Correlational studies examine, for instance, how changes or variations in teacher characteristics correspond to changes in teacher educational approaches. These correlational studies investigate such questions as: Do teachers with Characteristic A use Teaching Strategy A more than Teaching Strategy B? Or, do teachers and students who are similar with respect to Characteristic A like each other better, learn more from each other, or use similar modes of communication? What researchers gain from such studies is information about the degree to which one variable (a teacher characteristic) varies with, is related to, or predicts another (use of a particular teaching strategy). Studies of this nature are plentiful and have yielded valuable information. For example, correlational studies of teacher anxiety have shown that highly anxious teachers are less warm (Kracht and Casey, 1968), have more disruptive classes (Moskowitz and Hayman, 1974), and give lower grades to students (Clark, 1970).

An important advantage of correlational research is that a number of variables may be studied simultaneously in classrooms without disturbing the natural occurrence of events. It also suggests potentially fruitful relationships that deserve further clarification and thus leads to further research in a specific area. On the other hand, because of the way such studies are designed, researchers cannot use them to explain the underlying causes of certain relationships. That is, correlational research can statistically compute the relationship between teacher anxiety and students' ratings of teacher warmth, but it cannot determine whether high anxiety *causes* students to perceive teachers as less warm. Other factors relating to the teacher, the students, or the environment may contribute to the relationship, but the correlational approach does not determine causality.

Studies that determine cause and effect constitute a second major approach— *experimental research*. Such studies are based on hypotheses that show a relationship between one or more person characteristics and one or more treatment or environmental characteristics. More specifically, a hypothesis might predict that individuals who have a high degree of Characteristic A will benefit from Treatment 1, whereas subjects with a lower degree will profit more from Treatment 2.

The characteristics of persons investigated in experimental research have been shown to vary widely, as have experimental treatments. Both conventional measures of intelligence or personality and such obscure factors as preferences or expectations have been employed in research on persons. Similarly, treatments designed to adapt to differences in persons have been described in such terms as "degree of structure," "sensory modality," or "pacing." The results of experimentally adapting treatments to individual differences can be measured in terms of individual behaviors, attitude toward treatments, amount learned, and the number and quality of skills acquired.

An experiment by Koran, Snow, and McDonald (1971) illustrates the kind of information about matching environments to persons that one could expect to find in the literature. Using three separate treatments, these investigators tried to increase teacher trainees' skills in asking analytical questions. In the video-modeling (VM) treatment, trainees watched a video tape demonstration of an experienced teacher asking analytical questions of students. Trainees in the text-modeling (TM) treatment were given written copies of the video tape script but saw no visual demonstration. A control (C) group saw neither the video tape model nor the textual script. Trainees who scored high on a measure of perceptual-analytical ability (Hidden Figures Test, Part 1) learned to ask analytical questions more successfully after having undergone the TM treatment rather than the VM treatment. This effect was especially strong when these same trainees were found to be weak in the ability to remember photographically presented live action. The authors speculate that the competent trainees profited from a stimulus that allowed them to proceed at their own pace, to use those cues that were meaningful for encoding, and to be able to review the materials. For these trainees, the fixed-pace, concrete nature of the video medium may have run contrary to their usual strategies for processing skill-related information and thus interfered with their performance. In contrast, for trainees less skilled in analytical or perceptual processes, the video model may have compensated for their deficiencies by explicitly representing information that was more concrete and thus demanded less analysis from the trainees.

Empirical studies such as that of Koran and colleagues embody tradeoffs that are inescapable in real-life settings. Inherent in the process of scientific experimentation is the need to isolate and control. Because a researcher hopes to establish causal relationships, he or she must take steps to manipulate only those variables that are of interest to the experiment. In other words, the researcher is forced to reduce the natural complexity of the world to fit an experimental design. Unfortunately, this typically leads to the design of instructional treatments that are quite different from those used in actual instructional settings. A research treatment may, for example, be of shorter duration, be more rigorously structured, or employ a different sequence of content presentation than is usual in a real-life instructional plan. Thus, the artificial nature of the treatments may limit the researcher's capacity to generalize application of experimental results to actual practice. The use of experimental subjects, conditions, or tasks that are not representative of real teachers, contexts, and teaching tasks limit the utility of many studies. Also, when the variables studied seem obscure or irrelevant to practitioners, the likelihood is small that research can affect practice. And, finally, when individual differences are difficult to measure or seem limited in their effects on anything but a fairly narrow range of behaviors, their study probably offers little guidance for the practitioner.

To complicate matters even further, certain person characteristics may interact differently with different tasks, content, and outcomes. Imagine, for example, a teacher's or teacher educator's reaction to a prescription that reads: "Teacher A with Person Characteristic B should receive Type C instruction but only when Task Type D is used and only with Teacher Educator E." Although researchers are often unable to acknowledge the complexities involved in the application of research to real life processes, it is equally myopic for them to overcomplicate reality. Obviously, the most helpful empirical research is that which identifies teachers, environments, tasks, and outcomes in ways that can be meaningfully related to practice. The findings from a series or program of studies investigating a particular question are often useful in suggesting implications for practice, but those from a single study are usually not. "One-shot" studies that have not been replicated or used in further research tell the practitioner little. Findings from such studies may hint at potentially important effects, but further work is always needed to ensure their reliability and usefulness. Also, when research is generated from sources other than predictions made by theory, there is a danger that the results will be difficult to interpret and apply. By providing a conceptual framework, good theory can account for relationships which, on the surface, may seem arbitrary or unimportant. However, empirical research, when carefully designed and executed, may serve to build frameworks or theories of person-environment matching.

Theory-Based Matching of Persons and Environments

Practice and empirical research are both viable sources of information about individual differences; yet, they are each limited, as has been shown, in their own ways. Theory, or a logically organized framework of propositions and rules, represents a third source. Theory is derived from practice and research and serves a number of important functions:

1. A theory can explain occurrences. The criteria or requirements for this explanation function are straightforward: it must take into account the observable phenomena and it must be plausible. This particular quality of a theory is important because it helps to explain why one event is related to another, even when the connections are not intuitively or perceptually observable.
2. A theory provides a method for systematizing observations and research findings. It allows one to reduce the complexity of large amounts of data into simple, analyzable units.
3. A theory serves to generate research hypotheses. Because of the way theory organizes information, it suggests areas of inquiry that might be fruitful to pursue. This saves time, because in delineating these areas, theory eliminates others that may be less likely to yield useful information.

4. A theory allows one to predict outcomes from research. Thus, theory delineates questions that are useful to pursue and also suggests what will be found when the questions are researched.

Of course, even good theory has its limitations. These may result from the nature of theory or the ways in which people use it. Not all theory is equally practical. Bad theory fails to fulfill one or more of the four previously described functions. For example, although any theory can predict certain outcomes, some of these predictions will be more accurate than others. In the same way, not all theories lead to equally plausible hypotheses, and some are more likely than others to provide an adequate explanation of events. Naturally, theories that cannot be adequately tested have little usefulness, and theories that support and explain intuition are likely to have higher credibility with practitioners than those that seem too esoteric or narrow. Because there is no single comprehensive theory that can tell an educator how to deal with all persons, one must look to more than one theory in an effort to match persons and environments. As Hunt notes, a B-P-E framework (or, in a sense, a theory of theories) allows one to examine persons and environments from such a perspective.

Selecting the Most Appropriate Person Characteristics

In order to find those teacher characteristics that may be most useful for teacher educators to consider, it is necessary to follow some rules or criteria to assess the utility of various conceptions of the person. Unfortunately, a handy formula or set of rules for selecting the most useful personal characteristics does not exist. No body of knowledge points to certain characteristics that can tell teacher educators everything they need to know about teachers as persons. The selection of characteristics—and a suggested direction for teacher educators—may be guided by the following criteria:

1. Does the particular concept of the person have a substantial knowledge base? As opposed to guesswork, is it derived from some combination of practice, research, and theory of learning or instruction?
2. Is the characteristic of the person pervasive and salient; that is, does it influence a wide range of personal behavior and is it a prominent and lasting part of personal behavior?
3. Is there reason to believe that the characteristic is modifiable? Can it be quantitatively or qualitatively changed, as opposed to such personal attributes as sex or age?
4. Has the characteristic been investigated specifically in terms of its ability to explain teacher behavior?

The personal characteristics reviewed here meet these criteria in varying degrees. Some have had longer histories of examination and are therefore representative of a well-established knowledge base. Others are more relevant in their implications for teaching. Still others are more susceptible to change or modification. Some personal characteristics overlap or share, at least partially, the attributes of one another.

Intelligence/General Ability

One person characteristic that has a rich tradition of practical, empirical, and theoretical support is that of intelligence. Although Webster describes intelligence as "the capacity to apprehend facts and propositions and . . . to reason about them," over the years there have been numerous different working definitions of the concept. As early as 1890, Alfred Binet concluded that intelligence was "the tendency to take and maintain a definite direction; the capacity to make adaptations for the purpose of attaining a desired end; and the power of autocriticism" (Binet in Terman, 1916). Spearman (1927) was among the first to propose the existence of a general ability factor, g, which he contended was a measure of pure intellectual capacity. Later theories of intellectual functioning have distinguished between fluid and crystallized abilities (Cattell, 1971; Horn, 1968). Fluid ability is generally considered to be synonymous with Spearman's general ability or g. It is thought to be determined by neural-physiological structures and subject to decline during aging. Direct training is believed by some to have limited effect on this type of intelligence. Crystallized abilities, on the other hand, are less general, more related to specific tasks, and presumably more malleable. They increase as a result of education and experience.

So-called facet models of intelligence have evolved from sophisticated factor analysis techniques. Thurstone's (1931) use of factor analysis led to the identification of a set of seven factors, which he called "primary mental abilities." These initial seven factors were labelled verbal, number, spatial, memory, reasoning, word fluency, and perceptual speed. A more comprehensive facet model of mental organization has been proposed by Guilford (1967), whose "structure of the intellect" theory depicts abilities in terms of three dimensions—content, operations, and products. Crossing the three dimensions leads to a 120-cell configuration, with each cell representing a single hypothesized ability.

Regardless of the theoretical underpinnings, the acceptance of intelligence as a relatively stable, pervasive, and salient trait is widespread. Its prominence has ensured that some measure of general ability is administered in most research studies examining person-environment interactions. This seems to be fortunate, for as Cronbach and Snow (1977) conclude, much of the aptitude-treatment-interaction (ATI) research indicates that treatment dimensions have interacted more consistently with general ability (such as various measures of intelligence) than with specific abilities. Although few hard-and-fast conclusions can be drawn regarding intelligence, some findings suggest the following:

1. Low general ability learners are hindered more than high ability learners by instructional treatments that demand a great deal of self-organization or self-interpretation.
2. Low ability learners are helped by preinstructional organizers, providing they are not too elaborate. These have been found to be either useless or disadvantageous to those with high abilities.
3. Demonstrations intended to clarify what the learner is expected to do seem to help low ability learners, whereas complex elaboration in the form of verbal explanations appears to help those of high ability but hinders low ability learners.

In general, people with high general ability are more facile in adapting to intellectual problem situations. Perhaps they have more available strategies, are more efficient, or possess greater powers of concentration. They will likely profit from instructional situations that allow them to change modes of operation. Alternatively, instructional environments that reduce intellectual demands or the need to adapt will be more successful for lower ability persons.

Whether intelligence or general ability is modifiable has been hotly contested since various concepts first began appearing in the psychological and educational literature. The familiar nature versus nurture or heredity versus environment debates were concerned largely with this issue. The notion that general ability is fixed at birth has had unfortunate, if not dangerous, educational and political consequences, not the least of which have been the practices of stereotyping and "tracking." There is sufficient evidence to suggest that general ability is a function of both innate characteristics and environmental influences; indicating that it is at least in part modifiable.

The implications of investigation on intelligence have not resulted in blueprints for fail-safe educational environments. Much of the classical work on intelligence provides few guidelines to show how teachers may structure education to remediate, compensate, or supplement varying amounts of intelligence. When intelligence or general ability is conceptualized in less conventional ways, however, educational prescriptions seem more abundant. Mastery learning proponents such as Carroll (1963) and Bloom (1971) define aptitude or ability in terms of *rate of learning*. They maintain that what is learned will depend on the time the person spends in learning in relation to the amount of time he or she needs to spend. Time spent is determined by the willingness of the person to persevere and the time allotted for the learning task. The time needed, however, is determined by the person's aptitude for the subject, the quality of the instruction, and his or her ability to understand the instruction. The educational implication here is straightforward: allow the individual enough time and provide a variety of learning alternatives.

Viewing aptitudes or general abilities in terms of a person's level of prior achievement has been the basis for a line of research by Tobias and his associates. They have investigated whether an individual's level of prior knowledge of content to be learned affects his or her capacity to profit from different levels of instructional support. Tobias (1976) offers the following general hypothesis about a person's prior achievement in a content area and its relationship to instructional support:

> the higher the level of prior achievement, the lower the instructional support required to accomplish instructional objectives. Conversely, as level of prior achievement decreases, the amount of instructional support required increases.

In this context, prior achievement refers to the level of knowledge an individual possesses in a given content area before being exposed to instruction. Through pretesting, the level of knowledge relevant to a given content can be assessed. The concept of a pretest is obviously not unfamiliar in educational circles. From early childhood through adulthood, teachers regularly assess initial degrees of competence and knowledge as a precursor to instructional intervention. Parenthetically, in the classroom these pretests are probably most frequently informal in nature. That is, teachers talk with students to find out "where they are" in terms of a particular subject matter or set of skills, rather than using more standard paper-and-pencil measures.

As Tobias points out, the concept of instructional support requires more extensive clarification than the concept of prior achievement. Minimal instructional support might be defined by the teacher educator presenting the content to be learned—that is, lecturing or providing readings. Instructional support increases, however, as the teacher educator brings greater organization to the stimulus content to be learned and to the feedback provided learners. Thus, the teacher educator who provides teachers with learning objectives but eliminates extraneous, irrelevant material could be said to be providing more instructional support than the teacher educator who supplies only reading material. At the farthest end of the support continuum, one might imagine mastery-based learning environments in which the learner's progress is monitored by criterion questions. Thus, the more questions or checkpoints along the way, the greater the instructional support. This notion was illustrated in a study by Tobias and Ingber (1976) in which they found that students who were familiar with religious content to be learned needed less instructional support than those who were unfamiliar with it.

Although applying Tobias's work in instructional settings to the area of teacher development is risky, the possible implications of such work for teacher development may be quite important. Tobias's general hypothesis would suggest that teacher educators might usefully provide increased instructional support to teachers who are low in teaching-related knowledge and give less support to teachers high in prior knowledge.

Most likely, Tyler (1974) would support this broadened definition of general ability. She argues that traditional conceptions of intelligence have been severely limiting. She states that general intelligence scores adequately predict only success in school-related activity. Occupational success, for example, is not related to one's intelligence quotient (IQ). She suggests a need to broaden constructs about the meaning of abilities:

> What can be changed in our practice immediately, however, on the basis of what we now know, is our assumptions about the ways in which people differ from one another. We should regard each individual with whom we deal not as just an inheritor of less or more ability than others may show, and not as a point in multidimensional space, but as the possessor of multiple resources, developed and undeveloped, some of them more valuable to him than others. Whether or not we can measure these aptitudes by means of tests, if we start assuming that the aptitudes exist, we will make efforts to discover them; these efforts can take a variety of forms, such as observing the person in natural situations, interviewing him about his past experience, setting up tryout situations, and many others.

Examining differences in levels of prior achievement represents one approach to broadening the construct of intelligence or ability. Readings of the prior achievement and general ability of teachers are relatively easy to obtain. Because of performance- or competency-based teacher education efforts, pretests that are pertinent to teaching tasks already exist in many areas. Where they are not available, pretests may be constructed and administered. Once teacher knowledge is viewed as a function of task-defined abilities, higher levels of instructional support (for example, more criterion questions and greater pre-organization of materials) may be provided to those teachers who are low in prior achievement.

Stylistic differences in patterns of responding to intellectual tasks have also been identified. These appear to correlate with ways that individuals use their abilities rather than with the amount of ability an individual has. Although several distinct constructs have been investigated, they fall under the general rubric of cognitive styles.

Cognitive Styles

It may be important for teacher educators to determine not only what people know but how they acquire their knowledge. In the study of human characteristics, researchers have consistently found differences in the way people approach various types of perceptual tasks, or the way in which they process information. These personal characteristics, most often referred to as cognitive styles, are generally thought to be different from traditional ability measures and personality traits. Witkin, Moore, Goodenough, and Cox (1977) characterize cognitive styles in terms of four attributes:

1. Styles refer more to the form of cognitive processing than to the content of the material being processed. Individuals with different styles may use different strategies to deal with a same task or problem.
2. Styles are pervasive; they influence a wide range of behavior.
3. Styles are stable over time. There is evidence to indicate that patterns measured in childhood will be similar in adulthood.
4. Styles are generally viewed as bipolar, not unipolar. This means that one extreme is not necessarily valued more than the other. Consequently, both ends of a cognitive style continuum have various advantages and limitations.

As noted earlier concerning intelligence, there are numerous conceptions or theories of the nature of cognitive functioning.

Field Independence

Witkin's study of field independence represents a significant body of work on cognitive styles. *Field independence* refers to the degree to which individuals differ in their dependency on external cues when asked to make judgments in a complex, confusing situation. Some are able to analyze the situation in terms of its component parts and to ignore irrelevant information. When solving problems, people with such ability rely more on internal cues (those from their own bodily sensors) rather than on external cues. Several types of tests, such as the Rod and Frame Test, demonstrate consistent differences in style, and people can be identified by such tests as field independent or field dependent. As the phrase implies, field independent people are *independent* of the distraction of irrelevant cues. Alternatively, field dependent people *depend upon* contextual factors in making judgments.

Field independent or analytical people differ in a number of general ways from their field dependent counterparts. They are more intrinsically oriented, less likely to be sensitive in social and interpersonal settings, and less motivated by peer pressure or approval. In learning, they favor more abstract, analytically oriented subject matter. On the other hand, field dependent people are more highly influenced by context, tend to look to others in defining their own goals and values, and profit more from external reinforcement. They prefer socially oriented subject matter and seem more successful in mastering it than do field independent people.

Research on field independence can be separated into two major areas of inquiry, both of which have direct implications for teaching and teacher developmental activities. The first area deals with the characteristics and behaviors of teachers who demonstrate either field dependence or independence. That area of research has investigated such questions as whether or not differences in teachers on this single characteristic affect teaching strategies, philosophies of teaching, or attitudes toward classroom management. The second area of research has examined relationships betwen teachers and students who vary in terms of their preferred styles.

It appears that teachers' behaviors vary in some rather specific ways. Field dependent teachers appear to be more student-centered in their teaching approaches. They tend to favor discussion activities over either lecture or discovery methods (Wu, 1968). In other studies reported by Witkin and colleagues (1977), these teachers also stated their belief that students should set up a group standard for grading, whereas field independent teachers emphasized the importance of teacher-derived standards for performance. Also, field independent teachers prefer lecture or discovery methods, both of which leave much of the structuring of the learning situation up to the teacher. Differences have also been shown in preferences for methods of feedback to students. Field independent teachers favored corrective feedback (that is, informing students when their responses were incorrect and telling them why) as an effective teaching strategy, but the other group did not. Additionally, field independent teachers, but not the others, believed that expressing displeasure when a student performs poorly is important. Perhaps the greater orientation of field dependent individuals toward social approval or interpersonal harmony makes them resist the possible antagonism that might result from negative evaluative feedback.

Although field dependent and field independent teachers may behave differently, evidence indicates that these differences do not differentially affect student achievement. In an analysis of teacher characteristics data from the Beginning Teacher Evaluation Study, Stone (1976) found that although the two types of teachers differ in certain teacher behaviors, these did not correlate with the amount of student learning.

Research into the relationships of or interactions between teachers and students who are similar and dissimilar in cognitive styles provides further specific information. Two studies (DiStefano, 1970; James, 1973) found that when students and teachers shared the same cognitive style, they rated each other more positively than when they differed in cognitive style. In the James study, it was also found that teachers assigned high grades to students with cognitive styles similar to their own. In another study reported by Witkin and others, an additional variable, the sex of teacher and student, was added. Responses to postcourse interpersonal attraction questionnaires did not show a teacher-student cognitive style match-mismatch effect. However, an effect was found for sex. Students and teachers of the same sex valued each other more highly than those of the opposite sex. In this study, the possible effects of cognitive style appeared to be outweighed by those related to sex.

Witkin and colleagues cite three factors that probably contribute to this attraction between people with the same cognitive style. Students and teachers who share cognitive styles may also share similar interests. Also, they may have certain personality factors in common that allow them to appreciate or empathize with each other. Finally, it is possible that students and teachers of similar cognitive style may share similar preferences for modes of communication. W. D. Shows (1968), for example, found that field independent or dependent people tend to select verbal descriptions of pictures that judges rated as more likely to have been generated in accordance with each style.

Conceptual Level

As noted earlier, the work by Hunt and his associates on the construct of *conceptual level* represents one of the most well-developed and promising approaches to cognitive style. Hunt (1975) characterizes conceptual level in the following way:

> Conceptual Level is a person characteristic, indexing both cognitive complexity (differentiation, discrimination, and integration) as well as interpersonal maturity (increasing self-responsibility). A person at a higher Conceptual Level is more structurally complex, more capable of responsible actions, and, most important, more capable of adapting to a changing environment than a person at a lower Conceptual Level.

Thus, according to conceptual systems theory (Harvey, Hunt, and Schroder, 1961), a person's conceptual development is assumed to progress simultaneously along two dimensions: information processing abilities, or integrative complexity, and interpersonal orientation, or self-other relatedness.

The theory postulates a developmental sequence; that is, a person's conceptual capabilities progress from a concrete stage or low conceptual level (CL) through a series of increasingly abstract stages to a high CL. Early work (Harvey, Hunt, and Schroder, 1961; Schroder, Driver, and Streufert, 1967) formulated a developmental model consisting of four distinct stages or conceptual levels. Later modifications of the model by Hunt depict CL more in terms of a continuum of development rather than in terms of discrete stages. Hunt's matching model (Figure 4–1) posits a generally inverse relationship between CL and the degree of structure of the environment. Generally speaking, low CL individuals perform best in and prefer working under conditions of high structure. High CL persons, on the other hand, perform best in and prefer environments low in structure, or are unaffected by the degree of structure.

Theory, research, and practice suggest that CL is a relatively pervasive and stable human characteristic. It correlates in the 0.20s with intelligence, in-creases with age, and, at least in some instances, is related to social class, sex, and academic achievement. CL has been shown to influence behavior of children and adults in the classroom, administrative settings, summer camp, parental training conditions, and counseling relationships, among many other situations. Although it is relatively stable—that is, not situation specific or subject to fluctuations, except perhaps under severe conditions (Suedfeld, 1964)—there is reason to believe that CL, through direct purposeful interven-tion, can be modified upward (Oja and Sprinthall, 1978). If one assumes that development along the CL continuum is desirable, the challenge becomes one of moving a person from one stage to another. The task for the teacher educator, then, is one of determining how to structure environments so as to encourage growth from one level to the next.

The degree of structure of the environment has been defined in various ways (teacher versus student control, discovery versus didactic strategies, and rule-example versus example-rule presentations, to mention a few). Hunt suggests that movement from Stage A to Stage B will be facilitated by a carefully structured environment with clearly defined rules and expectations in an atmosphere that is "accepting but firm." Progression from Stage B to Stage C is encouraged by somewhat less structure and allowing more avenues of self-expression and autonomy.

Evidence also indicates that CL and the degree of structure of the environ-ment interact. In one often cited study, McLachlan and Hunt (1973) defined *structure* in terms of a discovery learning strategy (low structure) and a lecture approach (high structure). The abilities of low CL students to subjectively in-

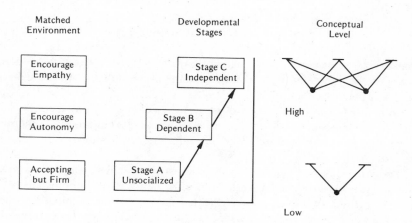

FIGURE 4–1. Developmental Matching Model. [Hunt, D. E. Person-environment interactions: A challenge found wanting before it was tried. *Review of Educational Research* (1975), 45 (2): 223. Reproduced by permission.]

tegrate the material to be learned were best facilitated by conditions of high structure. As one would expect from the developmental nature of the variable, high CL students, on the other hand, were unaffected by the degree of structure. In another study that investigated students' abilities to learn the concept of cognitive dissonance (Festinger, 1957), Tomlinson and Hunt (1971) defined structure in terms of providing examples only (low structure), presenting examples followed by rules (intermediate structure), and presenting rules followed by examples (high structure). Under conditions of low and intermediate structure, low CL students did not perform as well as high CL students. Also, low CL students in low and intermediate structure situations did not perform as well as low CL students in high structure situations.

Research on CL and teaching styles raises interesting implications for practice. Hunt and Joyce (1967), for instance, found high CL teachers to be more "interdependent" (that is, willing to help students theorize and think for themselves) in their teaching methods than were low CL teachers. Rathbone (1971) investigated how student CL affects teaching methods used by teachers. As noted earlier, the results of his experiment illustrate quite dramatically the notion of "student pull." That is, the CL of students forced teachers to modulate their teaching behaviors. According to Rathbone, when teachers, regardless of their own CLs, are faced with high CL students, they tend to read and adjust their behaviors to encourage students to think for themselves.

As teacher educators work to adapt their approaches to the needs and abilities of teachers, it appears that CL or other cognitive style variables may provide useful direction.

Ego Development

A teacher's level of ego maturity is another characteristic that may influence how she or he functions both personally and professionally. Loevinger and colleagues (Loevinger and Wessler, 1970a, 1970b; Loevinger, 1966) suggest that ego maturity can be conceptualized in terms of stages along a continuum. Just as with physical, psychosexual, or intellectual development, individuals at lower stages of development have different qualities from those at more advanced stages.

In Loevinger's scheme, the ego is a holistic construct that encompasses such processes as moralization, relatability, or conceptual complexity. It can thus be regarded as a master trait that influences a number of other traits. The ego has also been described as an organizing framework through which a person perceives and structures the world. This frame of reference or structure determines the meaning the world holds for an individual and how he or she will interact with it. The ego also influences those aspects of the environment to which the individual responds as well as the types of responses made. Loevinger calls the ego an "inner logic" that maintains itself and its identity by filtering out factors in the environment that are incompatible with its current level.

Ego development is characterized by increasing differentiation and complexity in impulse control, interpersonal style, conscious preoccupation, and cognitive style. As demands from the environment increase in amount and complexity, the individual must constantly adapt, and this causes the structures to progress from less to more complex. This process of change in structures has been conceptualized as a continuum that encompasses a sequence of ten stages, three of which are transitional. These stages are hierarchically ordered in terms of complexity. Although their sequence of occurrence is invariant, stages are not perfectly correlated with age. Adults can be found at most stages, although the modal level for American adults is near the middle of the continuum.

Presocial Stage. The presocial stage is perhaps the most difficult to study because measuring techniques that employ verbal language cannot be used. Two phases comprise this stage. In the presocial phase, the infant strives for the gratification of immediate needs. Because the child is unable to discriminate between himself or herself and other persons or things, an ego is not yet conceptualized. In the symbiotic phase, the child differentiates the mother or primary nurturing agent from others but still does not differentiate himself or herself from the mother.

Impulse Stage. At the impulse stage the formulation of the ego is apparent as the child is now able to differentiate himself or herself from others. Behavior is controlled by impulse and there is a preoccupation with the satisfaction of physical needs. The child is strongly dependent on others but in an exploitive and demanding way. Children at this stage view others in terms of their capability to punish or reward behavior. The child is oriented toward the present rather than the past or the future and views the world egocentrically.

Self-Protective Stage. The child at the self-protective stage begins to see relationships between actions and outcomes but is not yet able to accept the responsibility that his or her own actions are a causal agent for punishment. Blame is always placed on external factors. There is a recognition that rules exist, but the child (or adult) operates on the assumption that breaking a rule is wrong only if one gets caught. Although there is less dependence on others, interpersonal relationships are exploitive and manipulative. Impulses are coming to be controlled.

Self-Protective/Conformist Transition Stage. This transition is not carefully defined because, in some respects, it is an artifact of the Sentence Completion

Test. Responses that are not complex enough to be rated at the next higher stage or impulsive enough to be rated at the self-protective stage fall into this transition. Simple obedience and conformity to external social norms start to emerge here.

Conformist Stage.   In the conformist stage, the individual begins to associate his or her own well-being with that of a group, typically a family. Rules are obeyed primarily out of fear of disapproval by the reference group. Individuals at this stage are still not accepting of responsibility for their actions. Conforming to what is perceived to be the acceptable pattern of behavior by the group to whom the individual identifies is crucial because belonging is an important need during this stage. The individual is largely intolerant of people who seem different from himself or herself and often stereotypes them. Interpersonal relationships are conceived in terms of actions and concrete events rather than feelings.

Conformist to Conscientious Transition Stage.   Most adults in American society are located in this transition. Its major characteristic is that the individual starts to become less reliant on external "norms." He or she becomes more self-aware and begins to examine previously unexamined assumptions. Behavior is characterized as becoming more self-critical. The individual begins to acknowledge multiple perspectives and the value in individual differences.

Conscientious Stage.   At the conscientious stage, the individual begins to operate more in line with internal rules rather than external ones. He or she now has an internalized sense of responsibility for his or her own actions and behaviors. Reasoning operates at a more complex level. Feelings and motives now characterize interpersonal relations and the person develops the capacity for empathy and true mutuality in social interactions. The individual thinks in terms of obligations, ideals, and achievements.

Conscientious to Autonomous Transition Stage.   This stage is mainly characterized by increased complexity. The individual can better accept the ironies and paradoxes of life without needing to make them too simplistic. There is increased awareness of the inner conflict between dependency and independence. Interpersonal relations are highly valued in contrast with the ideals or achievement most highly valued in the previous stage. This person prizes individual differences rather than simply tolerating their existence. An increased appreciation of one's own individuality is an important benchmark of this transition.

Autonomous Stage.   At the autonomous stage, there is increased ability to cope with inner struggles over conflicting needs and patterns of behavior.

This individual is less judgmental and more tolerant of the choices made by others. Interpersonal relations are characterized by the recognition of mutual interdependence but also the acceptance of the autonomy of other people. Conscious thoughts center on self-fulfillment, complexity of reality, individuality, and role responsibilities.

Integrated Stage. Rarely are individuals who function at the integrated level identified. Consequently, less is known about this stage than others. However, it is believed that people at this stage have reconciled much of their inner conflict and cherish, rather than simply tolerate, individual differences. This person has an integrated sense of identity similar to Maslow's notion of the self-actualized individual.

Loevinger's stage model has undergone extensive empirical validation, in large part as a result of the availability of a highly reliable and valid measurement instrument—the Washington University Sentence Completion Test. This thirty-six item, semi-projective measure determines an individual's core functioning or stage of ego development based on the distribution of ratings to the items. This instrument was used in two studies (Bernier, 1977; Oja, 1979) that attempted to help teachers progress to higher levels of ego maturity, moral reasoning, and cognitive complexity. In both studies, elementary and secondary in-service teachers participated in workshops based on Mosher and Sprinthall's (1970) Deliberate Psychological Education Model. The general objectives for the model are to help people move along stages of cognitive-developmental growth and to encourage specific skill development. One major principle of operation is that cognitive restructuring or development is brought about through active experience and a structured opportunity to reflect on that experience. Bernier (1977) described the nature of the workshop intervention used in his study in the following way:

> an environment was created that enabled teachers to assume a position of responsibility in an atmosphere of colleagial relationships where one must take the perspective of others in making value and action choices and also regularly examine these decisions.

Intervention in the Oja study was in many respects a replication of the Bernier approach. The designers attempted, however, to make their workshop a more powerful treatment "in the sense of promoting principled autonomy and the assertion of one's individuality." Neither study was successful in moving people to more advanced stages of ego development as measured by the Sentence Completion Test. Most teachers were located at the conformist-conscientious transition level, both at the beginning and end of the treatment. Oja found significant differences on the post-test scores between experimental teachers who participated in the workshop and control subjects, but her examination of the data indicated that this finding may be an artifact of the instrument. The Sentence Completion Test shows a troublesome tendency to produce regressed scores when readministered after a brief interval. Perhaps at best, then, the workshop prevented teachers from showing post-test regression.

In discussing this failure to promote growth, Oja suggests that

> what may be called for to promote increased levels of ego maturity to 1–⁴/₅ (Conformist-conscientious transition) and 1–5 (Conscientious stage) are even more intensive, distinct role shifts out of the familiar classroom to major positions of leadership and responsibility in educational programs where the teachers would have significant autonomy and responsibility for control of their own destiny.

These studies suggest that ego maturity is a complex characteristic and not easily influenced by single, short-term interventions. This relative stability suggests that knowledge about a teacher's level of ego development may be important in the teacher educator's choice of strategies, however.

Moral Development

Many psychologists have dedicated their professional lives to the study of the human capability of making moral and ethical judgments. Most notable among these is Lawrence Kohlberg, whose work is especially important because he has conceptualized a comprehensive scheme of distinct levels or stages of moral maturity. In setting forth a developmental theory of moral reasoning, much as Piaget has done in cognitive development, Kohlberg lends direction to the matching of educational environments to differences in moral decision making.

Table 4–1 summarizes the three major levels of moral judgment and the stages within each level as presented in Kohlberg's theory.

A major defining characteristic of the first level, preconventional morality, is the importance of consequence and power in determinations of good and bad or right and wrong. Rules passed on by an adult authority must be followed to avoid negative consequences such as punishment or to obtain some desired reward. At the earliest stage (Stage 0), what is right is determined solely by what feels good or what one likes, and bad is anything that leads to unpleasant consequences. At Stage 1, the major determinant of "right" action is that which does not lead to punishment. Individuals at this stage defer to those who are perceived to be powerful because such people control rewards and punishments. Reciprocity is introduced at Stage 2, but it is unrelated to either loyalty or justice. The satisfaction of one's own personal needs lies at the basis of any attempt at sharing; an "I'll scratch your back if you'll scratch mine" principle operates. Meeting the needs of another is always contingent upon how that satisifes one's own needs.

TABLE 4–1
Kohlberg's Levels and Stages of Moral Development.

Levels	Stages
1. Preconvention.	0. Egocentric judgments.
	1. The punishment and obedience orientation.
	2. The instrumental-relativist orientation.
2. Convention.	3. The interpersonal concordance orientation.
	4. The "law and order" orientation.
	4½. The transition phase or "anti-establishment" orientation.
3. Postconventional.	5. The social contract legalistic orientation.
	6. The universal ethical principle orientation.

The conventional level of judgment depends less on immediate consequence. Societal groups such as the family or the nation become more meaningful in that they represent bodies of order that demand support and loyalty.
The capacity to recognize the intent of an action emerges here. In Stage 3,
the role of approval in determining right and wrong action is extremely important; a prevailing assumption at this stage is that one shouldn't cheat because nice people don't cheat. Stage 4 reasoning is rules-oriented. Everyone
must obey without question the rules or laws that are perceived to operate.
Moral judgments are made to reflect strict adherence to these rules. The next
stage (Stage 4½) has been described as transitional and "antiestablishment."
It lies somewhere between the convention and postconvention levels and
seems to reflect the individual's struggle to integrate his or her own emerging
needs with what he or she perceives to be the expectations and demands of
the social order.

The third and final level that Kohlberg describes is called the postconven-
tional or principled level. At this point, the individual is able to separate
moral values and principles from those who hold these values. Thus, the role
of authority is less pervasive in determining one's judgment of a situation.
Stage 5 is characterized by a social contract legalistic orientation. People
whose moral reasoning is typical of this stage hold that right behavior or action must conform to constitutionally or democratically agreed upon standards
but, beyond these, personal values and opinions should govern choice.
Changes in laws are welcomed when derived from rational considerations of
social need or utility. The last stage (Stage 6) is characterized by a much more
highly idiosyncratic system of ethical principles. Cooperation among individ-

uals is highly prized. Respect for the rights of others and for the dignity of the person should guide decision making.

Because of the developmental nature of Kohlberg's scheme, educational programs, courses, and curricular material whose objective is to increase the sophistication of students' moral reasoning capabilities have flourished (Rest, 1974b). Typically, the approach taken in these programs is the presentation of a series of hypothetical moral dilemma problems, followed by group discussions. During the discussion, issues are raised that challenge participants' present modes of thinking. By confronting other points of view and other sources of evidence, participants become aware of the limitations of their own processes of judgment. Throughout the activities, the teacher attempts to arouse within the student a level of cognitive confusion or disharmony which will eventually encourage movement to the next higher stage of moral judgment.

But for the teacher educator, of course, teacher growth rather than student growth is the primary objective. One must therefore ask, Is it reasonable to expect that the moral reasoning of different teachers will fall at different stages? Unfortunately, existing literature does not provide much information about the moral development of teachers. Data available on adults in general, however, suggest that considerable differences exist. Differences have been found for men and women in terms of the highest stage obtained. Erickson (1974) writes that although most of the adult population operates at the conventional level, adult women are typically at Stage 3 whereas adult men are at Stage 4. These differences between the sexes have not been found during childhood or adolescence but begin to show up during the college years.

Even if it can be shown empirically that certain teachers have less sophisticated approaches to making moral judgments, what difference does this knowledge make, and why would it be important information for the teacher educator? It is not known, for example, how the moral reasoning strategies of teachers affect their behavior in the classroom, the way they deal with conflict between children, or how they discipline students who misbehave. Little is known about the relationship between reasoning about hypothetical moral problems and how one actually behaves in real situations. Rest (1974a) summarizes the problem:

> The question of interest here would be whether moral judgment measures as presently conceived (i.e., using hypothetical dilemmas so as to arrive at a stage score) reliably relate to "moral judgment behavior" and whether the present scoring categories exhaust the important features of moral judgment behavior. Are the kinds of considerations which a person emphasizes in hypothetical situations in the test situation also emphasized in his deliberations on how to vote in the next election? Do the same concepts of authority, of distributive justice, of law appear both in the test situation and in his arguments for policy at his business? What is the relation between a politician's tested moral judgment stage

and his campaign speeches? After some 40 years of research it is amazing how little effort has been devoted to these questions.

To deal with this issue, many researchers have examined the degree to which people perform morality-oriented acts or behaviors. Studies of this nature have found modest but significant correlations between moral judgment stages and such behaviors as cheating, participating in politically oriented protests, or confession to crimes. But Rest points out that one class of activities that has not often been examined as an index of real life behaviors is that of verbal behaviors—that is, verbal opinions, arguments, or judgments expressed about moral issues in everyday life. His argument is that the expression of a moral judgment, whether it be in a courtroom, a classroom, or at a cocktail party, is a potentially powerful mobilizing force, which may have a strong impact on the shape and occurrence of external events. The ramifications of publicly stated judgments are undoubtedly heightened when they are expressed by authority figures or role models—both of which may often describe classroom teachers.

It would be an oversimplification to assume that a teacher's behavior in every situation can be predicted by his or her stage of moral reasoning. Despite a variety of contextual factors, however, the teacher educator will find it advantageous to be attentive to cues that might indicate the way a teacher thinks about moral problems. For example, the unsophisticated moral reasoner may demonstrate little tolerance for students who "refuse to follow the rules." Or a teacher with more advanced moral reasoning skills may become frustrated when his or her students do not manifest moral reasoning skills to the same degree.

Affective Characteristics

In conclusion, we will discuss three different but related teacher characteristics: attitudes, expectations, and concerns or anxieties. These attributes describe personal beliefs, feelings, and emotions to a greater degree than characteristics discussed earlier. Because research in these general areas of human behavior is plentiful, we will draw from those studies that contribute directly to the practice of teacher development.

Attitudes

Although research in this subject is relatively new, attitudes have long been thought to be strong determinants of human behavior. Variations on the construct of attitude, however, have become so complex and numerous as to defy simple definition. Thurstone (1931) described attitudes as affective for or against a psychological object. Allport (1935), on the other hand, described attitudes as states of readiness that influence kinds of behavior to related objects and events. Ostrom (1968) and others have advanced additional conceptions of attitudes. Khan and Weiss (1973) contend that despite the differences among definitions their commonality is shown by the fact that

> attitudes are selectively acquired and integrated through learning and experience; that they are enduring dispositions indicating response consistency; and that positive or negative affect toward a social or psychological object represents that salient characteristic of an attitude.

In particular, the attitudes of teachers have been of primary interest to many sociologists, psychologists, and teacher educators. As Loree (1971) indicates, investigation of (and the effort to actually shape) teachers' attitudes about themselves, their pupils, and teaching and learning in general have been prominent objectives of teacher education programs. Many programs have tried to identify "desirable" attitudes for teachers and have in turn encouraged their clients to assimilate them. Assumptions underlying these programmatic efforts are that (1) certain attitudes are characteristic of effective teachers, (2) at least some people do not possess these attitudes upon entering a teacher education program, and (3) it is possible to develop or modify attitudes in teachers.

As Loree also points out, teacher attitudes can be identified or measured in several ways. One of the most common techniques has been through a self-report inventory such as the MTAI, or Minnesota Teacher Attitude Inventory (Cook, Leeds, and Callis, 1951). Besides self-reporting, other methods of assessing teacher attitudes—such as systematic observation of teaching, projective techniques (open-ended response forms) and the semantic differential (seven-point scales bounded by pairs of adjectives opposite in meaning)—can be useful for enriching knowledge on teacher attitudes.

Obviously, all teachers do not possess the same attitudes toward themselves, toward pupils, and toward teaching and learning. Ryans's (1960) study of teacher characteristics supports this contention. He examined teachers' attitudes toward students, administrators, supervisory personnel, parents, and teaching practices. Ryan observed some of the following trends in teacher attitudes in his research:

1. The attitudes of elementary teachers toward pupils, administrators, fellow teachers, and nonadministrative personnel in the schools were markedly more favorable than were similar attitudes of secondary teachers.
2. Teachers judged superior by their principals have more favorable attitudes toward pupils than do teachers judged poor or unsatisfactory.
3. Attitudes of secondary teachers of greater experience tended to be slightly more favorable toward administrators and somewhat less favorable toward pupils than other experience groups.

4. More favorable attitudes toward pupils were expressed by women teachers in the secondary school, but among elementary teachers there was a tendency for men to possess more favorable pupil attitudes than women.
5. Teachers judged to be more warm, understanding, and more stimulating possessed more favorable attitudes toward pupils and administrators.
6. The educational viewpoints expressed by secondary teachers tended to be traditional or learning-centered in nature, whereas elementary teachers leaned more in the direction of permissiveness.
7. Teachers judged to be more warm and understanding in their classroom behavior (and to a somewhat lesser extent, those judged to be more stimulating) expressed more permissive educational viewpoints.

There is considerable support for the idea that the attitudes held by teachers influence how they behave in a variety of situations and that their behaviors in turn influence student behavior. Brophy and Good (1974) summarized a set of attitudinal studies pertinent to classroom practice. Some of the findings were quite consistent across studies. For instance, students for whom teachers felt an "attachment" were high achieving, conforming students who rewarded the teachers by showing desirable classroom behavior. Despite the positive attitude teachers expressed toward these students, however, there was no evidence to indicate that the teachers favored them behaviorally. On the other hand, teachers were generally less communicative and interactive with students about whom they felt "indifferent." Students about whom teachers were "concerned" were in general given a great deal of the teacher's time and effort. These students tended to seek out this help in a proactive fashion. "Rejection" students, or those whom teachers would remove from their classroom if given the opportunity, also generated a considerable amount of interaction or exchange with teachers. However, it was of a different quality; teacher concerns about these students had more to do with controlling their classroom behavior than with their academic achievement.

Not only do teachers hold different attitudes (and as a consequence behave differently), but Della Piana and Gage (1955) suggest that teacher attitudes also interact with pupil values. They tested the hypothesis that students' positive feelings toward teachers were determined by their own personal values in combination with teachers' attitudes. The results of their study indicated that teachers with favorable attitudes were better liked by students who exhibited strong affective values concerning teachers.

But can teacher attitudes be modified? Although the research does not yield a definitive answer, many studies suggest that they can be. Attitudes of prospective teachers toward curriculum reorganization, discipline, and attention to individual differences have been improved through education courses. Research on student teaching, however, has demonstrated that student teachers' attitudes often tend to become more negative and authoritarian. More investigation is needed to clarify the nature, strength, and duration of changes in teacher attitudes before this question can be answered with clarity.

Teacher attitudes, and in particular their differences, may prove to be important for teacher educators to consider as they formulate support environments. As Khan and Weiss (1973) point out, affective phenomena such as attitudes may interact with environmental factors:

> One of the important findings has been that main effects by themselves may not be adequate for understanding affective phenomena. It is likely that interaction effects such as teacher-program, teacher-instructional strategy, student-program, student-instructional strategy . . . may prove to be important sources of information in trying to understand how affective responses develop and how they may prove useful in developing classroom strategies. We would like to see the concepts of aptitude-treatment interaction (Cronbach and Snow, 1969; Gagne, 1967) broadened so that affective-treatment interactions become equally amenable for research. For example, a student's attitude toward an instructional strategy may prove to be more important for learning both cognitive and affective behaviors than either aptitude or past achievement.

We not only agree with Khan and Weiss but would also stretch this view of student learning to suggest that a teacher's attitude toward teacher developmental strategies may prove to be more important for his or her own growth and development than either aptitude or past achievement.

Expectations

Closely related to a teacher's attitudes toward a student are the teacher's expectations about that student. What are the implications of teacher expectations? Will they influence a teacher's behavior toward a student? Do teacher expectations affect student learning? Do different teachers show different patterns of expectations? A strong line of research addressing such questions was generated following the publication of Rosenthal and Jacobson's controversial *Pygmalion in the Classroom* (1968). The book reported a fascinating experimental study conducted in a single elementary school. The question investigated in the study was whether a teacher's expectations of individual students might generate "self-fulfilling prophecies." In other words, would a student live up to a teacher's expectations even when the expectations may be based on inaccurate information?

In order to investigate teacher expectations, Rosenthal and Jacobson erroneously informed each teacher in the study that several students in his or her classroom were diagnosed as "late intellectual bloomers" and could be expected to make large gains in achievement during the coming year. When the year was over, the group of students arbitrarily designated as "late bloomers" did make significantly greater progress than their same-grade-level counterparts. The difference was most pronounced for grades one and two and was stronger for girls than for boys. In general, the research on teacher expectations suggests that problems result when one or both of the following conditions exist: expectations are based on inaccurate data and expectations are inflexible. When the early, inaccurate perceptions of teachers about students change as the result of increased interactions, there is little likelihood of negative effects. However, an unwillingness or inability to adjust early expectations, when appropriate, often results in a negative, self-fulfilling prophecy for students.

The potency of expectation effects appears to depend on the characteristics of both teachers and students. Student characteristics that seem to affect expectation include sex, prior achievement patterns, and certain personality factors. Teacher variables include level of competence, coping styles, and defense mechanisms. These, and probably a myriad of other factors, affect how teachers form expectations and how these expectations guide behavior.

Although numerous studies have investigated this Pygmalion phenomenon in conjunction with children's achievements, some have examined the effects of expectations on adult performance. Findings from a series of studies by King (1971) indicate that supervisors' differing expectations of trainee capabilities are related to job performance. Supervisors were led to believe that certain members of each of five job training categories (welders, mechanics, pressers, assemblers, and nurses' aides) had special potential for their particular occupational trade. In all but one of the five categories, these "special potential" individuals demonstrated higher job performance than those in the control groups.

Rosenthal (1974) hypothesizes that the underlying explanation for the impact of expectations is reflected in four factors. A warmer, more supportive *climate* may be generated around high expectation students, and the level of *feedback* or information given to these students might be more extensive. Perhaps teachers use more difficult material with these students and teach more of it. Thus, the *input* that teachers give these "special" students may be greater. Teachers may also give the students more opportunity to produce *output*; that is, the students may be given greater encouragement to ask questions, to respond, or to practice. This conceptual action is supported by Garner and Bing (1973), who suggest that different teacher expectations lead to different teacher behavior and that these in turn foster differential student behavior, which may then result in different levels of student achievement.

In another model of expectancy effects, Brophy and Good (1974) conclude that one of three distinct patterns of behavior characterizes most teachers. *Proactive* teachers strive to establish and maintain the initiative in structuring interactions with their classes as groups and with their students as individuals. They use their expectations of students in planning educational treatments to individualize and optimize instruction for pupils by flexibly planning and altering instruction to account for changes in pupils. Proactive teachers, then, have clear ideas of what they want to do and attempt to minimize dysfunctional interference of their own expectations and student behaviors with their progress toward formulated goals.

The passive or *reactive* teacher is said to have generally accurate and flexible expectations that are adjusted to reach students' behavior. In contrast to the proactive teacher, the reactive teacher tends to allow students to control the patterns of teacher-student interaction in the classroom. The reactive teacher neither shows evidence of compensating for differences in student behavior nor of overreacting to these student differences, which leads to undesirable effects of teacher expectation.

The third type of teacher Brophy and Good characterized as an *overreactor*, or one who provides the most evidence of expectation effects that interfere with his or her teaching. The overreactor allows himself or herself to be conditioned by students' differences and accentuates or distorts differences by treating students more differently than they really are. This type of teacher is prone to favor students who exhibit acceptable, desirable behavior and reject or abandon students who demonstrate unacceptable or undesirable classroom behavior. More than the other teacher types, the overreactor is likely to stereotype students rather than view them as unique individuals; in general, according to Brophy and Good, this type of teacher is likely to be less competent than others.

In viewing these patterns of behavior as forming rather loose categorizations of general types of teachers, Brophy and Good do not claim that every teacher is one of these types in his or her transactions with all students. They point out that a teacher who is generally reactive may attempt to compensate for student deficiencies by working hard with one or two low achievers (but not all) and may also overreact with one or two others. In the same way, a proactive teacher may be conditioned by some students; but an overreactive teacher will not necessarily exhibit undesirable expectation effects with all students. The teacher educator who is aware of these kinds of teacher behavior patterns might begin to tailor his or her strategy to move a teacher away from excessive overreacting toward more proactive behavior.

Concerns and Anxieties

It is not surprising that teachers exhibit a variety of concerns and anxieties. They experience pressure from many directions. Students can be bored, disruptive, or blatantly hostile; parents frequently make demands that are impossible to meet; and the community generally expects teachers to keep up with the latest information, try out innovative teaching strategies, and have enough energy left over to "take a personal interest" in each and every student. Although the sources of concerns are many, it seems that in comparison to other person characteristics the concerns that teachers have about their work are more clearly related to their level of experience. This is reflected in a model by Fuller (1969), who has proposed a developmental conceptualization of teaching concerns. Fuller's model outlines three major phases or periods of concern: preteaching, early teaching, and late teaching.

The preteaching phase refers to that period in which the individual is enrolled in educational courses but has not yet had actual contact with pupils in the classrooms. During this time, students seem not to have a great number of specific teaching-related concerns. Because they have had no direct experience, their apprehensions about problems in teaching are based on hearsay or imagined problem situations. Pre-service teachers still identify more with the student role than with the professional role, and many of their concerns may not be different from other sophomores or juniors in noneducation settings.

Early teaching concerns are those expressed by student teachers and inexperienced in-service teachers. All of the vague uncertainties of managing oneself in the classroom are exposed when the individual begins to work in the schools. Survival concerns predominate here as the student worries about his or her adequacy. These concerns encompass fears about one's inability to control the class, doubts about one's level of mastery of subject matter, and a fear of being evaluated by supervisors.

Late concerns, or those typical of more experienced teachers, are the least understood of the three because fewer data are available. It appears, however, that teacher concerns become more pupil-oriented as teachers become more experienced. Most likely, as teachers acquire security in their own professional roles, they can focus more adequately on the needs of others. Another indication of this increased comfort level is the mature teacher's concern about meeting self-generated expectations for performance as well as those that supervisors might express.

A developmental pattern of concerns has also been identified when teachers are asked to work with any type of innovation. The Concerns Based Adoption Model, carried out at the University of Texas and based on Fuller's (1969) earlier work, described a continuum of concerns evident in teachers as they are introduced to certain innovations. Initially, concerns reflect issues about one's self, such as the impact of the innovation on one's professional status or role. Next, as they begin to use the innovation, teachers become more concerned with task-related problems, including adjusting one's teaching methods or acquiring a new management technique. Finally, as a teacher's comfort level increases over time, he or she becomes more concerned about understanding how the learner is affected by the innovation. Thus, the pattern of self-orientation to pupil-orientation parallels the developmental continuum of general concerns described by Fuller. Although experts do not necessarily agree about the exact nature of anxiety or its behavioral correlates, most would accept the fact that anxiety refers to those feelings of stress or tension that are aroused under situations perceived to be threatening.

Correlational research suggests that anxiety is related to several aspects of teaching. "Best" teachers were rated as being more relaxed (Moskowitz and Hayman, 1974) whereas high-anxiety teachers have been found to be less verbally supportive (Petrusich, 1967) and less warm (Kracht and Casey, 1968). Highly anxious teachers may, in general, be less effective in the classroom when effectiveness is defined in terms of student achievement. That is, several studies (Washbourne and Heil, 1960; Osborne, 1973) have shown that the greater a teacher's level of anxiety, the less students learn. Teachers who are fearful tend to be less warm, are often inconsistent in their behavior, and increase the anxiety levels of students.

That teachers have different concerns and anxieties and that these will likely depend heavily on the teacher's stage of professional maturity are important information for the teacher educator for several reasons. Until earlier concerns are resolved, the teacher's ability to attend to important student needs may be limited. Although the passage of time will likely increase a teacher's confidence about his or her ability to control the class, to deliver subject matter satisfactorily, or to meet the expectations of those in an evaluative role, other situational factors may operate more proactively. The probability that a teacher will resolve feelings of inadequacy may be enhanced, for example, by sensitive and supporting relationships with colleagues, principals, or supervisors. Consider a frustrated new teacher who is eager to implement innovative educational ideas encountered in methods courses but finds that the constant pressure of keeping order in the classroom requires most of his energy. In this situation, the wise teacher educator might first concentrate on helping the teacher master effective management strategies that can reduce classroom control problems before attacking other problems.

As concerns shift, the focus of the teacher educator's work with teachers should also undergo change. Perhaps with more advanced teachers, observation sessions will provide an opportunity to focus on particular strategies that teachers use to deal with specific learning problems in certain pupils. Or, they may serve as a vehicle for gathering information about the effectiveness of a teacher's adaption of an innovation to a particular content area. In contrast to the inexperienced teacher, the mature teacher may benefit most from help in refining skills and processes rather than in learning new ones.

SUMMARY

Teachers as persons and professionals differ from one another in a variety of ways. Some teachers may possess more general aptitude for teaching than others. Teachers' style of processing information and approaches to viewing knowledge also may vary. Whereas some teachers are intent upon advancing universal societal principles, other are more committed to maintaining "law and order." That different teachers worry about or are concerned with different problems is obvious to even the most casual observer. Accepting the premise that teachers are different in some important ways is, of course, a prerequisite to supporting their development differentially. Such differential support can only occur when the teacher educator is able to identify or discern important characteristics in each teacher and in turn adapt his or her strategies to compensate for or capitalize upon these characteristics.

Attending to differences among teachers may not be as overwhelming as it first appears. By becoming familiar with evidence on person-environment matching, teacher educators will have begun to equip themselves to adapt their approaches to different teachers. Being aware of what teachers know, how they think, the ways in which they make moral judgments, their attitudes, and their concerns will give direction to a teacher educator's actions.

↞ 5 ↠

Assessing Teacher Characteristics

I NFORMALLY, teacher educators often use practical insights, logic, and common sense to guide their decisions. But they must also be able to turn to scientific knowledge for direction in teacher development. The instruments presented in this chapter provide a more formal and systematic approach toward understanding the characteristics of teachers. With such increased understanding of how teachers reason, how they relate to others, and how they learn new skills, teacher educators should be better equipped to create truly responsive environments. The purpose of this chapter, then, is to assist those who would expand the base of empirical knowledge on teacher development.

Informal Assessment

Teacher educators gain much of their knowledge about teachers informally. Talking with or observing teachers is perhaps the most logical and practical way of assessing their needs and abilities. Chatting about a disruptive student, observing how a teacher organizes a lecture, or listening to a description of an incident at home may all reveal cues about a teacher's interests, attitudes, and so on.

Naturally, some teacher characteristics are easier to assess informally than others. Teacher anxiety, especially as it relates to a specific situation, such as a person's first teaching experience, may be relatively easy to detect. The novice teacher may openly express feelings of fear or demonstrate physical manifestations of nervousness. However, with characteristics that may be more complex, such as field independence, the assessment of behavioral cues is more complicated. Even when these cues are observable, the teacher educator must have the knowledge and skills to interpret them correctly.

The teacher educator who chooses to study certain specific teacher characteristics should understand that informal methods of assessment can be quite limited. Observing or talking with teachers will not produce precise delineation of their aptitudes, attitudes, or developmental stages. Typically, years of work go into the establishment of valid and reliable measures to determine the extent to which personal characteristics reflect those common to a group—and for good reason. Such constructs are not readily apparent in informal situations.

Formal Assessment

Compared to more informal strategies, formal assessment procedures offer several advantages. Because formal assessment is usually based on some type of test or scale, it ensures greater objectivity in the rating of behavior and facilitates comparisons among teachers. Also, because many instruments are based on educational or psychological constructs, scores can often be interpreted within a theoretical framework or perspective. Finally, instruments have undergone scrutiny for validity and reliability.

Teacher educators, however, might insist that teachers will object to being asked to complete formal instruments, and it is true that test taking can be time-consuming, expensive, and inconvenient. Many people are also skeptical about the value of tests or look upon them as an invasion of privacy. Moreover, policies about the use of such tests are sometimes dictated in part by negotiation or as part of a legal contract. Further, it is possible that the scoring and interpretation of such measures may demand a high level of expertise. For these reasons, it is important that tests, scales, or other formal measures be used only in conjunction with carefully conceptualized research designs or programs of teacher development.

Objective and Projective Measures

Two types of formal assessment instruments are in general use. *Objective tests and scales* are those measures whose scores are unaffected by the opinion or judgment of the scorer. In other words, anyone who follows the prescribed rules will assign the same score to the same items; thus, agreement among scorers is high. Familiar types of objective measures are aptitude or intelligence tests, achievement tests, personality measures, attitude and value scales, and interest inventories.

Objective measures use three types of items. Forced-choice or multiple-choice items require the examinee to select one or more responses from a given set. Agreement-disagreement items (true-false) require examinees to report their reactions to a number of statements using a scale of two or more possible responses or select from a list those adjectives that best reflect their attitudes, concerns, or traits. Rank order items require examinees to rank all items according to a specific criterion. Personality measures that utilize these item types are called self-report instruments.

Projective methods, on the other hand, are ways of studying personality by which the responses of the examinee are assumed to be projections of his or her unconscious attitudes, wishes, or conceptions of the world. The examinee is typically asked to respond to some ambiguous stimuli such as ink blots, pictures, or unfinished sentences. It is thought that the more unstructured or ambiguous the stimuli, the greater will be the examinee's projection.

An important difference between objective and projective measures is the procedure for scoring. Whereas scorers will always rate the same response the same way in objective measures, they can score the same data differently in projective methods. For this reason, the reliability and validity information on such instruments must be carefully examined.

Factors to Consider in Selecting Instruments

Before selecting any instrument to assess teacher characteristics, teacher educators should consider a number of factors, some of which are quite practical. For example, does an instrument exist that will measure the characteristic of interest? Is the instrument available for use? Is it easy to administer? Does it have clear procedures for scoring? What is the cost? Equally important, the teacher educator should review the instrument in terms of some basic principles of measurement. Two in particular—reliability and validity—are crucial because an instrument that does not meet these standards is of little value. The instruments discussed in this chapter exhibit a variety of different types of reliability and validity information. The major principles of measurement are as follows:

Reliability. Often used synonymously with the terms *stability, dependability,* and *predictability, reliability* refers to the consistency of measurement in a testing instrument. That is, a reliable test is one which, when it measures the same thing more than once, results in the same or similar scores. A number of conditions influence the reliability of a test, including its length, the difficulty of the items, the degree of objectivity in scoring procedures, whether the test is a speed test or a power test, similarity within the group of examinees, and the number of persons tested.

A number of approaches can be used to estimate reliability:

1. *Stability.* The test-retest method is used to estimate the stability of an instrument. If a test is stable, scores resulting from its first administration will predict scores resulting from its administration at other times.
2. *Equivalence.* Administration of alternative forms is the procedure used to predict how well different forms of a test are able to sample from the same domain of knowledge. If the tests are equivalent or parallel, scores from the two forms should correlate highly.
3. *Internal consistency.* Procedures for calculating internal consistency include the split-half method and the Kuder-Richardson formulas K–R 20 and K–R 21. These can be used to calculate the reliability of a test when only one set of test data is available. When items are not scored dichotomously (right or wrong), Cronbach's (1951) alpha is the appropriate measure.

Validity. Validity means whether or not a test measures what it purports to measure. Validity is of particular importance in educational and psychological research. Because such constructs as intelligence, anxiety, or conceptual level are more susceptible to errors of measurement than are such physical measures as height or weight, a score on a test serves as a proxy for the real thing.

In measurement, the concepts of validity and reliability are closely linked but have subtle differences. Tests that are unreliable can never be considered valid. In other words, an instrument that is inconsistent does not assess the same construct every time and therefore may not measure what the author *intends* it to measure (validity). Although the reliability of an instrument may be a necessary condition for validity, it is not a sufficient condition. A reliable instrument may consistently assess some construct or quality, but this may not be the same construct or quality that the test author *thinks* the instrument is measuring.

The *Standards for Educational and Psychological Tests and Manuals* (1966) discusses three types of validity: content, criterion-related, and construct.

1. *Content validity.* This refers to how well a measuring instrument samples the content, subject matter, or topics of concern. It addresses whether each item and the distribution of items as a whole cover the content adequately. This is a particularly important quality in tests designed to measure achievement. It is usually assessed by careful examination of items by subject matter experts.
2. *Criterion-related validity.* This refers to how well scores from a measuring instrument relate to some external, independent criteria. A teacher educator might reasonably wonder, for example, whether a teacher who scores high on a verbal ability test can communicate concepts clearly to students in a large group presentation. Many writers distinguish between two types of criterion-related validity—predictive and concurrent. To establish pre-

dictive validity, the criterion data are collected at a later date than the test data. The purpose is to determine how well test scores predict a future performance. With concurrent validation procedures, both the test data and criterion data are collected at about the same time. The purpose is to determine whether the test can be substituted for some external criterion that may be less convenient to administer, less efficient, or more expensive.

3. *Construct validity*. This refers to the degree to which variance in test scores can be explained by certain psychological properties or constructs. It is a primary concern for tests that purport to measure various mental processes or personality traits. Of all the types of validity, this is the most sophisticated because it attempts to determine not only whether people score differently on tests, but why. It emphasizes theoretical constructs and scientific inquiry as a method of validation.

One approach to construct validation involves administering an instrument to groups of people known to differ on the construct of interest. Assessing the effect of an experimental manipulation (for example, a training program) on scores is another approach. The third approach involves correlating the scores from the new instrument with scores from other validated tests that measure the same construct.

Selected Instruments

The following instruments are designed to assess person characteristics. Thousands of instruments exist, and those presented here do not represent the totality of tests, methods, or techniques for such assessment. In light of this limitation, we have tried to use several criteria as guides for selection. First, we have chosen those instruments relevant to the characteristics described in Chapter 4. Because these seem most promising in terms of understanding different teacher needs, it is important to identify relevant instruments. For some characteristics, many instruments are available. In these instances, we selected those in common use or most easily administered and scored. The Graduate Record Exam (GRE), for example, is not easily administered, but many teachers will have taken it in the course of applying to graduate programs.

Adequate instrument documentation is another criterion for instrument selection. Most instruments have a test manual containing information about development, administration, scoring, and reliability and validity data. If this information was sparse, an instrument may have been included because it seemed potentially useful.

Each instrument is reviewed in terms of (1) its purpose or the constructs it measures; (2) its general format, including item types, procedures for administration, and method of scoring; (3) reported normative data; and (4) references

TABLE 5–1
Teacher Characteristics and Corresponding Instruments.

Teacher Characteristic	Instrument
1. General Ability/Aptitude/ Intelligence	The Miller Analogies Test
	College Entrance Examination Board Scholastic Aptitude Test
	Graduate Record Examination Aptitude Test
2. Cognitive Style	
Field Independence	Embedded Figures Test
Conceptual Level	Paragraph Completion Method
3. Ego Development	Washington University Sentence Completion Test
4. Moral Development	Defining Issues Test
5. Attitudes	The Minnesota Teacher Attitude Inventory
	Teacher Preference Schedules
6. Anxiety	Manifest Anxiety Scale
	Teaching Anxiety Scale
7. Concerns	Stages of Concern About An Innovation Questionnaire
8. Implicit Theories	Role Construct Repertory Test

for further information. Not every description provides complete information because this is lacking in some test manuals. Table 5–1 lists the teacher characteristics described in Chapter 4 and the instruments included in this chapter that assess each characteristic.

An additional instrument is included that does not assess any of the teacher characteristics described in Chapter 4. This instrument, developed by David Hunt, is a variation of Kelly's Role Construct Repertory Test (REP). Hunt's version of the REP can be used to assess a teacher's constructs about students, teaching approaches, or learning outcomes. Assessing these may help one better understand what some researchers such as Gage (1978) refer to as a teacher's "implicit theories" of teaching. Because these theories reflect a set of implicit concepts about teaching and learning, they may be influential in guiding a teacher's thinking and behavior.

Because research on teachers' implicit theories is still new and relatively unfocused, there is little evidence linking what teachers think about teaching with their teaching practice.[1] There is reason to believe, however, that different teachers hold different belief systems, and that a teacher's implicit con-

---

[1] For an excellent review of research on teacher thinking, see Clark, C. M. and R. J. Yinger, Teachers' thinking. In P. C. Peterson and H. J. Walberg (Eds.) *Research on teaching: Concepts, findings, and implications.* Berkeley, Calif.: McCutchan Publishing Corporation, 1979, 231–263.

ceptualization of teaching and learning may be another useful characteristic to consider in planning teacher developmental activities.

The Miller Analogies Test

The Miller Analogies Test (MAT)[2] was developed to assess scholastic aptitude at the graduate level. It appears to be predominantly a measure of verbal ability for it correlates highly with other verbal ability measures. The MAT is composed of 100 analogy items, based on many areas of knowledge, including physics, mathematics, biology, chemistry, social sciences, literature, and vocabulary. The analogies are of the form A : B : C : D. Any one of the four elements might be excluded. The examinee selects the best of four possible options to complete the analogy. Fifty minutes are allowed for the test. Four alternative forms are available and one form is to be used for reexamination. The test can be administered either to groups or individuals but only at licensed centers.

Norms for the test have been established for a number of graduate and professional school groups and for industrial employees and applicants.

Two types of reliability data have been collected for all forms of the MAT. Odd-even reliability formulas have been calculated and are in the mid 0.90s for all six forms. Correlation between pairs of forms have also been calculated and are in the high 0.80s.

A number of significant correlations have been found between MAT scores and individual course grades, total GPAs, faculty ratings of student performance, and various types of success indicators in industrial or business settings. The manual provides correlation coefficients for MATs and numerous other measures. The MAT has also been validated by comparison with scores from groups that would logically be expected to differ in ability (such as high and low GPA students from the same school or those who finish or abandon doctoral programs).

Scores on the MAT may be sent out from the center where the test was administered.

Suggested Readings
DUGAN, W. E. *A study of the Miller Analogies Test with graduate students in education.* Unpublished master's thesis, University of Minnesota, 1939.
GLADING, J. C. *The Miller Analogies Test and its relationship to other tests and scholastic achievement at Springfield College.* Unpublished master's thesis, Springfield College, 1951.
MILLER, W. S. *Manual for the Miller Analogies Test.* New York: The Psychological Corporation, 1970.

[2] W. S. Miller. *Manual for the Miller Analogies Test.* (New York: The Psychological Corporation, 1970).

College Entrance Examination Board Scholastic Aptitude Test

The College Entrance Examination Board Scholastic Aptitude Test[3] (SAT) is a college entrance examination designed to measure aptitude for college work. It is the most widely used collegiate entrance test. Its main competitor, the American College Test Program (ACT) is used widely in the Midwest and South, whereas the SAT is used almost exclusively in the East and widely used in the West.

The test yields two scores, one for verbal reasoning (SAT V) and one for mathematical reasoning (SAT M). Verbal items deal with antonyms, sentence completion, analogies, and reading comprehension. Mathematical items involve arithmetic reasoning and ability to draw conclusions from tables and graphs.

There are ninety items in the SAT verbal and sixty on the SAT mathematics. All follow a five-option, multiple-choice format. A total of 180 minutes is allowed for the test.

The SATs are administered through the College Entrance Examination Board (CEEB) Admissions Testing Program. The test is given six times a year at centers established by the publisher. In addition to the aptitude test, a number of achievement tests are also included in the CEEB battery.

Scores for the verbal and math tests are each reported as a number on a scale ranging from 200 to 800, with a mean of 500 and a standard deviation of 100. According to a norming survey conducted in 1959, the average secondary school senior received a score of 360, with the standard deviation for the group approximating 120 points. For this group, a score of 800 would be 3.7 standard deviations above the mean, and a score of 200 would be 1.3 standard deviations below the mean.

Because the SATs are so widely used, extensive normative data are available. They are reported for groups separated according to a variety of factors including sex, amount of educational preparation, and schools attended (public versus independent).

Test-retest reliability coefficients range in the high 0.80s and the 0.90s for SAT V and slightly lower for SAT M. Intervals of up to 10 months have been reported. Internal consistency reliability estimates cluster around 0.91 and 0.90 for SAT V and SAT M, respectively. Parallel form reliabilities average two points lower for each. The correlation between SAT V and SAT M is in the high 0.60s.

Extensive validity data have been reported from studies involving both the most highly selective and least selective colleges, specialized curricula, spe-

---

[3] *A description of the College Board Scholastic Aptitude Test* (Princeton, N.J.: Educational Testing Service, 1956).

cific courses, males and females, and black and white students. College grades are often used as criteria. In general, the SAT V is a better predictor of freshmen grades in liberal arts colleges, whereas SAT M predicts performance better in engineering colleges. Some studies report that SAT scores predict college grades as well as high school grade point averages.

Suggested Reading
COLLEGE ENTRANCE EXAMINATION BOARD. A *description of the College Board Scholastic Aptitude Test*. Princeton, N. J.: Educational Testing Service, 1956.

Graduate Record Examination Aptitude Test

The Graduate Record Examination Aptitude Test[4] is a measure of overall scholastic aptitude, designed to predict success in graduate work. It yields two scores—verbal ability and quantitative ability. The verbal items measure knowledge of vocabulary and verbal and reading comprehension. Quantitative items involve arithmetical computation, algebraic problem solving, and interpretation of graphs and descriptive data. Currently, eight forms of the aptitude test are available. The total time allowed for the test is 180 minutes. The GRE package also includes twenty advanced achievement tests and three area tests. The advanced tests are comprehensive achievement tests in different fields of college study (mathematics, literature, and biology). The three area tests cover the social sciences, natural sciences, and the humanities.

These graduate tests can be administered through only one of two programs sponsored by the Educational Testing Service. The National Program for Graduate Student Selection has approximately 200 centers that offer the exam six times a year. On a single test day, the candidate may take the aptitude test only, one advanced test only, or the aptitude test and one advanced test. Scores are reported to the candidate, the candidate's college, and up to three prospective graduate schools. This program is designed primarily for securing scores on particular people to decide on their qualifications for admission to graduate school. The Institutional Testing Program is used to assess the effectiveness of undergraduate instruction at specific institutions, for comparative studies of institutions, and for counseling undergraduates. The area tests are administered in this program only.

The initial norms for the GRE were established for a group of 5,200 college seniors in seventy-five colleges. Since 1967, norms have been based on samples from three consecutive years. The manual provides extensive norms reported in percentile form. GRE test scores are reported in a system of scaled scores based on a mean of 500 and a standard deviation of 100.

Reliability data for the GRE Aptitude Test are strong. Odd-even coeffi-

[4] *Guide to the use of Graduate Record Examinations*. (Princeton, N.J.: Educational Testing Service, September, 1980).

cients yield reliability ratings from the mid to upper 0.90s for the verbal test and from the high 0.80s to mid 0.90s for the quantitative test.

In contrast to the quality of the reliability data, the test publishers have been criticized for reporting little validity data. Subsequently, the Educational Testing Service (ETS) has issued several reports that summarize existing validity data through 1967. Correlations of GRE aptitude scores with GPA have ranged from high to 0. Other indicators of success in graduate work, such as ratings by faculty members, completion of degree, or length of time needed in graduate studies, would yield additional validity information.

Suggested Readings

BORG, W. R. GRE aptitude scores as predictors of GPA for graduate students in education. *Educational and Psychological Measurement* (1963), **23:** 379–382.

ROBERTSON, M., and W. NIELSEN. The Graduate Record Examination and selection of graduate students. *American Psychologist* (1961), **16:** 648–650.

STAFFORD, J. W. The prediction of success in graduate school. *American Psychologist* (1951), **6:** 298–307.

STRICKER, G., and J. J. HUBER. The Graduate Record Examination and undergraduate grades as predictors of success in graduate school. *Journal of Educational Research* (1967), **60:** 446–448.

Embedded Figures Test

The Embedded Figures Test (EFT)[5] assesses an individual's ability to locate simple stimuli within complex visual arrays. It is the most widely used measure of field independence. The defining characteristic of field independence is the consistent pattern of one's mode of perception. People with analytical tendencies or those who separate out parts of a field from the surrounding field as a whole are field independent. They are able to attend to relevant perceptual information and disregard that which is irrelevant. Field dependent people, on the other hand, perceive a stimulus field globally. This tendency reduces their ability to recognize the discrete identity of stimulus elements within the total perceptual field. These people tend to be highly influenced by irrelevant detail; thus, the more complex the array, the less likely they are to identify embedded components.

Field independence, although an indicator of perceptual style, has been found to be a pervasive and stable aspect of broader forms of psychological functioning. It appears to influence a variety of behaviors, including receptiveness to different types of reinforcement, sensitivity to social cues, use of internal frames of reference, or preferences for educational-vocational areas.

Both a short and long form of the EFT are in use. The long form consists of twenty-four complex geometric figures and eight simple figures. Each simple

---

[5] H. A. Witkin, P. K. Oltman, E. Ruskin and S. A. Karp. *A manual for the embedded figures test.* (Palo Alto, Calif.: Consulting Psychologists Press, 1971).

figure is embedded in several of the complex ones. Items increase in difficulty as the test progresses. Complex and simple figures are printed on separate cards.

The test is administered individually. First, the examinee is asked to study a complex figure for fifteen seconds. This is then covered by a corresponding simple figure, which the examinee studies for ten seconds. After its removal, the complex figure is again presented. The subject is then asked to locate the simple figure within the complex one. There is a five-minute time limit for each item (three minutes for short-form items). Scores are based on the amount of time taken to locate the simple figures. The shortened form, which contains the first twelve items of the longer form, correlates in the mid 0.90s with the longer version.

Reliability estimates, based on data from three major age groups, ranges from the low 0.60s to the mid 0.90s.

Construct validity has been established by a strong correlation of EFT performance to that on other perceptual tests designed to assess ability to disembed (for example, Rod and Frame Test, Block Design, Object Assembly). Criterion-related validity has been established by studies that show performance on EFT is related to other aspects of intellectual functioning that involve differentiation.

Suggested Readings.
WITKIN, H. A., P. K. OLTMAN, E. RASKIN, and S. A. KARP. *A manual for the embedded figures test.* Palo Alto, Calif.: Consulting Psychologists Press, 1971.
WITKIN, H. A., C. A. MOORE, D. R. GOODENOUGH, and P. W. COX. Field dependent and field independent cognitive styles and their educational implications. *Review of Educational Research* (1977), **47**(1): 1–64.

Paragraph Completion Method

The Paragraph Completion Method[6] assesses conceptual level (CL). Derived from a theory of personality development (Harvey, Hunt, and Schroder, 1961), this person characteristic refers to an individual's level of cognitive complexity and interpersonal maturity. Stages of development are identifiable on both of these dimensions. High CL persons are more cognitively complex. In processing information, they are better able to "differentiate, discriminate, and integrate" than are low CL persons. High CL persons are also better able to adapt to a changing environment and, in terms of interpersonal maturity, they tend to be more independent and self-reliant than those at lower stages.

Hunt proposes that individuals at different stages of CL need different amounts of structure in their environments. Structure may be defined in terms

---

[6] D. E. Hunt, L. F. Butler, J. E. Noy, and M. E. Rosser. *Assessing conceptual level by the paragraph completion method.* (Toronto: Ontario Institute for Studies in Education, 1977).

of whoever is responsible in the environment for making decisions. In high-structure environments, the training agent has major decision-making responsibility; in low-structure environments, the student makes many decisions about his or her own learning. Hunt's "matching model" proposes that high CL individuals will function best in low-structure environments whereas low CL individuals will do best in high-structure environments.

The test consists of six open-ended topic stems: three assess how the individual thinks about conflict or uncertainty; the other three tap how respondents think about rule structure and authority. The subject is asked to respond to each stem by writing down his or her own opinion and ideas, using a minimum of three sentences. A three-minute time limit is placed on each response. Scoring involves assigning a single numerical value, ranging from zero to three, to each of the six responses. The total score is based on the average of the three highest responses. The number of points assigned to each response reflects the degree of complexity and maturity evident in the thought structure that underlies the response. To discriminate among responses, raters must be well versed in the characteristics of the various stages of CL. The manual provides training exercises for raters.

The manual reports interrater reliability coefficients from more than twenty studies, with the median $r = 0.86$.

Test-retest coefficients of reliability for a one-year period, using samples of students in grades six through thirteen, are in the 0.50s and 0.60s.

The validity of CL has been established in several ways. Construct validity has been shown in a number of studies where students with different levels of CL profited most from instructional programs that were matched in terms of degree of structure. Developmental growth of CL is greater when students are involved in matched rather than mismatched programs. Teachers at higher levels of CL have been shown to be more flexible, creative, and adaptable in their teaching styles. That CL does not correlate highly with measures of intelligence, ability, or achievement indicates its viability as a distinct construct.

Suggested Readings

HARVEY, O. J., D. E. HUNT, and H. M. SCHRODER. *Conceptual systems and personality organization.* New York: John Wiley & Sons, Inc., 1961.

HUNT, D. E. *Matching models in education.* Toronto: Ontario Institute for Studies in Education, 1971.

HUNT, D. E. Person-environment interaction: A challenge found wanting before it was tried. *Review of Educational Research* (1975), **45:** 209–230.

HUNT, D. E., L. F. BUTLER, J. E. NOY, and M. E. ROSSER. *Assessing conceptual level by the paragraph completion method.* Toronto: Ontario Institute for Studies in Education, 1977.

Washington University Sentence Completion Test

The Washington University Sentence Completion Test[7] assesses stages of ego development. In Hauser's (1976) words, Loevinger's approach is best characterized as one that takes account of the individual's integrative processes and overall frame of reference. Ego development can be considered as a continuum of stages that display increasing levels of differentiation and complexity. Seven stages and three transitional phases have been suggested by Loevinger. Although these form an invariant hierarchical order, adults may stop at any given stage. They would demonstrate the characteristics or character styles typical of that stage. The test assesses an individual's stage or core level of ego functioning.

The test is comprised of thirty-six sentence completion items. The examinee's responses are assigned to one of the nine levels (the presocial level is excluded because it is nonverbal) on the basis of how closely it matches the description provided in the manual.

Three methods can be used to score the test. The most commonly used procedure is the automatic total protocol rating. From a table of values constructed by Loevinger and Wessler (1970), the scorer is able to calculate a total score based on each examinee's cumulative frequency distribution of scores. The second procedure is more subjective in the sense that the observer must make more judgments about the data. The third system, called "item sum rating," is used when ego development is to be treated as a continuous variable in a regression analysis.

Estimates of reliability for the Sentence Completion Test are strong. Test-retest, split-half, and internal consistency (alpha) coefficients have been calculated. On the test-retest, intervals consisted of one or two weeks. Coefficients ranged from 0.44 to 0.91, depending on the scoring system used. Split-half reliability coefficients and internal consistency coefficients are in the 0.80s and 0.90s.

The Sentence Completion Test scores have been reported to correlate 0.45 and 0.47 with intelligence test scores and 0.74 and 0.69 with chronological age.

Moderate correlations have been found between ego development and moral development. The correlations between ego development and conceptual complexity, social desirability, Machiavellianism, and attitudes toward women have also been assessed; they offer limited evidence for construct validity. It appears that these relationships may be affected by the age of the individual.

Some studies have reported relationships between scores on the ego devel-

[7] J. Loevinger and R. Wessler. *Measuring ego development, Vol. 1.* (San Francisco, Calif.: Josey-Bass, Inc., 1970). Also, J. Loevinger, R. Wessler, and C. Redmore. *Measuring ego development, Vol. 2.* (San Francisco, Calif.: Jossey-Bass, Inc., 1970).

opment test and specific interpersonal behaviors. Hauser reports one study found that pre-conformist and post-conformist students had different levels of involvement in extracurricular activities.

Suggested Readings

HAUSER, S. T. Loevinger's model and measure of ego development: A critical review. *Psychological Bulletin* (1976), **83**: 928–955.

LOEVINGER, J., R. WESSLER, and C. REDMORE. *Measuring ego development* (Vol. 2). San Francisco: Jossey-Bass, Inc., 1970.

LOEVINGER, J., and R. WESSLER. *Measuring ego development* (Vol. 1). San Francisco: Jossey-Bass, Inc., 1970.

LOEVINGER, J. *Ego development.* San Francisco: Jossey-Bass, Inc., 1976.

Defining Issues Test

Based on Kohlberg's theory of six stages of moral reasoning, the Defining Issues Test (DIT)[8] assesses moral judgment development. According to Rest (1974a), "moral judgment scores attempt to tap the basic conceptual frameworks by which a subject analyzes a social-moral problem and judges the proper course of action." It is assumed that people who are at different developmental levels will perceive moral dilemmas differently.

The DIT is an objective test that uses a multiple-choice rating and ranking system. Both a long form and short form are available. The long form contains six stories. After reading each one, the examinee must select one of three resolutions for the dilemma. Next, he or she reads twelve statements that reflect concerns or issues that might be raised in the resolution of the dilemma. For the most part, the twelve statements represent reasoning typical of one of the six stages of moral reasoning. A few of these are labelled "m" statements: "lofty sounding but meaningless items." The examinee is asked to rate the importance of each of twelve concerns in the decisions he or she makes. Each statement is rated on a scale from 1 to 5 (1 = no importance; 5 = great importance). Finally, the examinee must indicate which of the twelve concerns or issues he or she considers to be first, second, third, and fourth most important in making a decision.

Scoring involves calculating a *P* score or principled morality score for each subject. This indicates the "relative importance attributed to principled moral considerations" in making moral decisions across a number of moral dilemmas. The author also explains how the data can be used to classify examinees in specific stages. Tests can be scored by hand or by computer.

Test-retest reliabilities reported in the manual are r = 0.81 for a group of ninth graders for a two-week period and r = 0.65 for a group of undergraduates for an eighteen-day period.

---

[8] James R. Rest. *Manual for the defining issues test: An objective test of moral judgment.* (Minneapolis, Minn.: University of Minnesota, 1974).

The validity data for the DIT are convincing. The test shows strong correlations with standard Kohlbergian measures. It has also been shown to correlate highly with several attitude measures designed to assess political-moral stances on issues, and it discriminates among people whom one would logically expect to be found at different levels. In one large study, the DIT was administered to four student groups including junior high students, senior high students, college students, and two types of graduate students (seminarians and students majoring in political-science and philosophy). The study showed that the P score, more than any of the other stage scores, most clearly differentiated the groups. That the DIT taps moral reasoning rather than generalized logical reasoning capabilities is supported by the finding that moral instruction, but not instruction in logical reasoning, led to more sophisticated moral reasoning judgments.

Suggested Readings

REST, J. *Manual for the defining issues test: An objective test of moral judgment.* University of Minnesota, 1974.

REST, J. R. New approaches in assessing moral judgment. In T. Lickona (Ed.), *Man and morality.* New York: Holt, Rinehart and Winston, 1974.

REST, J. R. The cognitive developmental approach to morality: The state of the art. *Counseling and Values* (1974), **18**(4): 64–78.

REST, J. R., D. COOPER D. R. CODER, J. MASANZ, and D. ANDERSON. Judging the important issues in moral dilemmas—An objective measure of development. *Developmental Psychology* (1974), **10**: 491–501.

The Minnesota Teacher Attitude Inventory

The Minnesota Teacher Attitude Inventory (MTAI)[9] "is designed to measure those attitudes of a teacher which predict how well he will get along with pupils in interpersonal relationships and indirectly how well satisfied he will be with teaching as a vocation" (Cook, Leeds, and Callis, 1951). The intent of the instrument is to help those responsible for teacher education programs to predict the type of classroom atmosphere various pre-service teachers will foster. The authors of the instrument suggest that a high score on the instrument points to a teacher who has many positive attributes. He or she is a socially secure person who runs the classroom in a cooperative manner and makes the students in the classroom feel secure enough to act, think, and speak out freely. Such a teacher has subtle methods of discipline, and teacher and students enjoy working together enthusiastically on a daily basis. Conversely, the atmosphere created by the teacher who scores low on the scale would be one of distrust and domination. A low score would also indicate preoccupation

---

[9] Walter W. Cook, Carroll H. Leeds, and Robert Callis. *Minnesota Teacher Attitude Inventory.* (New York: The Psychological Corporation, 1951).

with subject matter to the detriment of student needs and an emphasis on heavy-handed discipline.

The instrument consists of 150 items that discriminate between two groups of teachers who are rated either "superior" or "inferior" by their principals. Criteria measure a teacher's ability to win student affection, maintain desirable forms of discipline, and understand children. Respondents use a five-point scale ranging from "strongly agree" to "strongly disagree." The test is printed in eight-page reusable booklets and can be group administered. There is no time limit. The possible range of scores is from +150 to −150.

Norms have been computed for high school seniors, college freshmen, elementary and secondary education students, and several groups of experienced teachers.

The split-half reliability coefficient reported in the manual is 0.93.

Validity of the MTAI was investigated through correlation with other measures of teacher behavior. One study (Leeds, 1952) found that ratings of teachers by principals, students, and classroom observers correlated with the MTAI. One study (Della Piana and Gage, 1955) found that when students came from classrooms designated "least cognitively oriented," their ratings of teachers were related to MTAI scores, but not when students came from "most cognitively oriented" classrooms.

In the studies establishing norms, the authors found, at the high school level, that teachers of academic subjects had more positive attitudes than did teachers of special subjects such as music or physical education. Length of teaching experience was not a factor, but school size was positively related to MTAI scores.

Suggested Readings

Cook, W. W., C. J. Hoyt, and A. Eikaas. Studies of predictive validity of the Minnesota Teacher Attitude Inventory. *Journal of Teacher Education* (1956), **7**: 167–172.

Cook, W. W., C. H. Leeds, and R. Callis. *Minnesota Teacher Attitude Inventory*. New York: The Psychological Corporation, 1951.

Della Piana, G. M., and N. L. Gage. Pupils' values and the validity of the Minnesota Teacher Attitude Inventory. *Journal of Educational Psychology* (1955), **46**: 167–178.

Leeds, C. H. A second validity study of the Minnesota Teacher Attitude Inventory. *Elementary School Journal* (1952), **52**: 398–405.

Teacher Preference Schedules

The Teacher Preference Schedules [10] assess an individual's unconscious motivations for teaching. Two scales are involved: Form G assesses personal gratifications derived from teaching and Form A assesses the attitudes that un-

---

[10] G. G. Stern, J. Masling, B. Denton, J. Henderson, and R. Levin. Two scales for the assessment of unconscious motivations for teaching. *Educational and Psychological Measurement* (1960), **20**: 9–29.

derlie these motivations. Motives in each of the two forms are defined as practical, status-striving, nurturant, nondirective, critical, preadult-fixated, orderly, dependent, exhibitionistic, and dominant.

In the first phase of the development of the instrument, the authors constructed eighteen teacher role descriptions. Next, a panel of six teachers met to discuss each hypothetical role in detail. The panel identified a total of twenty-nine teachers who seemed to exemplify these roles. Then these teachers underwent in-depth interviews and completed an eighty-item Q sort, the Sterns Activity Index, and ten Thematic Apperception Test cards. Case studies for each teacher grew out of the data obtained from these various sources. The types of satisfactions or gratifications expressed by teachers in each role, as well as expressed attitudes that seemed to correlate with these job-related satisfactions, formed a pool of items which were then used to compile the scales for the two forms.

The two scales each consist of 100 items, or ten per role category. Both tests use a six-point scale ranging from "strong dislike, disapproval" to "strong liking, preference, approval" for the gratification form, and from "strong disagreement" to "strong agreement" for the attitude form. Both forms take from twenty-five to forty minutes to complete and are machine scorable.

Norms are reported in the form of means and standard deviations for a group of 105 freshmen from Cortland State Teachers College and for fifty-two seniors in the School of Education at Syracuse University.

Test-retest reliability coefficients ranged from 0.65 to 0.83 for the attitude form and from 0.68 to 0.86 for the gratification form. These were computed on fifty-three teachers enrolled in a summer school course over a three- to four-week interval. Procedures designed to assess the level of internal consistency of each scale were also calculated. Consistent significant differences were found between the various scales within and between the two forms.

Differences between a group of Syracuse seniors and Cortland freshmen were found for both forms. The Syracuse students, who had either completed or were currently involved in student teaching, were more student-oriented than teacher-oriented. They scored lower on certain scales and higher on others than the Cortland students. The instruments also discriminated between elementary and secondary teacher candidates.

Suggested Readings

DAVIS, O. L., JR., and K. YAMAMOTO. Teachers in preparation: Professional attitudes and motivations. *Journal of Teacher Education* (1968), **19:** 365–369.

STERN, G. G., J. MASLING, B. DENTON, J. HENDERSON, and R. LEVIN. Two scales for the assessment of unconscious motivations for teaching. *Educational and Psychological Measurement* (1960), **20:** 9–29.

Manifest Anxiety Scale

The Manifest Anxiety Scale (MAS)[11] assesses an individual's level of anxiety by way of a self-report of the presence or absence of overt symptoms. It has been widely used as a tool for selecting subjects for research studies. In constructing the instrument, Taylor asked experienced counselors and clinicians to select from a list of 200 items taken from the Minnesota Multiphasic Personality Inventory (MMPI) those items that best described symptoms of anxiety. Sixty-five items were rated as such by 80 percent of the five judges. These, along with 135 items classified as nonindicators of anxiety, were administered to a group of undergraduates. Modification of the instrument based on this trial and a number of subsequent administrations led to the present scale of 225 items. Fifty of the original sixty-five items are included. The 175 buffer items include 134 items from the L, K, and F scales of the MMPI and forty-one items from a rigidity scale. The MAS is administered under the title "Biographical Inventory."

Examinees respond with true or false to each of the items. A single score for the scale is based on responses to the fifty anxiety-related items.

Norms for the newest scale have been established on 220 undergraduates in an introductory psychology course. More extensive norms are available on the next most recent version, including more than 2,000 undergraduates and 500 Air Force personnel in training.

Test-retest reliabilities have been calculated on undergraduates. For a three-week interval, r = 0.89; for a five-month interval, r = 0.82; and for a nine- to seventeen-month interval, r = 0.81.

In a later revision, twenty-eight items were rewritten to provide greater clarity. The test-retest reliability coefficient for this revised scale is r = 0.88 after a four-week interval.

To determine criterion-related validity, anxiety scale scores from a group of 103 psychiatric patients were compared to those from a group of normal individuals. The patient group showed significantly higher scores on the scale.

The scale has also been correlated with other measures of anxiety. One of these was the Autonomic Perception Questionnaire, which encourages subjects to report somatic symptoms characterizing their anxiety experiences. The MAS was positively correlated with the anxiety scale from this instrument and negatively correlated with the ego strength scale.

Suggested Readings

AHANA, E. A study on the reliability and internal consistency of a manifest anxiety scale. Unpublished master's thesis, Evanston, Ill.: Northwestern University, 1952.

[11] J. Taylor. A personality scale of manifest anxiety. Journal of Abnormal and Social Psychology (1953), 48: 285–290.

KORCHIN, S. J., and H. A. HEATH. Somatic experience in the anxiety state: Some sex and personality correlates of autonomic feedback. *Journal of Consulting Psychology* (1961), **25:** 398–404.

TAYLOR, J. A., and K. W. SPENCE. The relationship of anxiety to performance in serial learning. *Journal of Experimental Psychology* (1952), 44: 61–64.

TAYLOR, J. A. A personality scale of manifest anxiety. *Journal of Abnormal and Social Psychology* (1953), **48:** 285–290.

Teaching Anxiety Scale

The Teaching Anxiety Scale (TCHAS)[12] attempts to assess anxiety directly related to teaching. Some of the items are aimed at general attitudes about teaching and others focus on emotional reactions toward specific situations that arise in teaching. About half of the items are phrased positively and half negatively.

Several forms of the scale have been developed, but Form (1)–29 appears to be the most flexible in that it can be used with both pre-service and in-service teachers. It contains twenty-nine items. Respondents rate their reactions on a five-point scale (1 = never; 5 = always).

A total score is calculated by summing the individual item ratings. To prevent an acquiescent response set, positively phrased items are scored in reverse. A high total score indicates a high degree of self-reported anxiety.

Norms are reported for 200 pre-service and 407 in-service teachers. The manual reports alpha coefficients of reliability for Form (1)–29 in the 0.90s. Pre-service teachers at elementary and secondary levels are included in the sample. A test-retest coefficient of reliability, with retest intervals from one to three days, is 0.95.

A special concern with this instrument is whether or not what it measures differs from general anxiety. Many correlations of the various forms of TCHAS with the Taylor Manifest Anxiety Scale, a commonly used measure of general anxiety, indicate that to some degree the two do measure similar constructs. However, stronger correlations have been found between TCHAS and the Anxiety Self-Report, another scale designed to measure specific teaching anxiety. This suggests that TCHAS accounts for variance from sources other than general anxiety. Further evidence comes from the author's report that a procedure suggested by Cronbach indicates that from 0.76 to 0.86 of what the instrument measures is reliably unique from that measured by the Manifest Anxiety Scale and the Test Anxiety Scale, respectively.

TCHAS scores also discriminated between groups of pre-service interns who were labelled by their supervisors as either high anxious or low anxious.

[12] J. S. Parsons. *Assessment of anxiety about teaching using the teaching anxiety scale: Manual and research report.* (Austin, Texas: Research and Development Center for Teacher Education, the University of Texas, 1973).

Ratings of a select group of TCHAS items by pre-service interns and their respective supervisors were also consistent.

Suggested Readings

PARSONS, J. S. *Anxiety and teaching competence.* Unpublished doctoral dissertation, Stanford University, 1970.

PARSONS, J. S. *Assessment of anxiety about teaching using the Teaching Anxiety Scale: Manual and research report.* Austin, Tex.: Research and Development Center for Teacher Education, The University of Texas, 1973.

Stages of Concern About An Innovation Questionnaire

The Stages of Concern About an Innovation Questionnaire (SoCQ) is designed to assess teachers' concerns about change.[13] The instrument is based on a seven-stage developmental model which grew out of the work by Fuller and associates (Fuller, 1969). Earlier stages in the model are characterized by disinterest in the innovation or by concerns that are informational, but impersonal in nature. In other words, the teacher may be curious about the innovation, but not interested in his or her own involvement with it. As one moves along the developmental continuum, concerns become more personal. The teacher becomes concerned about the implications of his or her own role in adopting the innovation. The demands of adopting and using the innovation are measured against possible rewards. As these person-oriented concerns are resolved, attention is focused on the specific tasks, or processes, involved in actually incorporating the innovation into the setting. Concerns at these stages have to do with issues like efficiency, management, and organization. Later stages of concern focus on the overall impact of the innovation on students and the educational process. The authors describe developmental progression from unrelated concerns to those that relate to the self, the task, and finally to the more general impact of the innovation.

The instrument consists of three parts. The first part, an introductory page, explains the purpose of the questionnaire and provides directions. The second part is a list of 35 items, each designed to reflect concerns relevant to one of the seven stages of the model. Respondents rate the degree to which each item reflects their feelings using an eight point scale that ranges from "Irrelevant" to "Very true of me now." The third part of the instrument is a one page demographic information sheet.

The SoCQ can be administered individually or in a group, though it has also been administered successfully by mail. Hand scoring and machine scoring are possible. Scores can be interpreted in three ways. The simplest

---

[13] G. E. Hall, A. A. George, and W. L. Rutherford. *Measuring stages of concern about the innovation: A manual for the use of the SoC Questionnaire.* (Austin, Texas: The University of Texas, 1979).

method is to identify the highest stage score. A second method is to look at the highest and second highest stage scores. The third and most detailed method involves an analysis of the complete seven stage profile. The manual provides complete descriptions for all three methods.

Test-retest reliability coefficients for the seven stages of concern scales range from .65 to .86. Internal consistency estimates (alpha coefficients) for each of the seven scales range from .64 to .83.

The validity of the 35 item SoCQ has been established primarily through the use of correlations with interview data from respondents. Interview protocols that encourage respondents to describe their concerns were used to obtain this information. These studies have shown strong correlations between the stage scores on the questionnaire and the types of concerns expressed in the interviews. Researchers have also found that when teachers participated in a five-week workshop to prepare them to adopt an innovation in their reading program, they scored at higher stages of concern than their colleagues who were unable to attend the workshop.

Suggested Readings

FULLER, F. Concerns of teachers: A developmental conceptualization. *American Educational Research Journal* (1969), 6(2): 207–226.

GEORGE, A. Development and validation of a concerns questionnaire. Paper presented at the annual meeting of the American Educational Research Association, New York, 1977.

HALL, G. E., R. D. WALLACE, JR. and W. A. DOSSETT. A developmental conceptualization of the adoption process within educational institutions. Austin: Research and Development Center for Teacher Education, The University of Texas, 1973.

HALL, G. E., A. GEORGE, and W. L. RUTHERFORD. Measuring stages of concern about the innovation: A manual for the use of the SoC Questionnaire. The University of Texas, Austin, Texas, 1979.

Role Construct Repertory Test

The Role Construct Repertory (REP) Test [14] measures the complexity of an individual's system for describing other people. As originally developed by Kelly (1955), it is based on a theory of personal constructs. Briefly, Kelly's theory asserts that each individual has a personal set of constructs by which he or she views the world. One's constructs are like hypotheses in that they are put to the test in environmental interactions. When constructs allow one to make accurate predictions, they are maintained; otherwise, they are discarded. To understand how a person thinks, one must understand his or her constructs about other persons and events. The REP Test assesses the types of constructs individuals have about various roles. The broader the diversity of

---

[14] D. E. Hunt. *Conceptions of persons, environments, and behaviors (Exercises 1–3) and manual for scoring concepts of persons, environments, and behaviors.* (Unpublished manuscript. Toronto: Ontario Institute for Studies in Education, 1976).

constructs that a person generates, the more complex he or she is conceptually.

Hunt (1976) devised a version of the REP Test to use especially with teachers. It solicits constructs of students (persons), teaching approaches (environments), and learning outcomes (behaviors). Briefly, the procedures for administering the REP Test are as follows:

1. Materials consist of twelve 3 x 5-inch cards that subjects number from one to twelve.
2. Subjects are given a list of twelve different role titles and asked to write the names of different students (persons) they know or have known on the cards, one name per card. The names on the cards correspond with the role titles.
3. After identifying each role person, the subject is instructed to consider three of the persons (delineated by the examiner) at a time. Constructs of persons are formed by the subject's indicating in what way two of these persons are alike and different from the third. Following this, a second triad of persons is considered, then a third, and so on. Processes for eliciting subjects' constructs of teaching environments and learning behaviors are similar.

Hunt's manual lays out a scheme for scoring the information in the responses. For each of the three construct areas, he suggests a number of attributes. There are seventeen for the person component, thirteen for the behaviors component, and twelve for environments. On the person component, for example, attribute areas or themes include sociability, ability, motivation, and responsibility, to name a few. For each attribute, specific examples are given of words or phrases that might be found in protocols.

Frequencies or percentages of themes detected in the protocols can be calculated. Conceptual fluency might be thought of as the sum of all the attributes mentioned.

The only reliability data found for Hunt's version of the REP Test was reported by McNergney, Bents, and Burcalow (1979). They found interrater reliability for the scoring of the constructs of behaviors, persons, and environments ranging from 0.80 to 0.90. In this study, a total of twenty-eight pre-service elementary teachers completed all three scales of the REP Test.

No validity data have been reported.

Suggested Readings

HUNT, D. E. Conceptions of persons, environments and behaviors (Exercises 1–3) and Manuals for scoring concepts of persons, environments and behaviors. Unpublished manuscripts. Toronto: Ontario Institute for Studies in Education, 1976.

HUNT, D. E. Teachers are psychologists, too: On the application of psychology to education. Canadian Psychological Review (1976), 17: 210–218.

KELLY, G. A. *The psychology of personal constructs* (Vol. 1). New York: W. W. Norton & Company, Inc., 1955.
McNERGNEY, R., R. BENTS, and J. BURCALOW. *Effects of training on teachers' abilities to generate constructs.* Unpublished manuscript, University of Minnesota, 1979.

SUMMARY

If teacher educators are to enrich their interactions with teachers, they must learn more about teachers—what they value, need and expect. In this chapter, two approaches to assessing teacher characteristics were discussed. Informal assessment, the first approach, occurs when a teacher educator casually observes teacher behavior or converses with teachers to further his or her knowledge about teacher needs. These informal strategies are widely used as the only source of information about teachers. Unfortunately, although such strategies are practical and unobtrusive, providing the teacher educator with important insights into the needs of his or her teacher colleagues, they have limitations.

Formal assessment of teacher characteristics, the second approach, involves the use of instruments such as those described in this chapter. Standard instruments offer the advantages of being reliable and valid measures of teacher characteristics. Many are linked to theory and research which provide the teacher educator with a framework for understanding teacher responses. By using such instruments the teacher educator may also contribute to the empirical base of knowledge on teacher needs and abilities.

❧ 6 ❧

Teacher Developmental
Environments

I F WE could identify the very best teachers, we might well find them to be an extremely diverse group of people with radically different backgrounds and interests. It would be safe to assume that they had not become the best teachers by reading the same books, receiving the same training, or spending the same amount of time in the practice of teaching. The best teachers, as those who are mediocre or poor, are unique people with differing capabilities who have been exposed to different conditions affecting their professional learning.

Any educational environment is a set of external conditions designed to help people learn. When the learner happens to be a teacher, this environment may be defined in terms of those conditions that promote his or her professional development. For this reason, teacher educators should not hold up a single, exemplary teacher educational environment as a model for imitation. Instead, they must recognize that even the best teachers are different and that supporting their development calls for planned variations in educational environments that complement teacher capabilities.

This chapter is intended to help teacher educators *begin* to create planned variations in educational environments for teachers, or environments that are adapted to the needs of different teachers. We stress *begin* only because we are aware of the difficulties of trying to meet individual needs. It is one thing to be committed to the value of individualized or personalized education and quite another to put it into practice. Even given an abundance of resource-rich environments, the most highly skilled teacher educator cannot enable all teachers to become effective and satisfied professionals. Yet it is possible—even with somewhat less than the richest resources—to help most teachers

177

change and grow. To assist teacher educators in this process, we propose a teacher developmental environment that can be varied to form many different kinds of environments.

Environmental Scope

The primary consideration for any planned environment is its scope. How large (inclusive) or small (exclusive) an educational environment should be is important for two reasons. The first involves practicality. Large, long-term educational environments for teachers place quite different demands on the teacher educator's resources than do those of smaller dimensions. Understanding the potential scope or size of an environment, then, allows teacher educators to plan realistic responses to the needs of teachers. Second, it is our hypothesis that the optimal scope from which to begin thinking about and formulating developmental environments is one that includes classroom observation and feedback to teachers. Therefore, an optimum environment for planned teacher development would be one of medium scope and not so inclusive as programs of teacher development or so exclusive as activities designed for development of minute skills.

Our reasons for discussing teacher developmental environments primarily in terms of classroom or clinical activities are not based on convenience alone. If the processes of teacher development are to be better understood and ultimately effected, they need to be applied on a teacher-by-teacher, classroom-by-classroom basis. When teacher development occurs at the classroom level, the chances for integrating theory and research on teacher development with the actual practice of teaching are greatly improved. As teacher educators get into classrooms, they necessarily take their direction for research and development activities from practical, problem-solving experiences. The general characteristics of teacher developmental environments are therefore ideally related to clinical practice.

Snow (1968) and Hunt and Sullivan (1974) are among several researchers who have drawn attention to the importance of scope in formulating and investigating an educational environment. How much of the environment should be described and examined? The answer, at the risk of sounding glib or vague, is that an environment should be as inclusive or as exclusive as is appropriate. Some educational environments must involve many events and issues over long periods of time. Others are by necessity narrow and brief. But to say that there is no given set of specifications for the scope of educational environments is not to say that scope is unimportant. Defining or setting the limits of an environment is necessary for planning and investigating instructional procedures as well as for communicating what such an environment is trying to achieve.

To illustrate the "appropriateness" of environmental scope, it may be useful to consider a familiar example of an environment in politics or government—that of a village mayor. The mayor's environment primarily addresses the problems within the borders of a township. Among other things, the typical mayor must decide which of the town's streets will need repair, formulate recommendations for property evaluation and tax assessment, decide on a bond issue for a new school, purchase oil to run the power plant, or speak to the high school civics class on the rights and responsibilities of community leaders. If one were to draw a ring around the mayor's primary sphere of influence and concern, it would correspond to the township.

Although the demands on a mayor's energies are largely local, this official can ill afford to be parochial. An increasingly well-informed electorate and state and federal issues that have implications for local communities necessitate a broader view. At times, managing a town successfully requires that the mayor be able to deal in larger units of environment as well. For example, this might include negotiating with an intra- or interstate construction company for street repair, recommending property evaluations and tax assessments consistent with other municipalities or state and federal requirements, talking to school board members about attracting new businesses and industries, finding the best price for oil and investigating alternative sources of energy, or comparing leadership on the local, state, and national levels for the high school's civics class.

On some occasions, however, a mayor must also be concerned with fairly narrow and immediate concerns. For instance, a particular citizen's home may have become flooded when heavy rains forced the town's drainage system to back up, and the mayor might take a personal interest in helping the victim find temporary housing or apply for a low-interest loan to rebuild. In this situation, the mayor is concerned with creating a set of conditions that will respond to a single, isolated problem.

A village mayor, then, may deal with environments that vary in scope. The optimal unit of environment appears to be the town, but this is true only as the town exists in the context of more inclusive environments such as the state and nation and the more exclusive environments of its citizens.

In teacher development there is a similar environment of optimal scope. A teacher educator is concerned first with helping classroom teachers grow in their performance of various tasks in the classroom. Among other things, this could mean that a teacher educator may need to help teachers present lessons that hold the students' interest, lower teacher anxiety about speaking to large groups of students, or help teachers initiate a pupil evaluation and reporting system. If one were to draw a ring around a teacher educator's primary sphere of influence and concern, it would probably correspond to a classroom or collection of classrooms.

Teacher educators often need to manage larger units of environment as well. In school districts where student interest in science is high, for example, a teacher educator might organize a science curriculum review committee, write a proposal to the National Science Foundation for funds to develop an environmental studies program, recruit and organize parents to serve as classroom aides, or establish a series of in-service workshops on science teaching.

At times, however, a teacher educator, like a mayor, must attend to isolated issues or deal in smaller environmental units. For instance, there may be one or two days during the year when helping a particular teacher with the student rehearsal for a class play will make the difference between success or failure in the teacher's own eyes and in the eyes of the larger group of teachers or the public. The teacher educator must then help create a set of conditions that supports one teacher's fairly limited concerns.

At different times, teacher educators must be able to create and manage environments that vary in scope. They may need to engage in large-scale consultation or create educational programs to support teacher growth. At other times, a response to an individual teacher's concerns may be appropriate. In general, however, teacher educators can support teachers and help them grow in the performance of personal and instructional classroom tasks by creating environments that directly address life in the classroom—environments that fit the typical activities of classroom teaching and learning. This would seem to be the optimal place to begin teacher development.

Characteristics of Teacher Developmental Environments

Teacher developmental environments are the means by which teacher educators help teachers accomplish personal and instructional tasks in the course of teaching. They are designed to support teacher growth. But unlike many teacher educational environments, developmental environments are intended to systematically accommodate differences among teachers and their teaching situations. The responsiveness of educational programs to the needs of

TABLE 6-1
The Characteristics of Teacher Developmental Environments.

1. Objectives
2. Procedures
3. Support System
4. Management Strategy
5. Provisions for Evaluation

classroom teachers can be measured in terms of five characteristics that are present in all teacher developmental environments, regardless of scope. These may be adapted from one situation to another as needs arise (Table 6–1).

Teacher Developmental Objectives

As discussed earlier, teacher developmental objectives, or more specific goal statements, may be seen in terms of *demands* (simple or complex) and *focus* (personal needs or instructional needs). Teacher developmental environments, then, may be organized around the following four types of objectives:

1. Accomplishing simple personal tasks.

   Simple personal tasks are immediate activities intended to enhance the personal characteristics of teachers. These tasks are "simple" in the sense that they involve relatively few behaviors and in general may be accomplished in relatively short periods of time. Such a simple personal task might involve broadening one's knowledge about a particular concept, such as the four basic food groups necessary for good nutrition. In this case, a teacher might be encouraged to talk with the school nurse or to read a chapter from a health education text in order to enhance his or her knowledge of nutrition.

2. Accomplishing simple instructional tasks.

   Simple instructional tasks are activities intended to enhance a teacher's methods of teaching. Like simple personal tasks, these involve relatively few behaviors and in general can be accomplished rather quickly. But, in contrast to simple personal tasks, they are concerned more directly with the techniques and procedures of instruction. For instance, learning how to thread a film projector or how to give clear directions for the procedures to be followed during a fire drill could be considered simple instructional tasks. A teacher educator might facilitate these activities by providing opportunities for teachers to practice particular kinds of behavior.

3. Accomplishing complex personal tasks.

   Complex personal tasks are activities which develop teacher characteristics that are pervasive, or those that may influence many aspects of teaching. Because they encourage internal change, the accomplishment of these tasks involves performing a variety of behaviors over an extended period of time. For example, helping a teacher advance through Hunt's stages of conceptual level could be characterized as a complex personal task. This might involve lowering a teacher's dependence on external authority, helping the teacher develop a set of internal standards, or encouraging the teacher to view problems and solutions as multidimensional.

4. Accomplishing complex instructional tasks.

Complex instructional tasks may be thought of as networks of activities directed toward the acquisition of a particular teaching skill. They are complex because they require the demonstration of many behaviors over an extended period of time. For example, if a teacher were to develop the skill of teaching through social action, he or she might need to perform such behaviors as finding and helping students to find learning resources outside the school, taking students to town meetings on community issues, participating as a team member on a local planning commission, or becoming involved in developing proposals for state or federal funding. Accomplishing the complex instructional task of teaching through social action or accomplishing other complex instructional tasks such as implementing a new curriculum package obviously requires that teacher educators provide a number of experiences for teachers.

Environmental Procedures

The term *environmental procedures* refers to the sequence of activities in which a teacher educator engages to create a developmental environment for teachers. The developmental environment associated with the teacher's classroom instruction has four phases or procedural steps: pre-planning, a preobservation planning conference, observation and analysis of classroom behavior, and a post-observation conference. Each of these procedural phases, discussed briefly here, is described more completely in Chapter 7.

Pre-planning

In the classroom-oriented, clinical environment, the first procedural phase involves the teacher educator only. It allows him or her to prepare for a clinical encounter with the individual teacher. As part of this pre-planning phase, the teacher educator may want to review earlier clinical episodes with the teacher to recall on-going tasks and the amount of progress made in earlier sessions. If specific plans were made for tasks to be addressed in the next clinical episode, the teacher educator must think about how best to facilitate the teacher's efforts.

Another function of pre-planning is to encourage the teacher educator to reflect on the teacher's individual characteristics. Reflection allows the teacher educator to adapt strategies that accommodate the teacher's individual needs. Recollecting, for example, that a particular teacher is highly organized and independent, the teacher educator might want to choose a management strategy that encourages the teacher to initiate topics and activities in the conference.

Pre-observation Conference

In this second procedural phase, the teacher and teacher educator plan together for the upcoming classroom observational session. Pre-observation conferencing is an important part of the clinical model for several reasons. It helps the teacher educator reestablish communication with the teacher, not only as a teacher, but as a person and self-developer. Because both have busy schedules, teachers and teacher educators may have time for only quick exchanges in the corridor or intense discussions over some school crisis. The deliberate act of holding the conference gives participants the chance to renew their relationship. Also, the teacher educator can use the conference to become familiar with the teacher's methods of instruction and instructional evaluation. The two might also discuss future learning activities for students and review relevant materials. Or they might decide upon important student learning outcomes and plan methods of assessment. The need to review the specifics of a teacher's instructional plans will depend on such factors as the teacher's experience, the complexity of the skills involved, and the amount of time available for conferencing. Finally, the conference encourages teachers and teacher educators to cooperate in selecting the kinds of teacher and student behaviors to be observed and to specify how observations will be recorded. These will be guided largely by developmental objectives specified earlier in the planning conference. Because the teacher educator may be more aware than the teacher of the range of available observation methods, he or she will frequently suggest how observations might be recorded. But teachers may also offer suggestions about modifications to make the system more appropriate. For some tasks, both teacher and teacher educators may find that a tailor-made system will produce the most useful information.

Collecting and Analyzing Classroom Observational Data

In this phase, the teacher educator begins with a last-minute check to ensure that the teacher's instructional plans for the observation period remain as agreed upon in the pre-observation conference. Such a check is especially important when the observational session does not immediately follow the planning conference. It allows the teacher educator to adjust his or her expectations and, if necessary, the types of data collected.

During observation, the teacher educator's main task is to collect information about classes of behavior that have been mutually agreed upon. The teacher educator can also use the observational session as an opportunity to learn more about the teacher's aptitudes or attitudes. This knowledge can help the teacher educator better meet the teacher's needs.

Once the observational session is over, the teacher educator must organize the data and prepare them for the teacher. As a general rule, the most important task is to prepare a data summary that addresses mutually selected teacher developmental objectives. Suggesting ways in which the data confirm or contradict hypotheses about the usefulness of particular strategies is an important interpretive function of the teacher educator's feedback to the teacher.

Post-observation Conference

Two activities are important in this last major procedural phase of the clinical environment. The first is to share information and perceptions, and the second is to work out future directions. As mentioned earlier, this feedback conference should occur only after the teacher educator has examined and organized the data acquired from observation. Teachers, too, must have the opportunity to share opinions and insights about their own behavior and that of the students during the observational session.

Discussing the data from observational sessions often suggests future directions that should be pursued. If the teacher appears to need further help with some personal or instructional task, plans might then be discussed for dealing with the problem. Or if the teacher needs to undertake new tasks, these can also be specified. Before the post-conference ends, the teacher should feel that feedback from the observational session has been adequate and that plans have begun for working on teaching skills.

Environmental Support Systems

The term *environmental support systems* refers to the internal and external resources a teacher educator calls upon to help teachers master different objectives. The idea of support system comes from Joyce and Weil (1980), who include it as one of five dimensions in their models of teaching—one they regard as "necessary for the existence of the model." The resources that teacher educators provide for teachers might also be viewed as necessary conditions for the existence of teacher developmental environments.

Teacher educators can look to themselves as one source of support. One's own knowledge of research on the teaching of mathematics or skill in empathic listening are personal resources that might be tapped. Equally important are external sources of information and expertise. The competence of a respected, experienced teacher, a set of curriculum materials, or a two-day science workshop all represent potentially viable external sources of support for teachers.

In terms of personal resources, teacher educators can draw upon what they know (knowledge base), what they know how to do (skills), and what they feel or believe (attitudes) to provide direction for structuring environments to help teachers move from lower to higher levels of proficiency.

Personal Resources: Skills, Knowledge, and Attitudes of Teacher Educators

In a broad sense, teacher educators must acquire knowledge in four main areas of their work. First, they should be familiar with what research, theory, and practice say about person characteristics—specifically, how teachers teach as well as how they think, feel, and behave as persons. (See Chapter 4 for a full discussion of this subject). Second, teacher educators must understand the various tasks teachers may be expected to encounter, the behaviors that teachers must perform to demonstrate mastery of these tasks, and the task demands placed on teachers by teacher educators, by students, by the educational community, and by the public. (See Chapter 2 for a discussion of the sources of teacher tasks.) Third, teacher educators must be knowledgeable about the kinds of behaviors teachers may be expected to perform. Thinking pluralistically, the teacher educator must be aware of and accepting of multiple behaviors that may satisfy the same objective. Fourth, teacher educators must be aware of various approaches or strategies for helping teachers grow—that is, how to build teacher developmental environments.

Aside from knowledge about teachers, tasks, and behaviors, a major skill required of the teacher educator is the ability to apply this knowledge to the design of effective environments. Although a rich knowledge base is important, it is practical only to the extent that it can be applied to the problems of helping teachers grow. Of course, this distinction between "knowing about" (knowledge) and "knowing how" (skill) is neither specific to teacher development nor to the field of education as a whole. The structural engineer faces the same problem of translating theory, or knowledge, into practice with the design of each new bridge. The design is a product of the engineer's knowledge of the principles of physics, the composition of different construction materials, the implications of traffic flow patterns, and climatic conditions. Although a working knowledge base in each of these areas is essential, the engineer's major contribution is his or her skill in bringing all of them together so that each bridge will be safe and functional. In the same way, the teacher educator's design—the teacher developmental environment—must reflect a command of all relevant areas of knowledge, but most important, it must ensure that the teacher changes along the desired dimensions.

Many individual skills will contribute to the teacher educator's overall ability to help teachers master their various tasks. Consider, for example, those skills needed to systematically accumulate information about an individual teacher. Being a good listener is an important skill that can offer valuable clues to the needs, abilities, and interests of the teacher. Being a good observer is another way to determine such things as a teacher's motivational level, concern for students, or competence in a teaching skill.

The attitude of teacher educators toward teachers and toward their own roles may, however, be as important as their fund of knowledge or level of skill. Because attitudes often affect behaviors, a teacher educator's attitudes will shape the quality of the environment he or she provides for teachers. For the best developmental environments, certain general attitudes in teacher educators are desirable. It is especially important that teacher educators recognize and respect the individuality of the teachers with whom they work. If the teacher educator accepts each teacher as unique in the sense of having distinct needs, motivations, curiosities, and capabilities, it naturally follows that he or she will create an environment that reflects these differences. The logical outgrowth of such an attitude is the teacher educator's commitment to building a repertoire of strategies for flexibility.

It is also important for teacher educators to recognize that teachers may and should be expected to do things differently. Not every teacher will be able to master every teaching task, but for any single objective, different behavioral results may be appropriate. Consider the task of assessing student outcomes. Despite the requirements of school testing programs, there is often room for variations among teachers. Some teachers may prefer to develop their own testing instruments. Others may become skilled at identifying published instruments that they can modify to meet specific needs. Some may discover that they learn most about student achievement from paper-and-pencil tests. Others may prefer to hold interviews with students. Given the objective of helping teachers improve their abilities to assess learner achievement, teacher educators must recognize that teachers may respond in various acceptable ways. The best starting place for the teacher educator may be in helping the teacher identify the approach or set of approaches that seems most suitable.

Teacher educators should also possess some sense that teachers can and will change in positive ways. Statements such as "Helen has never been able to manage her class and never will!" reflect an attitude that militates against teacher growth. Although it is necessary to be realistic in one's expectations, the optimistic prophecy is the most advantageous in teacher development—as in teaching.

External Resources: Other Persons and Materials

To create environments for teachers, teacher educators must often turn to resources beyond their own knowledge, skills, and attitudes. These may include people, materials, or technical services and facilities.

Within the school or outside of it teachers can gain valuable support from other people. Teachers are important human resources within the school. Often they may complement or supplement one another's skills. A teacher who is unable to control class discussions, for example, might profit from observing another who skillfully manages student interaction by soliciting opinions, probing student responses, and keeping the group on target. Helping teachers draw upon one another's skills and abilities calls for teacher educators who are familiar with the strengths and needs of each of the teachers with whom they work. When the teacher educator identifies a problem of poor management, he or she can turn to those teachers who have demonstrated competence in managing their classrooms and call on them to help the teacher in question.

Bringing the two parties together, of course, may not solve the problem. If, for example, one teacher is to observe another, the focus and scope of the observational activity should be clarified. Vague instructions such as "Watch how Mary Smith teaches—she's terrific!" may not help at all. At worst, the teacher who is observing may be left to wonder exactly what is so "terrific" about Mary's teaching. Both observer and observee would benefit from a common understanding of the purpose of the observation. Teacher educators may also help teachers work together while providing observation skills training or suggestions for giving feedback to others about their performance. If teachers are to help other teachers in the context of their classrooms, then teacher educators must arrange adequate conditions for them to become involved.

Although often overlooked, other personnel within the school are also potential sources of support. Curriculum specialists can help teachers explore new materials and teaching approaches within specific content areas; media specialists can offer expertise in the design of such instruction and the use of technology; and school counselors can suggest ways of working with problem students. Because there is often a tendency to overlook the expertise of those in one's own backyard, teacher educators should be especially careful to seek out the knowledge and skills of these in-house people whenever appropriate.

Many people outside the school may be called upon to support teachers as well. These resource people may be found in colleges and universities, state departments of education, or business and industry. Teacher educators might, for example, call upon a designer of computer-based educational materials to help a teacher set up a computerized mathematics program.

Materials represent another source of external support. One type consists of curricular or instructional materials teachers use in working with students. Keeping current on the latest developments in materials for all the disciplines would be more than a full-time occupation and represents an unreasonable goal for the teacher educator. Fortunately, curriculum specialists and librarians can offer suggestions for the selection and use of materials within specific content areas.

Other kinds of resource materials are those designed to help teachers improve specific teaching competencies. Those most commonly used include books, films, tapes, self-instructional modules, kits, and computerized instructional units. They can represent an invaluable aid for the teacher educator whose own expertise in these areas may be limited. However, before selecting materials for use with teachers, a number of criteria might be considered:

1. Relevance to target tasks and behaviors. Do these materials speak directly to the tasks and behaviors on which the teacher is working?
2. Use. How will the teacher use these materials? Can they be taken home? Do they stand alone or are they part of some larger package or sequence? Will equipment or other resources be needed?
3. Cost. If these materials must be purchased, can the cost be justified? Are they reusable?
4. Quality. Have materials been validated? Do they reflect current knowledge in the area? Are they well written and well produced?

Another category of external resources upon which teacher educators can draw is that of technical services and facilities. Some of these go hand-in-hand with microteaching, which requires videotape equipment and experienced personnel, or experimental teaching based on computer technology, which requires other forms of technical support. Teachers who want to use the computer for diagnosis and prescription, for delivering instructional lessons, or for storing information about students will also have to be trained, and equipment must be purchased, updated, and maintained.

Facilities appropriate for carrying out various teaching tasks may also have to be secured by the teacher educator. The teacher who wants his or her students to sponsor a science fair will need a large enough space to accommodate exhibits, participants, and visitors. In some cases, helping teachers make more effective use of shared space may also be necessary. A storage closet may have to become a listening center, or a hallway may become a temporary art gallery for student artists. A willingness to help teachers find and use facilities to make their jobs easier will help them benefit from and value teacher developmental environments.

Environmental Management Strategies

The term *environmental management strategies* refers to how decisions are made in the environment. Essentially, there are three strategies or methods for making decisions—teacher-directed, teacher educator-directed, or shared/negotiated.

Teacher-Directed Strategy

In teacher-directed environments, teachers have the major responsibility for controlling and managing their own learning. Working with teacher educators, they take the initiative in raising issues for discussion, selecting personal or instructional tasks to be worked on, and suggesting how their performance might be assessed.

In this environment, the teacher educator may be viewed as functioning inductively: he or she encourages teachers to encounter various teaching/learning events and to formulate their own general rules. Although empirical research has not subtantiated all claims, several strengths and weaknesses of inductive strategies are frequently cited. According to advocates of inductive strategies, because those who learn inductively are active rather than passive participants in learning, their autonomy and problem-solving strategy (seeking information rather than receiving it) supposedly enables them to attack unfamiliar problems with some confidence. Proponents of inductive methods also believe that this extra personal effort enhances the learner's attention and increases the value of the task in the learner's eyes.

An opposite view holds that teacher-directed or inductive trial-and-error strategies may not only be inefficient and time-consuming but also require that the learner possess some initial degree of motivation to make inferences—a condition that may not be true in all cases. Further, learners who are impulsive are likely to short-circuit the learning process by making so many errors that they collapse in frustration or prematurely settle on an inappropriate conclusion.

Supporting personal growth through teacher-directed environments raises several questions. For example, does teacher directedness assume that the teacher educator becomes totally passive or is there some direct action that he or she can or should take to assist the process? If teachers are to be encouraged to make their own decisions and act upon them, what sorts of decisions must they make? Is a teacher educator who functions inductively really playing a mind reading game to force the teacher to infer some generally accepted premise? Are some tasks in which teachers engage more amenable to teacher-directed management structures than others? Answers to these questions may help clarify what is meant by teacher-directed development.

Looking at teacher-directed environments in light of conferencing activity might clarify some aspects of this approach. As teachers plan a lesson that is to be observed by the teacher educator, they face a number of logical and fairly predictable decisions. They must first decide how to characterize or assess the needs of their students. For example, teachers might logically think about past achievement so as to predict the most appropriate teaching environment for supporting student growth. They must also establish goals or behaviors they can reasonably expect students to achieve by the end of the lesson. One function of the teacher educator in the teacher-directed management strategy is to allow teachers to make their own decisions about such issues as student characteristics, behavioral outcomes, and teaching environments. Teacher educators can also encourage teacher exploration by helping to identify problem solutions that the teacher has overlooked or may not know about. If in planning a math lesson, for example, the teacher intends to assess student learning only in terms of the amount of time it takes the student to recall multiplication facts, the teacher educator may help this teacher consider other indicators of learning. Can students apply principles of multiplication in problem-solving activities? Have students discovered any rules that govern multiplication operations (for example, $A \times B = B \times A$)? Has the teacher tested the strength or conviction of student learning by trying to confuse students? Identifying alternative student outcomes by posing such questions during the planning conference may increase the teacher's awareness of useful alternatives. It is important to point out, however, that teacher educators are not duty-bound to offer alternatives for every aspect of teacher planning. Instead, they should do so only when they think the teacher would benefit from additional information upon which to base a decision.

Teacher Educator-Directed Strategy

Contrary to the inductive strategy, the teacher under this strategy adjusts to the environment established by the teacher educator. The teacher educator is the primary source of control for the organization of teacher learning and assumes major responsibility for the quantity and quality of decisions made in a teaching episode. The teacher educator-directed environment guides the teacher toward the performance of certain teaching processes or behaviors by providing direction or unifying concepts that the teacher may be unable to provide alone.

The very nature of a teacher educator-directed environment places a teacher in a position primarily of receiving information rather than solving problems. Teacher educator-directed (or didactic) strategies, however, do not demand that a teacher be totally passive. That is, an idea expressed by a teacher educator may spark independent exploration on the part of the teacher.

Trying to support teachers by making decisions for them and organizing their learning also raises its own set of questions. For instance, do teacher educator-directed approaches work better with some types of teaching material and some tasks than with others? Are there recognizable, general concepts of "good" teaching upon which teacher educators may draw to organize teacher learning? What decisions are most appropriately made by the teacher educator and what decisions should be left to the teacher? Although there may be partial answers to these questions, often they are neither complete nor satisfying.

The pros and cons of didactic strategies are essentially a reverse of inductive or teacher-directed approaches. As with inductive strategies, the strengths and weaknesses of didactic approaches are to varying degrees substantiated by research, theory, and practice. Didactic approaches, according to proponents, are more efficient than trial-and-error methods because they require less time to accomplish a goal. They also point out that such strategies reduce chances of frustration and failure because guidance better prepares persons to face new and challenging situations. Opponents argue that didactic approaches smother incentive, increase dependence on external authority, and encourage passivity.

Negotiated or Shared Strategies

It is unrealistic and probably unreasonable to expect that either teacher educators or teachers will maintain absolute control over decision making in teacher developmental environments. Only in rare instances in their interactions with teachers can teacher educators be expected either to make or to defer all decisions. A more accurate portrayal of most environments would reveal some form of shared or negotiated decision making in which both parties demonstrate initiative and provide direction.

Shared decision making suggests that in the context of a planning conference, for example, the teacher, teacher educator, or both will make decisions about the teacher's needs and abilities, the teaching behaviors to be accomplished during the lesson, and the kinds of tasks that the teacher will undertake during and after instruction. The teacher may be aware of his or her limitations in keeping some students actively engaged in seatwork while simultaneously conducting small group instruction with others. The teacher educator might make some recommendations to the teacher about physical classroom organization and his or her behavior toward students who will be working independently. At the same time, the teacher may assume major responsibility for structuring the small group work. Once the lesson is completed, the teacher educator may be expected to take the lead in providing information or feedback about teacher actions, student actions, and teacher-student interactions pertinent to seatwork activities, but to do so with some attention to the classroom as a whole. The teacher, in turn, may be expected to assume primary responsibility for sharing his or her perceptions about the conduct of the small group session. Together, they may be able to speculate about why things occurred as they did and to formulate a new set of recommendations for a future lesson.

As these examples imply, this process of shared or negotiated decision making may extend beyond the immediate relationship between the teacher and teacher educator to the relationship between teacher and students. For instance, a teacher may have the requisite preparation and confidence to diagnose student needs, abilities, knowledges, and attitudes. The same teacher, however, may be less inclined or able to set appropriate outcomes for his or her students. In that case, the teacher educator might well defer decisions regarding diagnosis of student characteristics to the teacher but assume more responsibility for establishing student objectives.

Before electing to use a shared decision-making strategy, teacher educators should consider their own feelings about its potential strengths and weaknesses. Is the process of negotiation democratic or really just confusing and inconsistent? What decisions must be made and which, if any, are better deferred or neglected altogether? Should some decisions be made only by the teacher? Should some be made only by the teacher educator?

A negotiated or shared strategy should guide teachers when they would benefit from direction but also encourage teachers to make those decisions that they can make themselves. The process of negotiation should be characterized by thoughtful examination of the qualitative dimensions of decision making. That is, both teacher and teacher educator must actively engage in critical, honest appraisals of their own and each other's perceptions as well as the assumptions upon which their decisions are based.

Provisions for Environmental Evaluation

Provisions for environmental evaluation refers to the methods a teacher educator employs to gather information about the effects of the environment. Because teacher developmental environments are personalized, different teachers may be encouraged to pursue different objectives. Each environment must be judged in terms of its success in helping each teacher meet his or her own needs, whether simple or complex, personal or instructional.

Three groups of participants can be examined for information about the effects of environments: teachers, students, and teacher educators.

Using Teacher Outcomes to Assess Environments

Evaluating the achievement of personal and instructional tasks means examining what teachers do and say. Observing teachers as they perform behaviors in their classrooms is the most direct method of assessing outcomes. Teacher educators can easily judge a teacher's progress when the focus of observation is a simple task. For instance, when a teacher is trying to distribute class materials more quickly, only a few behaviors need to be examined. Does the teacher hand materials to one student at a time or ask several students to assist in passing them out? Such behaviors can usually be demonstrated in a brief period of time. The number of observable behaviors is also limited for personal tasks. A teacher's increased confidence in handling a problem student, for example, may be indicated by such physical behaviors as an increase in the amount of direct eye contact or a more assertive tone of voice.

When teacher developmental objectives focus on complex instructional or personal tasks, observation and gathering data of teacher behavior require more time and effort. Consider the demands inherent in learning how to manage classrooms effectively. Kounin's (1970) studies indicate that it is crucial to eliminate unproductive managerial behavior patterns. "Overdwelling," for example, occurs when the teacher nags or preaches at students. Other indicators of poor management include a teacher's spending too much time emphasizing the obvious, wasting time distributing materials, or overexplaining directions. Becoming an effective classroom manager may require unlearning a variety of unproductive behaviors, as well as practicing new ones. The teacher educator will need to observe a teacher's management behaviors over a relatively long period of time to determine if the task is being carried out effectively, and thus whether or not the developmental environment has been helpful.

In addition to direct observation of classroom behavior, tests might be used to determine the teacher's ability to perform certain tasks. A teacher's mastery of some complex personal tasks, for example, can only occur gradually. For such tasks, a test may be a more valid indicator of progress than observation. (Instruments that can be used to examine growth on complex personal tasks are examined in Chapter 5.)

Another method of assessing the effects of environments on teachers is to solicit their opinions and attitudes concerning the clinical process. The teacher educator might encourage the teacher to express his or her satisfaction or dissatisfaction with the developmental environment. This type of information can help the teacher educator make changes as the cycle of planning, observing, and discussing data continues. Once the cycle is completed, the teacher educator may ask the teacher to comment upon specific aspects of the process.

Other sources of information about teachers' reactions to the developmental environment might come from teacher logs or attitude and opinion surveys. Logs can record the reactions of teachers to sessions with the teacher educator and activities in which they engage while working on particular objectives. Keeping a log, however, makes additional demands on a teacher's time, and its rationale must be clearly laid out. Teacher attitude or opinion surveys can be useful if the teacher educator wants to identify areas in which he or she could perform more effectively.

Using Student Outcomes to Assess Environments

What students achieve, how they behave, and what they think are other kinds of useful data for assessing the effects of teacher developmental environments. Although student achievement is generally thought to result from a combination of factors, most educators assume that it is affected by what teachers do. Although research gives this assumption only partial support, several process-product studies suggest that some teaching behaviors relate to student achievement.

Student learning, of course, is always under scrutiny, whether through a progress check at the end of an instructional unit or a comprehensive achievement test at the end of the year. McGuire (1974) offers four questions about student performance that one should ask in evaluating an instructional program.

1. How much gain was made by the total and by relevant subgroups of students under this teacher?
2. What are the characteristics of the students who appear to gain the most (or least) from this teacher?
3. What are the specific areas of greatest and least gain?
4. What specific misconceptions (or other forms of inadequacy) are still relatively common among students at the end of working with this teacher?

Using each of these questions to examine student achievement in relation to teacher performance may suggest additional areas in which the teacher educator can help the teacher.

Another way to assess the effectiveness of the developmental environment is to observe specific student responses to new behaviors demonstrated by the teacher. Although they may not be directly related to achievement, these responses may indicate changes in attention, level of participation, or in the atmosphere of the classroom. For example, observing a high school teacher's attempt to manage simultaneous small group discussions, the teacher educator might focus on how students behave in small groups. How many seem involved in the discussion? How many appear to be daydreaming, talking about unrelated things, or working on other assignments? What types of questions do students ask? Do they behave differently when the teacher leaves their group to work with another one? Some of these may alert the teacher to possible modifications in the small group discussion format.

Student opinions about or attitudes toward teachers are further gauges for assessing the effects of teacher developmental environments on teachers. Student opinion forms, attitude rating scales, questionnaires, or interviews can be used to solicit information from students. Although effective teaching should not be equated with popularity, most teachers value student approval. Care should be exercised in the interpretation of students' opinions, because they are influenced by so many factors. A teacher who is a good entertainer, has a quick sense of humor, or is an easy grader may receive high ratings but be ineffectual in helping students learn to calculate math problems or understand Renaissance literature. Student opinions and attitudes are important but should not be viewed as the sole indicator of teaching improvement.

Using Teacher Educator Outcomes to Assess Environments

In addition to teachers and students, teacher educators can also provide information about the effectiveness of teacher developmental environments. Their judgment in this respect is based on their knowledge, experience, attitudes, and awareness of the effects of their own behaviors on teachers.

A teacher educator draws upon personal expertise and experience to assess a teacher's progress toward teacher developmental objectives. The teacher educator's knowledge about teacher characteristics, tasks, and behaviors not only assists the selection of appropriate objectives but helps to evaluate how effective the environment has been in helping a teacher meet these objectives. The scope and quality of information that the teacher educator can assimilate on a teacher's performance will be determined by the educator's knowledge of assessment methods and skill in applying them. An ability to collect and use observational data, test results, and verbal feedback is an essential part of the teacher educator's skills, and the accuracy with which the educator judges the effectiveness of the environment will be directly related to the richness of this information.

Teacher educators' attitudes also determine their perceptions of the effectiveness of teacher developmental environments. These can be influenced by several factors, one of which is the teacher educators' organizational perspective. A study by Blumberg and Amidon (1965) shows that supervisors and teachers do not always perceive the quality of their relationship in the same way. Supervisors in the study saw their own behaviors towards teachers as being less directive and their work with teachers as being more productive than did the teachers. However, as teachers and teacher educators work together more closely on mutual objectives, the differences in their perspectives may be reduced.

A teacher educator's attitudes are also affected by an understanding of his or her own needs. Blumberg states that analyzing one's own interpersonal needs may be helpful in assessing why a relationship with one teacher feels comfortable but another is not. If the teacher educator recognizes, for example, that he or she enjoys being in control, then it becomes easier to understand why it is a struggle to work with a teacher who also wants to exercise control. Of course, teacher educators must recognize that not all of their interpersonal needs can be met in every relationship. An educator may prefer to engage in a nondirective style of interaction, but that approach is likely to be inappropriate when applied to a teacher who is new or insecure. Although it is not always feasible to accommodate one's needs or preferences, an awareness of them can make the teacher educator more comfortable in his or her working relationship with many different teachers.

The skill with which a teacher educator responds to problems that arise in working with a teacher may also contribute to his or her attitude. Some forms of conflict occur when an emotional issue (such as a power struggle) underlies disagreements over content (Blumberg, 1974). The remedy for this situation may ultimately lie in resolving some interpersonal conflict between teacher and teacher developer. Cogan (1973) suggests that certain "professional conventions" be followed if conflict between a teacher and a supervisor cannot be resolved. Because the teacher is ultimately responsible for delivering the actual instruction, the supervisor should defer to the teacher's plan of action when agreement about how to proceed cannot be reached. However, the teacher should try, where possible, to take the supervisor's position into account. Then data should be collected that document the extent to which the teacher's proposed solution has been effective. If this solution or strategy does not work as planned, the teacher must be willing to accept responsibility and make adjustments in his or her approach.

SUMMARY

Teacher developmental environments are planned variations of support for different teachers undertaking various personal and instructional tasks. These environments may vary in terms of activities and time allotted.

Teacher developmental environments may be described in terms of five characteristics. They have specific objectives that may include helping teachers accomplish personal or instructional tasks of either a simple or complex nature. Also, teacher developmental environments follow procedures. For example, an environment designed to work with teachers in the context of their prescribed classrooms would begin by joint planning in a pre-observation conference, observing classroom teaching, and discussing observational data in a post-conference. Third, they have support systems that may include the skills, knowledge, and attitudes of the teacher educator and other external resources such as training materials. Further, teacher developmental environments are characterized by a management strategy to place responsibility for decision making about what activities are to be accomplished, when they are to be done, and how progress shall proceed. Finally, teacher developmental environments provide for their own evaluation. Teacher educators may look to themselves, to teachers, or to students to assess the effectiveness of the support they have provided teachers.

❧ 7 ❧

A Clinical Environment
for Teacher Development

THIS chapter presents a clinical process best characterized as a set of recommendations for establishing a working relationship between teachers and teacher educators in the context of the teacher's classroom. The *clinical process for teacher development* refers to the organizing framework for teacher development activities, or a guide that teacher educators can follow as they work with teachers in classrooms. The clinical process should not only raise questions about the interaction between teachers and teacher educators but should also provide a more specific example of the environmental model discussed in Chapter 6. This clinical process is similar to Dewey's (1896) notion of a laboratory approach. Dewey thought of the classroom as a laboratory of teaching and learning in which theoretical ideas could be examined by classroom teachers and psychologists. The results of such investigations could then be applied directly for the improvement of instruction (Wirth, 1966). In the clinical process, the classroom is a laboratory in which primary investigations can further the development of teachers' personal and instructional skills.

In advocating the use of the classroom as a laboratory for teacher development, it is important to raise a note of caution. This idea is in direct conflict with the largely prevailing view that the classroom is not (1) for research, (2) for improving teachers, or (3) the place for outsiders to observe instruction. Those who hold such a view believe that teacher education should go on elsewhere and that teachers should improve on their own time, not on "company" time.

Before discussing the clinical process in detail, another word of caution is in order. The methods presented here are not intended to be simple, step-by-

197

step exercises that if followed guarantee success in teacher development. In fact, the clinical process that we propose may even complicate existing teacher educational practices by asking people to perform in ways they may find at least partially unfamiliar. Although the clinical process tries to account for many ideas and events in the complex interactions between teacher educator and teacher (and to a certain extent between teacher and students), it does not attempt to represent an empirically validated model of how teachers grow. The process should be viewed, instead, as a reasonably flexible and systematic way for teacher educators to think and act so as to reflect concern for the behaviors of teaching and learning, the characteristics of different teachers, and the multiplicity of tasks in which teachers must engage.

Following a brief overview of the clinical process, this chapter will discuss each of its steps and draw attention to some practical dos and don'ts. The discussion concludes with an extended example showing how the process might operate in practice.

Overview

The clinical process is composed of four phases: pre-planning, pre-observation conference, observation and analysis, and post-conference (Figure 7–1). Each phase (with the exception of pre-planning) is broken into *action steps* and *reflection steps*. These are separated in the illustration by a dotted line to indicate that they occur concurrently during the clinical episode.

Action steps are patterned closely on the model of clinical supervision presented by Goldhammer (1969); they are intended to be sequential guides for the teacher educator's overt behaviors in a particular episode. That is, action steps lend direction both to the focus and flow of activity between the teacher educator and teacher as the two exchange information and ideas in a clinical episode. Reflection steps, on the other hand, are less easily observed. They guide teacher educators in informally assessing teacher characteristics and in adapting teacher developmental environments so they can better support teachers. Reflection steps describe the teacher educator's conscious effort to become aware of teacher needs and abilities, to reflect on them, and to respond by adapting the clinical environment to the teacher's needs.

In the clinical process, *pre-planning* is initiated by the teacher educator *before* encountering the teacher. This pre-active phase serves as an opportunity for planning and organizing a developmental environment for the teacher. It is a time to reflect on the teacher's characteristics and to formulate directions to suggest to the teacher in the later pre-observation conference. The *pre-observation conference* marks the first face-to-face meeting of teacher educator and teacher in a given episode. It is the point at which the teacher educator reestablishes communication with the teacher, determines

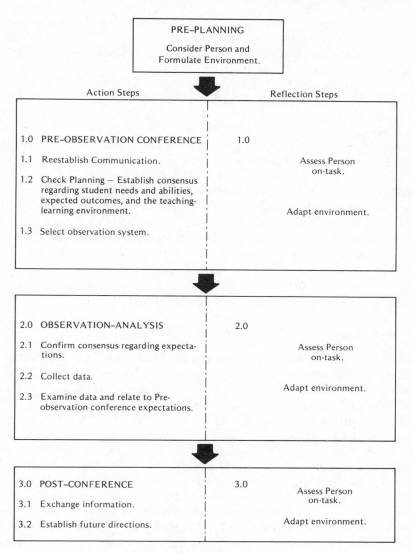

FIGURE 7–1.   Clinical Process for Teacher Development.

the nature and extent of the teacher's planning for the upcoming lesson, and decides about the approach to be followed while observing the instructional activity. This phase is also a time for the teacher educator to bring the pre-planned teacher developmental environment in line with the immediate needs of the teacher. That is, the pre-observation conference is a chance to consider the teacher's abilities, perhaps to revise the plan of action, and to anticipate possible problems and opportunities that may arise during the course of the lesson. During *observation and analysis* the teacher educator gathers information on teacher and student behaviors through classroom observation and then analyzes these data to reconcile earlier expectations with the realities of the lesson. This phase offers further opportunity to revise the clinical environment. Informal impressions of teacher aptitudes, as well as the more formal results of data acquired through systematic observation of instruction, may suggest further revisions of the teacher developmental environment prior to the post-conference. The last phase, the *post-conference*, is an opportunity for the teacher educator and teacher to discuss their perceptions of the completed lesson. The teacher educator solicits the teacher's reactions and judgments and shares the data collected along with his or her perceptions of their meaning. The teacher educator tries to present information in such a way that the teacher will perceive it as having genuine value. Then he or she formulates directions for future activities based on the teacher's needs.

The Clinical Process: Step by Step

Pre-planning: Consider Person and Formulate Environment

Before initiating the clinical process, teacher educators must think about the teachers with whom they are going to work and plan developmental environments based on teacher needs. Of course, a teacher educator may not know a particular teacher well. If the focus of developmental activities is a student teacher and the teacher educator is an in-service teacher, they may have met informally and probably spent some time together in the classroom. If the teacher educator is a principal and the teacher an in-service person, they will probably have interacted in a variety of settings—in committees, faculty meetings, the classroom, and the faculty lounge. It is possible, of course, that both participants are fellow in-service teachers and partners in a team-taught classroom. Regardless of the degree of familiarity with the teacher, a pre-observation conference should not be attempted without first considering the characteristics of the teacher, for these impressions will form the basis on which a teacher developmental environment is constructed.

As suggested in Chapter 4, the teacher educator's reflection on a teacher's personal characteristics can take a number of forms, some more useful than others. The particular approach to reflecting on and assessing teacher characteristics will be determined primarily by the salient needs and abilities of the teacher and the abilities of the teacher educator to recognize and process relevant cues. For example, from knowledge born of past contact with the teacher, the teacher educator might develop some impressions about such things as the teacher's reliance on the principal, other teachers, or the teacher educator for direction, as compared to his or her reliance on a set of internal standards. One might also have some sense of how the teacher reacts to stress and ambiguity—does the teacher take things in stride or get angry and upset under pressure? Having interacted with the teacher in various settings, the teacher educator may also have acquired a sense of the teacher's ability to think abstractly and the relative ease with which he or she views a situation from more than one vantage point. Does the teacher view questions and answers or problems and solutions as having more than one dimension? Can he or she view people and events from the students' point of view, or those of other teachers, or the principal? How flexible is he or she in dealing with others? In short, teacher educators could have some general idea of the *conceptual level* of the person with whom they are working. These impressions, however limited, provide some initial basis for tentatively planning the environment to be created during the upcoming session.

As noted in Chapter 4, a generally inverse relationship exists between a person's conceptual level and the degree of environmental structure (Figure 7–2). That is, a person of low conceptual level profits most from and prefers to work in an environment that is highly structured. A person of high conceptual level, on the other hand, can work effectively in an environment of either high or low structure but prefers the latter. Translating this relationship between conceptual level and environmental structure into teacher developmental terms, the teacher educator formulates an appropriately matched clinical environment. That means if a teacher is flexible, confident, and able to make decisions while managing instruction, a teacher educator would provide less structure or less direction. If, on the other hand, a teacher is rigid and seemingly incapable of viewing teaching and learning from various van-

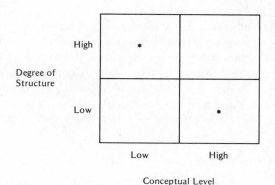

FIGURE 7–2. Optimal Match of Persons in Terms of Conceptual Level and Environment in Terms of the Degree of Structure.

tage points, a teacher educator would then provide more structure in both the amount and nature of directions. If a teacher is confident about and skilled at handling some things but not others, as is often the case, then a teacher educator would plan to negotiate the structure of the environment. He or she would attempt to provide directions only in those instances where the teacher appears to need them.

Whatever initial plans the teacher educator might make about the clinical environment, they will not be etched in stone. Depending on the exchange between teacher and teacher educator as they meet, the teacher developmental environment may be adapted to teacher needs as the session progresses.

Appropriately matching the developmental environment and the teacher is of critical concern to the teacher educator. Cogan (1973), discussing supervision, observed: "Carefully tuned strategies must be designed to achieve individualized objectives in the teacher's professional development. . . . The program has to 'fit' the teacher." Hunt (1971) has used the phrase *optimal mismatch* to describe the kind of relationship between environment and person that is necessary for growth. That is, the environment should be slightly more challenging and more complex than the person's present level of development. By creating an environment that is just above a person's present capabilities, the teacher educator tries to encourage teacher growth in small increments. If the environment were too complex or too challenging, then the teacher educator would risk rejection of developmental activities because of what might appear to be overwhelming demands. If the teacher educator were to match the environment perfectly to the teacher, the result might be complacency rather than stimulation of teacher growth.

Pre-observation Conference

Once the teacher educator has considered the needs and abilities of the teacher and has formulated tentative plans for the environment, he or she is ready to initiate the pre-observation conference. That conference is composed of three different action steps (1.1 Re-establish communication, 1.2 Check planning, and 1.3 Select observation system) and one reflection step (1.0 Assess person on-task and adapt environment). These steps are repeated from session to session, but they may deal with new and varied concerns each time.

Re-establish Communication

For both the teacher and teacher educator, the initial exchange of amenities and some informal chitchat are as much a part of the need for human contact as they are tension relievers. There is some happy medium between chatter and embarrassingly personal contact. In re-establishing communication, the teacher educator works to attain a balance between these extremes.

Writing about supervision, Goldhammer (1969) points to the need for supervisor and teacher to spend a few initial moments "to review habits of communication, their familiarity with one another's intellectual style and expressive rhythms . . . to eliminate problems of mutual adjustment and reduce anticipatory anxiety." He sees the first few moments that the supervisor and teacher spend together as a time for setting a tone that will create a relaxed atmosphere.

The re-establishment of communication is more than a time for nurturant ambiance. Among a teacher educator's practical concerns is establishment of a schedule for observation and post-conference. It is not uncommon for a clinical episode to be interrupted by other activities. With in-service teachers, this seems to be the rule rather than the exception. A pre-observation conference may be held in the early morning, followed by observation several hours later, with opportunity for post-conferencing not arising until the close of the school day. During this action step, then, the teacher educator and teacher may take a few moments to lay plans about when and where the clinical episode will be played out.

Check Planning

That teachers plan instruction in different ways and to varying degrees is apparent when one examines their lesson plans. From the elaborate goals, objectives, procedures, materials, and evaluation required for methods classes to the cryptic scrawl in a daily plan book, teachers exhibit different ways of conceptualizing instruction. Indications of a teacher's ability to plan, however, are not always revealed in writing and much of a teacher's instructional planning is probably never transferred to paper. But obtaining evidence of the sorts of tasks teachers undertake, whether written or spoken, is crucial for teacher educators if they are to help reconcile teaching practice with teaching intent.

The teacher educator who expects to gather useful and appropriate information during observation must understand three elements in the teacher's thinking: (1) the students who are to be taught, (2) what they are supposed to learn, and (3) how the teaching environment will be organized to accomplish this learning. Translating these three variables into B-P-E terminology, the teacher educator needs to know the behaviors that teachers expect students to demonstrate (B), the teacher's diagnoses of student characteristics (P), and the teaching environment (E) that the teacher plans to establish so that students will demonstrate the intended behaviors. These elements of information about the projected lesson have been depicted by Hunt and Sullivan (Figure 7–3).

E	P	B
Different ways of teaching	Different types of students	Effects

FIGURE 7–3. Components in Planning. [From Hunt, D. E. and E. V. Sullivan. *Between psychology and education*. The Dryden Press, 1974, p. 277. (Reproduced by permission.)]

Whether or not they formulate their plans in B-P-E terminology, each teacher might be expected to address these components. As teachers elaborate their ideas about the upcoming lesson, their plans might begin to expand (Figure 7–4). It is important to note, however, that a teacher educator would not expect even the most flexible teacher to provide a different environment for students in all teaching situations. The characteristics of each student multiplied by the number of students in a room and the number of instructional activities would make the task of adapting instruction to all individuals for all purposes too staggering. Instead, there is probably some pattern of groups of various size and characteristics that the teacher can reasonably be expected to plan for and manage. For example, a teacher's use of reading groups or skill groups in mathematics are attempts to recognize and attend to the varying needs of students. Such groupings, when organized on the basis of student characteristics and reorganized periodically as needs and abilities change, are efforts to meet the needs of individuals.

To clarify and establish consensus on the expectations for a lesson, the teacher educator might ask the teacher some of the following questions about expected behaviors, learner characteristics, and the planned teaching environment.

E	P	B
Text	Verbally oriented students	To understand relation between climate and soil
Map overlay	Spatially oriented students	

FIGURE 7–4. Alternative Plans for Teaching Students Varying in Aptitude. [From Hunt, D. E. and E. V. Sullivan. *Between psychology and education*. The Dryden Press, 1974, p. 279. (Reproduced by permission.)]

1. What are the students expected to learn from this lesson? What are the goals and objectives? How will you know if students have accomplished them? (B)
2. What are the abilities, knowledge, and past experiences of students in this area? Do they seem to need a good deal of direction or are they better left alone? Are there particular values students hold that might influence how they will approach this particular kind of content? How interested or motivated are they? Are they anxious or confident about this area of work? (P)
3. What *content* will you use as a vehicle to achieve goals and objectives? What *learning activities* will be employed, and with which students (for example, lecture, small or large group discussion, self-directed learning centers, peer instruction, silent reading, library work, singing, listening, films)? How will the activities be *sequenced?* How much *time* will be allocated to each activity? How much of the focus and flow of activity will be controlled by the teacher? How much will be controlled by the students? What *materials or machines* will be used? What follow-up assignments or out-of-class work will be assigned, and to which students? (E)

Select Observation System

Once the teacher and teacher educator are clear about the characteristics of students to be taught, what students are expected to learn, and how the teacher will proceed with instruction, the teacher educator is ready to move to the final action step of the pre-conference—that of selecting a method of observation. This is a critical step in the clinical process, for the observation instrument or system will govern the nature of the information that is collected, analyzed, and eventually shared during the post-conference. As the observation systems previously discussed illustrate (Chapter 3), teacher educators can (1) note occurrences of behavior according to pre-established categories at regular intervals of time during a class session, (2) note specific behaviors only as they occur, (3) take verbatim notes of what they see and hear during a lesson, (4) make audio tapes of sessions, or (5) videotape teachers and students. Various observation schemes follow different procedures and yield different kinds of information. Selecting an appropriate observation system or combination of systems depends upon being able to project what sorts of teacher or student behaviors will be demonstrated in the upcoming lesson.

It is important that teacher educators share their thoughts about methods of observations with teachers. As the projected teacher or student behaviors in the lesson plans become apparent during the pre-observation conference, the teacher educator will begin to decide on the instrumentation most suitable for the observation session. Being knowledgeable about a few common, general systems of observation, such as those in Chapter 3, should give teacher educators some idea of how they might begin to observe with validity, reliability, and usefulness. But whatever decisions are made about instrumentation, they should be discussed with the teacher before concluding the pre-observation conference. This allows the teacher an opportunity to provide useful direction about persons and events to be observed, and it also serves to allay teacher anxiety.

Assess Person, Adapt Environment

As teachers discuss their plans, the teacher educator begins to acquire not only information about the upcoming lesson but also an immediate reading of teachers' needs and abilities. As they discuss the content of the lesson, specific learning activities, the pace or timing of the lesson, materials to be used, assessment of student characteristics, expectation for outcomes, or the amount of teacher versus student control, teachers are "telling" the teacher educator about themselves. In discussing their plans, they are providing information about themselves that may enable further refinement of the teacher developmental environment.

The teacher educator can adapt the environment during the pre-conference by mirroring and guiding a teacher's thinking about students, objectives, and procedures to be implemented in the upcoming lesson. For instance, if a teacher is apprehensive about things getting out of hand when students are allowed to select from a number of learning activities, the teacher educator might begin to probe the teacher's thinking about his or her students' characteristics. Is it possible that some students can handle freedom of choice while others cannot? Do student behaviors have anything to do with their interests in this area? How might the teacher recognize and differentiate among students' interests and abilities? Is it reasonable to expect Bruce and Bob to solve the same problem as Judy and Matthew? Maybe things get out of hand because some students cannot read the materials or because they had the same lesson last year with another teacher. Why not ask students which activities they like best and which seem to help them most?

In asking questions and giving suggestions, the teacher educator offers and negotiates alternatives where they might be appropriate, and provides definitive direction where it appears to be needed. In these ways, he or she adapts the environment to the needs and abilities of the teacher.

Observation/Analysis

Once the pre-observation conference steps of action and reflection have been accomplished, the teacher educator is nearly ready to begin observation and analysis. The process of observing, recording, and interpreting student actions, teacher actions, and student-teacher interactions is central to the clinical practice of teacher development. It is possible, of course, to hypothesize about teaching and learning, but until one actually observes teachers and students, these hypotheses will remain untested and unvalidated. Collecting data through observation allows teacher educators to support or reject their intuitions and thus refine their own impressions of teaching and learning. This particular action step is a time to be fully engaged in collecting information about the behaviors of teachers and students and involved in teaching-learning activities. Data collection, however, is only part of the task. The teacher educator must also try to make sense of the data, relate information to the expectations set in the pre-observation conference, and organize the data in a way that will be understandable to the teacher in the post-conference.

Confirm Agreement

Before teacher educators begin observation, it is important that they make one last effort to ensure that the pre-conference agreement is set. As noted earlier, sometimes it is not possible to establish an agreement during a pre-observation conference and immediately begin to fulfill it. The teaching episode to be observed does not always occur right after the pre-observation conference. When a teacher educator has several observations to make in one day, the processes of pre-conference, observation and analysis, and post-conference must be juggled to accommodate the schedules of several teachers. When it is necessary to hold a pre-conference with a teacher and return at a later time to observe a session, the step of confirming the agreement is a useful checkpoint for both teacher and teacher educator.

Confirming the agreement means that immediately prior to observation, teachers should be asked if they have made any last-minute changes in planning that were not discussed during the pre-observation conference. As the time between pre-observation conference and actual observation increases, the chances of alteration in plans increase, particularly if a teacher attempts to respond to the immediate moods and interests of students.

It is inevitable—and, it could be argued, even appropriate—that deviations from the agreement will occur during a lesson. As Hunt (1976) estimates, teachers read their students and adapt their teaching to fit student needs somewhere on the average of 100 times an hour. It is highly unlikely, therefore, that all the interactions between teacher and students could be predicted in the pre-conference. Even though some final changes may be agreed upon during this action step, teachers must still feel free to adapt their instruction as they go along. Such changes can always be discussed in the post-conference. The purpose of confirming the pre-observation conference agreement, then, is not to discuss every detail of anticipated teacher/student performance so as to raise the agreement to a point of law. Instead, the act of confirmation is intended to clarify the expectations of both teacher and teacher educator.

Collect Data

Having confirmed the pre-observation conference agreement, the teacher educator is ready to observe and collect data pertinent to the implementation of the lesson. As noted, possessing data about teacher and student behaviors encourages raising one's judgments about teaching and learning from a level of conjecture to one based on demonstrable performance. If the data substantiate intuitive perceptions and warrant conclusions, then conclusions may be drawn. Without supporting data, verifying one's judgments is a difficult and risky business. Furthermore, teacher educators who fail to collect data may overlook some of the more subtle, yet potentially important, patterns of teacher-student behavior. Things that appear obvious in teaching or learning at a casual glance may be less influential for both teachers and students than nuances of behavior that become apparent upon examination of concrete data on performance. Also, records of classroom transactions, when kept on each session, allow both teacher educator and teacher to consider behaviors contemporaneously as well as over time.

Although records of classroom behavior can provide useful insights, the process of data collection can be a somewhat unnerving experience for both teachers and students. Being WATCHED—or, even worse, having one's behavior recorded and codified—is threatening for many people, especially if the observer is an "outsider." Ideally, if a teacher educator functions as Smith did in Geoffrey's classroom (Smith and Geoffrey, 1968)—as a participant-observer over an extended period of time—a teacher's anxiety could be reduced, and the threat of the Hawthorne effect (false changes in the teachers' and students' behaviors because they know they are being observed) could be diminished as well. In reality, however, time rarely permits this luxury. Even if the teacher educator is a familiar figure in the classroom, he or she should take pains to be sensitive to the apprehensions of students and teachers under observation.

Obviously, if the sampling of classroom behaviors is to be of any value it must reflect teacher-student behaviors as they actually occur. This attempt to capture reality inevitably leads the teacher educator to ask how often observation must occur before accurate assessment of performance can be assumed. Erlich and Borich (1976) addressed this question in estimating the effects of observation across various types of lessons at the second- and third-grade levels. They concluded that many variables of teacher and student behavior must be observed and measured more than three times before they can be judged to be sufficiently reliable. Three, of course, is not a magic number; however, the Erlich and Borich study suggests a rule of thumb that is useful for the question of frequency of observation: make *frequent* observations of *shorter* duration across various types of class content or in various contexts, as opposed to *fewer* observations of *longer* duration. Teacher educators who follow this rule will more likely develop a well-rounded conception of what really occurs in the classroom, and one that is more reliable. As this picture of the classroom emerges, one should be better able to address meaningful issues of instruction rather than dissipating personal time and energy—as well as the teacher's—on random, isolated, and relatively inconsequential events.

One last point on data collection is useful to keep in mind. Brophy and Good (1974) note that teacher behavior directed toward the class as a whole or toward subgroups of students is not usually representative of behavior directed toward individual students. For this reason, they recommend that although data should be collected on a representative sample of students or on the whole class, separate records should also be maintained for individual students to provide a representative picture. By collecting data on some individuals, a teacher educator may address issues of particular interest and concern to teachers as well as draw attention to the needs and abilities of individual students. Some observation systems lend themselves better than others to observation of individuals. Depending on instrumentation, therefore, sometimes data on individuals will be easier to collect than at other times.

Examine Data and Relate to Agreement

As discussed earlier, selection of instrumentation and processes of observation must be handled thoughtfully in order to yield information of high quality. But the process of analyzing and reporting results can also be skewed by teacher educators and thus affect both the conclusions drawn from a clinical teacher development episode and their utility. Awareness of the following guidelines should help one analyze data accurately and draw reasonable conclusions that may be shared with the teacher.[1]

1. Examine and relate data from teacher and student behaviors to the objectives discussed in the pre-observation conference agreement. Treat this information as being of primary importance. If other data are collected that are tangential to the pre-observation conference objectives but possibly important, treat such information secondarily.

   Teacher educators must be careful not to read too much into data when they have not decided beforehand how the data are to be analyzed and fitted to objectives. Possessing an abundance of unanticipated information may lead one to focus on data that support expectations and neglect data that appear incongruous with the teacher educator's assumptions or biases.

---

[1] Items 1 through 3 are derived from Theodor X. Barber. *Pitfalls in human research: Ten pivotal points.* Elmsford, N.Y.: Pergamon Press, Inc., 1976.

This may be a particular problem with ethnographic procedures of observation, such as the Goldhammer note-taking procedure discussed earlier.

2. If information exists that fails to confirm or contradicts teacher educator expectations established in the pre-conference agreement, then plan to share it.

Another problem may occur when observers fail to share information that does not support—or indirectly contradicts—their earlier expectations. Consider, for example, the teacher educator who, over the course of several sessions, has been working with a teacher to smooth out her transitions from one activity to another to increase student work involvement and decrease disruptive behavior.[2] In the most recent session, the teacher educator may observe several examples of the teacher incorporating suggested techniques from past sessions but simultaneously observes a continued level of student misbehavior. If, in the course of examining the latest data, the teacher educator chooses to ignore instances of teacher transitional behavior that were smooth but accompanied by student misbehavior, such action jeopardizes an accurate assessment of the lesson.

3. Keep the results in perspective. Concentrate on patterns of behavior as opposed to random isolated events.

Closely associated with the failure to share pertinent or contradictory information with a teacher is a tendency to misrepresent the magnitude of concerns. In the previously mentioned situation, this might occur when a teacher educator concentrates on one or two weaknesses in teacher transitions and simultaneously de-emphasizes the otherwise positive behavior of teacher and students. As Goldhammer (1969) and others point out, and as reason dictates, the focus should be on salient patterns of behavior, not random, isolated events.

4. Analyze, try to understand, and build on the things that work well for teachers.

Overanalysis of observational results that fail to confirm or contradict expectations may divert a teacher educator from teacher successes. If things are going well, or, to continue the same example, if teacher transitions are smooth and students are actively involved, then one might usefully analyze this apparent success for greater understanding. Heightened awareness of why things work well may enable a teacher educator to build on or extend the successes attained by teachers, not dwell on their absence.

5. Put collected and analyzed data in a form that will be understandable to the teacher in the post-conference.

Clarity is essential in data reporting. If teacher educators expect teachers to understand and act upon the results of observation, it is imperative that they organize results with brevity and clarity. Elaborate or complex analyses and reporting schemes are often appropriate for research, but they will be of little direct benefit to the teacher.

---

[2] In Chapter 3 we discussed the work of Jacob Kounin (1970) related to classroom management and discipline. One argument he presents is that in general smoother teacher transitions lead to greater student work involvement and fewer instances of inappropriate behavior.

Assess Person, Adapt Environment

Once the lesson has been observed and the data analyzed, the teacher educator is better prepared to bring the pre-observation conference strategy in line with the immediate needs of the teacher. New information acquired from direct observations of teaching should help in the adjustment of the environment before encountering teachers once again in the post-conference. If teacher development is to be effectively adapted to individuals for short-term and long-term objectives, the need for fresh information about teaching and learning is extremely important. The stability of certain person characteristics, such as intelligence or cognitive style, has been well established. Other characteristics, such as teachers' anxieties or their knowledge of particular tasks, may vary considerably within relatively short periods of time. Recognizing and providing for variations within a single teacher, or among different teachers, will depend not only on the quantity but also the quality, or freshness, of information about teacher needs and abilities.

A study by Tennyson and Rothen (1977) in computer-managed instruction illustrates what can be accomplished when instruction is based on up-to-date, task-specific information about a learner's capabilities. They investigated the relationship between a person's ability to learn a concept and the quantity and quality (freshness and relevance to task) of information used to adapt instruction to individual students. Subjects were randomly assigned to three treatment conditions: full adaptive, partial adaptive, and nonadaptive. The full adaptive treatment was designed to account for students' general aptitudes or abilities as determined by a pre-measure and their on-task performances. The partial adaptive treatment consisted of an instructional model based only on the pre-measure of student aptitude. The nonadaptive treatment was designed to be uniform for all students regardless of individual differences they might exhibit before or during instruction. Results revealed that the full adaptive treatment was superior to the partial adaptive and nonadaptive treatments in terms of the time students spent on the learning tasks and the degree to which they succeeded in mastering the material. In turn, the partial adaptive treatment was superior to the nonadaptive treatment on all outcome measures.

Diagnosing learner aptitudes to design computer programs to teach a single concept is, of course, a long way from the processes of reading personal characteristics and adapting environments for teacher development. Conceptually, however, the Tennyson and Rothen study points out the importance of constantly updating information to make decisions that guide the focus and flow of instructional support. The results of their experiment illustrate what can be accomplished when support is adapted to persons based on an incremental knowledge of their capabilities, particularly when a portion of that knowledge is drawn from on-task performance. The more information that is available, the fresher it is, and the more relevant to ultimate objectives, the greater are the chances of adapting instructional support to the needs of the individual.

Post-conference

The post-conference is an important occasion for both teacher educator and teacher. During the post-conference, information can be exchanged about the teaching episode, perceptions of student and teacher behaviors shared, and speculations made about future courses of action. It is, in a very real sense, an *instructional event* for both teacher and teacher educator. The post-conference is a time for evaluating the effectiveness of a teacher developmental environment, but it is also a time for honesty and plain speaking—talking about what worked and what did not.

Although the post-conference in a sense brings "closure" to the clinical process, it is not really a conclusion. Some issues may be laid to rest during the post-conference; more often, however, loose ends that resist interpretation or explanation remain. The post-conference, then, is not just a convenient ending to the immediate process, but it is also the point at which the teacher educator begins to form thoughts about the teacher developmental environment to be created in a future session.

Time is a key variable in the life of a teacher educator, and that is certainly no less true for teachers, particularly when it comes to post-conferences, or setting aside time to talk about something that is already completed. Finding time to discuss the lesson, however, is crucial if the results of observation are to have any practical value.

It is not unlikely that a post-conference will be squeezed in during lunch, part of a planning period, or in class while the pupils are doing seatwork. If observations regularly yield useful information, however, both teacher educator and teacher may establish a priority for post-conferences.

Exchange Information

The exchange of information between a teacher and an observer in the post-conference is a relatively unexamined area of behavior. Based on a study conducted on conferences in elementary schools, Kyte (1962) recommended an optimal number and sequence of issues to be discussed but did not consider how this might be modified by differences among teachers. In a somewhat different vein, Blumberg and Amidon (1965) investigated teachers' abilities to discriminate among various types of supervisory behavior. They then compared these supervisory styles to teachers' perceptions of their own learning as well as to their perceptions of the supportiveness and productivity of conferences. These researchers concluded that consistent patterns of supervisory behavior exist, at least in the minds of teachers, and that different styles have varying effects on teachers' perceptions of the utility of conferences. As teacher educators approach a post-conference, then, they must decide what information to share with a teacher and must formulate plans for how that information might best be presented to a particular individual. In the post-conference, teacher educators face essentially the same three strategy options posed by the pre-conference: they can direct the discussion, allow the teacher to direct it, or share information reciprocally.

As teacher educators implement their chosen post-conference strategies, they both consciously and unconsciously reveal their own biases or preconceived commitments to particular points of view. Even though they may constantly try to remain open throughout the entire clinical process—taking various precautions against threats of subjectivity—their biases may nonetheless adversely affect the objectivity of the results. This will ultimately be reflected in the post-conference. As Dunkin and Biddle (1974) suggest about any kind of educational research, researchers must try to recognize their commitments to preconceived ideas and theories and not allow these to color their methods or interpretation of data.

The same propositions undoubtedly hold true for teacher educators. But it is naive to expect people to divest themselves totally of their commitments to what constitutes effective teaching in order to be purely objective. As noted earlier, relying on hard empirical facts about "good" teaching versus "bad" teaching leaves teacher educators with some, but not nearly enough, direction. Reliance on practical knowledge, therefore, seems not only acceptable but desirable. Throughout the clinical process—and especially at the point of exchanging information in the post-conference—teacher educators should be deliberately open about the origin of their own beliefs and not try to mask them in sanctimonious testaments to theory and research. Whether the strategies teacher educators have planned are directive, nondirective, or shared, none of these options preclude the honest, yet discrete, disclosure of personal commitments or assumptions.

Establishing Future Directions

This final action step is intended to leave the participants with some sense of what can be accomplished after the post-conference. If minor difficulties or major problems in teaching have been identified in the session, plans must be formulated to address these concerns in upcoming lessons. It may be that concentrating on a few simple details, such as organizing different reading groups, setting up a study corner for science, or changing the seating arrangement, can clear up post-conference concerns. By identifying a few things to work on in upcoming instructional sessions, both teacher and teacher educator can leave the post-conference with some positive direction.

It is important to remember, however, that establishing future directions does not mean that the teacher educator should try to find things that have gone wrong and encourage the teacher to correct them. Many sessions leave both teacher and teacher educator satisfied that student and teacher goals are being realized or perhaps even exceed expectations. Establishing future directions in these situations is a matter of helping a teacher understand why things are going well and giving further encouragement. As we have continually stressed, supporting teachers to build on their successes is every bit as important as strengthening areas of weakness. Teacher developmental environments can and should be tempered to teachers' strengths and interests, just as they can be designed to correct weaknesses. Or, as Salomon (1972) suggests, not only can environments be adjusted to compensate for and remediate learner deficiencies but they may also be designed to capitalize on the kinds of things persons prefer to do and do well.

As teacher educators recognize the unique strengths and needs of individual teachers, it is inevitable that they will be drawn toward commonalities among persons as well. As we pointed out in the Action Step of Reestablishing Communication, the actors in the clinical process are, after all is said and done, ordinary people with some very ordinary things in common—not the least of which is a need to preserve their own dignity. It is imperative that teacher educators be sensitive to this need throughout the clinical process, and especially at the conclusion of a session. Studs Terkel, the peripatetic interviewer and observer of life, writing of an encounter with a fireman, states it well:

> On occasions, overly committed, pressed by circumstance of my own thoughtless making, I found myself neglecting the amenities and graces that offer mutual pleasure to visitor and host. It was the Brooklyn fireman who astonished me into shame. After what I had felt was an overwhelming experience—meeting him—he invited me to stay "for supper. We'll pick something up at the Italian joint on the corner." I had already unplugged my tape recorder . . . I remember the manner in which I mumbled. "I'm supposed to see this hotel clerk on the other side of town." He said, "You runnin' off like that? Here we been talkin' all afternoon. It won't sound nice. This guy, Studs, comes to the house, gets my life on tape, and says 'I gotta go' . . ." It was a memorable supper. And yet, looking back, how could I have been so insensitive?" (Terkel, 1972, pp. xxii–xxiii.)

Of course, every post-conference will not end with a take-out dinner, but at least a few could. Teacher educators and teachers need moments to share something of themselves as people, even if it risks some self-conscious bumbling or the appearance of contrived informality.

Assess Person, Adapt Environment

Throughout the clinical process the teacher educator will have made a conscious effort to assess and respond to the teacher as an individual. In fact, the characteristics of the teacher have ideally been the guiding concern for action. Teacher educators look for behaviors that indicate teachers' abilities to accomplish various tasks in order to adapt environments to fit their needs. This final reflection step of assessing the teacher and adapting the environment during the post-conference is an extension of teacher educator behavior begun early in the clinical process. As teacher educator and teacher conduct what Goldhammer (1969) has humorously referred to as a post-mortem on a lesson, the teacher educator must continue to read teacher behavioral cues in order to respond in ways that will be supportive.

Processes of assessing teacher characteristics and adapting the environments during the post-conference are much the same as in the pre-observation conference. That is, the teacher educator seeks to clarify, guide, and in some instances, direct the teacher's attempts to evaluate certain aspects of the now concluded teaching episode. In two special ways, however, processes of assessing and adapting during the post-conference may differ from the same activities in the pre-observation conference. First, the post-conference is an occasion for looking backward as well as ahead. It is a time to consider in retrospect the behaviors of teacher and students in relationship to pre-observation expectations. Even though there are those who believe evaluation differs from planning only in point of time, that may not be true to the teacher in a post-conference. Looking back on his or her own behaviors, as well as on those of the students, in the company of an outsider who has just witnessed them, may arouse quite a different set of feelings and reactions. Such differences in a teacher's feelings of adequacy should further guide the teacher educator in adapting the environment during the post-conference.

The second difference between pre- and post-conference assessing and adapting lies in the fact that one faces a teacher in the post-conference who in at least some ways is more experienced than he or she was in the pre-observation conference. In short, the process of teaching, however brief, can be expected to influence the teacher. Fuller (1969) supports this by citing a study (Newlove, 1966) which determined that after only fifteen minutes of teaching a public school class, prospective teachers expressed concerns about teaching. Given even a single brief encounter, it would appear that persons who function as teachers can be affected by the experience. But if this is true of neophytes, one would expect that a person in later phases of development as a teacher would also be affected by teaching, although perhaps in different ways.

The work of Fuller and her colleagues, discussed in Chapter 4, raises the possibility that teachers who differ in terms of experience may be expected to perceive and express different sorts of concerns about teaching. Such differences could have important implications for assessing teacher characteristics and adapting the clinical environment to teacher needs. For instance, pre-service teachers who are concerned mainly with their own survival could be expected to benefit more from stronger suggestions and more direct feedback than in-service teachers who are concerned with elements of teaching mastery. The teacher educator who is aware of such differences among teachers will be better equipped to respond in useful ways than one who is not.

An Applied Example of the Clinical Process

The example presented here[3] suggests how the clinical process might operate in practice. It consists of a brief summary of the phases and steps of the clinical process as they were carried out by a teacher educator (Linda) with a beginning teacher of French (Elizabeth). To facilitate reader understanding, the example is presented in roughly the same graphic form as Figure 7–1. In addition, we draw attention to the components of a teacher developmental environment (purpose, procedures, management strategy, support system, and provisions for evaluation) noted in Chapter 6 by highlighting them in the margins of the text.

At the conclusion of the clinical episode, Linda asked Elizabeth to assess her performance as a teacher educator and to evaluate the overall value of the session. Elizabeth's reactions appeared to be quite candid. She stated that in the conference situations she had felt free to express herself. Initially, however, Elizabeth found the pre-observation conference confusing because she

Purpose—Linda establishes some preliminary teacher developmental objectives—the first a long-term personal task, the second, a short-term instructional task.

Pre-planning: Based on her past knowledge of Elizabeth (teacher), Linda developed the following profile to guide her own behavior during the upcoming pre-observation conference:
Person: Elizabeth is independent with a high need to achieve. Confident in German but somewhat anxious about her conversational abilities in French. Able to recognize difficulties with her teaching methods. Willing to take risks. Enthusiastic and creative (uses various media). Person-oriented and desirous of encouraging student-student, student-teacher exchange in class.
Projected teacher developmental environment:
Objectives: (1) To encourage Elizabeth to gain confidence about her own use of French. (2) To help Elizabeth identify a few types of activities that encourage student involvement. Linda planned to allow Elizabeth major responsibility for determining student objectives, lesson content, learning activities, sequence, and pace of activities. She would also serve as a possible resource in planning but make few if any direct suggestions unless specifically requested. During observation, Linda intended to concentrate on Elizabeth's use of French, particularly in periods of free conversation.

Procedures—Pre-planning is the first major procedural step.

Management Strategy—Based on her analysis of Elizabeth's characteristics, Linda chooses a teacher-directed management strategy.

[3] The example presented here was taken from R. F. McNergney, C. A. Carrier, L. Leonard, and B. Harootunian. Teacher development: An interactive approach. Paper presented to the annual meeting of the American Educational Research Association, San Francisco, California, April 12, 1979. It has been modified slightly for use in this chapter.

Procedures – The pre-observation conference is the second major procedural step.

1.0 Pre-Observation Conference:
1.1 Reestablish communication: Conference was conducted over breakfast and during walk to school. Plenty of time for informal talk as well as discussion of upcoming lesson.
1.2 Check planning: Elizabeth exhibited very little awareness of differences among students in terms of their abilities/needs. She was aware of general level of class competency with verb tenses but largely unaware of comprehension, vocabulary, and phrase structuring abilities of class as a whole and as individuals. She established the following general objectives for all students: (1) Selected students will describe, in French, the actions in the cartoons. (2) All students will write a paragraph in French describing one cartoon of his or her choice. (3) Selected students will read their paragraph to the class. In order to accomplish objectives, Elizabeth planned three activities: (1) Presentation of cartoons via an overhead. (2) Class writing activity in small groups. (3) Reading and class discussion of paragraphs. It was not clear how much time would be devoted to each activity.
1.3 Select observational system: Linda decided to make an audio tape of the lesson and to take stenographic notes.

Reflection Step 1: As they confer about the upcoming lesson, it became apparent to Linda that Elizabeth's previous concerns about her own conversational abilities were clearly subordinate to her concerns regarding student involvement. Because Elizabeth appeared generally unaware of student abilities in grammar, vocabulary, written/oral skills, and was vague about time to be spent on each activity, Linda decided to concentrate on Elizabeth's methods of responding to students more than on her use of French. As Linda adapted the pre-planned environment to meet Elizabeth's immediate needs, her objectives changed: (1) to help Elizabeth determine how her verbal and nonverbal behaviors encourage or restrict student work involvement; (2) to encourage Elizabeth's confidence about her own use of French, especially in free conversational situations; (3) to help Elizabeth establish an appropriate pace for learning activities.

Revised Purpose – Linda refines the objective to be pursued.

Support System – Linda uses an external resource (tape recorder) and draws upon her own personal skills in note-taking.

Procedures – Observation/analysis is the third major procedural step.

2.0 Observation/Analysis
2.1 Confirm expectations: This step was not necessary because observation occurred immediately after pre-conference.
2.2 Collect data: The following selected notes represent those taken during class. (T=teacher, S=student, FS=foreign students, r=respond or repeat):

8:25 Elizabeth introduces Linda and explains why she is there. T: introduces overhead with Qu'est-ce que c'est? (turns out lights, closes door). T: Qu'est-ce que c'est "drole" S: strange (no eraser at board T goes on). T: What is he doing? S uses past tense w/error. T models answer. T encourages thinking in French. T: a le repas; catches and corrects own error. T asks ques/Sr/Tr. T points to items on pic Vous avez dit... (Ss smile and lean forward). T: Est-ce que vous pouvez l'ecrire... gestures to S. S: I don't understand. T: I want you to... T: Je cherche une description ... T translates. Ss go to board and write class example. They correct their own errors.

8:30 T counts students off in pairs in French and uses gestures to group them. T gives instruction in French. S volunteers to get dictionaries. FS: I think maybe I don't have to do this exercise. T: you can be a resource person. T: Apres les descriptions on les fera ensemble. T: Parlez en francais s'il vous plait. S: Can we do this in English? T: Non en francais. T walks around: Qu'est ce qui se passe? Ss work and 2 girls at back speak in English.

Reflection Step 2.0: Linda's observation was guided by the objectives outlined in the pre-observation conference. She found it useful later in the period, however, to adapt her observational behaviors in order to document a brief episode of unanticipated instruction on the use of dictionaries.

Observation/Analysis (Continued)

2.3 *Examine data and relate to expectations:*
Analysis of data yielded the following:
(1) Students selected to respond to overhead did so
fluently with the exception of two girls who used
more English than French.
(2) All students were able to write several sentences
about their selected cartoons. They did so with enthusiasm, in some cases referring to dictionary.
(3) Paragraphs read aloud were comprehensible.
Discussion, however, lacked focus and closing was
awkward, i.e., no summary or direction for further
work. Papers were collected for further analysis.
(4) Elizabeth exhibited variety of nonverbal techniques for gaining and holding student attention:
continuous movement about room with pauses to
help individuals, rearranged furniture to facilitate
small group activity, animated hand gestures, covered eyes to demonstrate "aveugle," pats on shoul-
ders to reinforce.
(5) Elizabeth verbally encouraged foreign student
to serve as resource, demonstrated courtesy with
many instances of "s'il vous plaît," corrections of
students done in casual, unoffending manner, repeated correct responses for reinforcement, some
joking and personal interest shown.
(6) All students on-task until closing of lesson.
Pace appropriate up to that point.
(7) Elizabeth's use of French was appropriate and
did not appear strained.
(8) Elizabeth took advantage of an opportunity for
unplanned instruction (incidental learning) on the
dictionary—explaining how and why to look up
words both ways (French to English and vice versa).

Procedures — The post-conference is the fourth major procedural step.

3.0 *Post Conference:*
3.1 *Exchange information:* Discussion of lesson
was shared—neither Linda nor Elizabeth dominated
the session. Linda concentrated on Elizabeth's
variety of verbal/nonverbal techniques for involving
students and drew attention to the need for more
effective closure. She also noted Elizabeth's useful
but unplanned instruction on the dictionary.
Elizabeth noted that her own confidence with
French was enhanced by using the foreign student
as a resource for other students (also unplanned).
3.2 *Future Directions:* Planned closures. More
specificity in instructions. Build on cartoons; students liked them as evidenced by high degree of
work involvement. Become more aware of the
needs of individuals (two girls in back of room).

Reflection Step 3.0: During the post-conference,
Elizabeth encouraged frank criticism of her teaching.
She wanted specific details of her behavior related
to student involvement. Where Linda provided little
direction in the pre-observation conference so as to
avoid restricting Elizabeth, she adapted her behavior
in the post-conference to point out what she believed to be the obvious strengths/limitations of the
lesson. She perceived Elizabeth to be quite open to
specific suggestions for upcoming lessons. Linda
made a mental note to supply even more specificity
in upcoming sessions with Elizabeth, expecially as
related to planning for lesson closure.

was not well planned for the upcoming lesson. But after they had talked, Elizabeth said she began to work things out (the purpose of the planned writing
activity was clarified in her own mind). According to Elizabeth, Linda's explanation of the data collected helped her realize the impact of some of her actions on students. But examining Linda's notes directly was not particularly
helpful, except for those pertaining to lesson closure. Elizabeth was especially
pleased with the post-conference because Linda seemed to listen closely and
answer her questions directly, giving concrete suggestions for improvement.

In general, Elizabeth felt that Linda was extremely helpful, but at times not sufficiently "critical."

SUMMARY

The clinical process of teacher development is a framework upon which planned variations in developmental environments for teachers can be constructed. Delivering support to teachers in conference situations built around instructional episodes allows teacher educators to plan and refine their approaches in accordance with the needs and abilities of teachers. The characteristics of teachers as they are revealed in their transactions with students and teacher educators serve as benchmarks that guide the quality and quantity of support offered.

The clinical process of teacher development is not a simple cookbook approach for meeting teacher needs, however. There are too many demands placed on teacher educators in clinical settings for any recipe to guarantee results. Teacher educators to be successful must be knowledgeable about the kinds of tasks teachers face and how teachers might behave. They must also be aware of the characteristics of teachers and be able to respond to them in complementary ways. In a sense, then, the clinical process requires teacher educators to do for teachers what teachers are expected to do for students. Such demands are complex, and as teachers would undoubtedly testify, not easily met. But if in extending themselves to recognize and respond to problems and opportunities in the classroom, teacher educators do no more than provide a good model for teachers, they will have accomplished a great deal.

⤙ 8 ⤚

The Challenges of Teacher Development

THE preceding chapters should leave little doubt that the effort to develop the unique capabilities of teachers is, at the very least, a difficult proposition. There would seem to be much to know about teachers and teaching and much to know how to do in order to support teacher personal and professional growth. The problems may seem overwhelming, but, even to the cautious, these problems are not so much obstacles as they are challenges or opportunities for learning more about the development of teachers.

This chapter explains more fully some of the challenges facing teacher educators. Some of these are ethical; they involve formulating principles of conduct that govern the behaviors of teacher educators and teachers. Others are more broadly professional; they relate to developing the requisite skills, knowledge, and attitudes of teacher educators. Still others are economic or political; these are pertinent to the development and utilization of resources. And, finally, some challenges—those that are relevant to asking and answering questions about teaching and teacher development—revolve around research. This final chapter concentrates on a few selected challenges and describes opportunities for responding to them to support development of teachers.

The Challenge of Formulating Principles of Conduct

Teacher development is a value-laden activity. Teacher educators routinely face decisions about the needs and capabilities of teachers and the kind of support that will allow them to accomplish certain activities. Making the right decisions is not simply a matter of diagnosing teachers and prescribing support according to some inviolable, value-free theory. Instead, teacher educators must exercise their own best judgment; and, quite naturally in the course of making judgments, teacher educators face a number of ethical issues.

One of the first of these ethical problems is to decide when and under what conditions teacher educators are justified in intervening in the development process to change teacher behaviors. This text has both implied and expressed the idea that teacher change in personal and instructional behaviors is crucial if teachers are to become responsive to students and to fulfill their own aspirations. Nowhere may change be more important than in the profession of teaching. Too often teachers become settled in habits and routines that can make them unresponsive to new teaching opportunities or classroom experiences. As Medley (1979) states, "The poorest risk is the teacher who is set in his ways—who cannot or will not change. How can such a teacher adapt to society's goals, methods, values, expectations that take place all about him?" Some might claim that the argument for the support of teacher change might provide a further excuse for people who seek to enlarge their own positions. It could raise new concerns for teachers—concerns that might demand more money or jobs. Teacher educators could, in effect, become one more layer in an educational bureaucracy that seeks, in Parkinsonian fashion, to perpetuate itself.

Before intervening in the lives of teachers, it is imperative that teacher educators examine their own motives. Without careful self-examination, they may fail to distinguish between interventions that are justifiable and those that are self-serving. As suggested in Chapter 2, when teacher educators perceive that (1) the task is important, (2) teachers in need are capable of making changes, and (3) resources for support are available, they should be reasonably assured that intervention is warranted. But such conditions, quite obviously, do not always exist. Many teachers develop their own capabilities with little or no encouragement from others. They demonstrate new instructional techniques and accomplish personal goals quite easily and naturally. When teachers are already growing—in a sense serving as their own teacher educators—the need for outside intervention is greatly diminished.

Treating different teachers differently in itself raises another serious issue—that of stereotyping. Differentiation of people in terms of types, stages, or levels of development might be translated into practice in such a way that some teachers are labeled "good" and given "more" or "better" treatment, and others might be described in less favorable terms and treated accordingly (Hunt, 1973). The tracking of teachers in educational programs could be similar to the tracking or streaming of students. Teachers might be diagnosed in terms of their motivation, teaching skills, or some other characteristic, and given intractable prescriptions of course work or other learning activities. More likely, however, teachers might suffer the effects of informal relegation to types or categories that are accompanied by little or no environmental support. For example, the recent concerns about teachers growing old or stale on the job might lead to a reliance upon such labels and an unwarranted ostracism of those teachers who are viewed as beyond hope.

It is true, of course, that labels can carry either positive or negative connotations and, to a certain extent, the act of labeling teachers, like that of labeling students, is inevitable. Labels, in and of themselves, are not harmful. What is important, as Hunt (1973) suggests, is how people use them. Labels can serve a valuable function by helping teacher educators organize and consolidate information about teachers; they may allow teacher educators to respond more efficiently and effectively than otherwise. Furthermore, as Cronbach and Snow (1977) point out, there are ways to safeguard against the misuse of labels. Instead of standing as rigid stereotypes, for example, labels can be considered flexible categorizations when they are periodically reassessed. In this way, they can be used as temporary descriptions, not permanent stereotypes.

Another—and perhaps even more important—strategy for safeguarding against the misuse of labels is to work on those teacher characteristics that contribute to the labels (Cronbach and Snow, 1977). That is, if a teacher is considered deficient in a particular aptitude or characteristic, the teacher educator might concentrate directly on developing that aptitude or characteristic. The teacher who is at a particular stage of conceptual development, for instance, might be given help in progressing to the next stage. Or the teacher who is inordinately negative might be encouraged to develop more positive attitudes. Deliberate efforts to develop teacher characteristics that contribute to labels may be one of the most promising courses of action open to teacher educators.

Another issue central to the conduct of teacher development is that of deciding if, and under what conditions, information about teacher needs and abilities is to be shared with teachers. For example, if a teacher educator perceives that a teacher is particularly deficient in a given set of skills or perhaps exhibits a certain prominent dysfunction in relating to others, then the teacher educator must decide whether or not to share his or her perceptions with the teacher. When these perceptions are positive and the job is one of building on teacher strengths instead of remediating deficiencies, the decision to share or not to share perceptions is an easy one. Frequently, however, a teacher educator's perceptions of teachers' strengths are balanced by other perceptions of teachers' needs. Then, the decision to communicate one's thoughts and feelings about teachers to teachers is more difficult.

No doubt some would assert that if relationships between teachers and teacher educators are to be open, genuine, and productive, teacher educators must always express on the outside what they think and feel on the inside. Others would argue that sharing one's perceptions of teachers as persons and professionals threatens working relationships and might border on tactlessness. Common sense suggests that to a certain degree both positions have merit. Transmitting a message about one's perceptions of a teacher to the teacher could be productive or damaging, depending on the nature of the message, the skills of the sender, and the capabilities of the receiver.

Before communicating one's perceptions with a teacher, it is crucial to evaluate the quality of those perceptions. In practice, teacher educators base their impressions of teacher capabilities largely on what teachers tell them and on their observations of teachers in action. They then try to interpret teachers' needs in terms of theory, research, or their own practical experience. The more one observes and communicates with a teacher, the better one's information is about his or her needs and abilities. Thus, perceptions developed over time and based on repeated observations might be worth sharing with teachers. Perceptions or impressions that are based on infrequent observation and communication, on the other hand, are of questionable value and might better be left unspoken.

If teacher educators are confident that their perceptions, whether positive or negative, are valid and worth sharing, they should communicate them with care. For most people, it is easy to talk with others about their strengths, but even these messages may be lost or garbled if they are not stated carefully. When sharing their perceptions of teacher needs, however, teacher educators must be especially cautious. Recklessly communicating impressions of the other's needs can hurt, frighten, anger, or inhibit and is likely to render open and honest communication in the future virtually impossible.

But sharing one's perceptions of teachers' needs, when done sensitively, can have positive results. When teachers have the opportunity to clarify their intentions and actions, they may provide further information that can help teacher educators refine their perceptions. Until these perceptions are verified with teachers and, if necessary, altered, teacher educators may operate on misperceptions that prevent them from being helpful. In addition, when teacher educators express their perceptions of teacher needs openly and sensitively, teachers are given a chance to help themselves grow. Becoming aware of one's capabilities, as viewed through the eyes of another, might enable teachers to make better decisions about their own development.

Another question for teacher educators emanates from the idea of differential treatment. Is it really fair to create different environments for different teachers? No doubt some would argue that treating individual teachers differently, regardless of the terms used to characterize teachers and the methods employed to support them, is patently unfair. They would argue that working differently with different teachers denotes inequitable and unjust treatment. According to this reasoning, all teachers should be afforded the same treatment in all situations. For those who object to differential treatment, the creation of educational environments of equal quality, whether for students or teachers, is a matter of spreading the available human and material resources evenly across those to be served.

The idea that all people must be treated in the same way so as to be fair is deeply ingrained not only in education but in our society at large—and for good reason. For too many years and in too many ways, a few groups have been given "different," "special," or "preferential" treatment, while others have had to settle for much less. The inequities that can result from treating different people differently are all too familiar, painful, and numerous to chronicle here. Nevertheless, offering the same educational environment to all people may not be the most just approach when there is reason to believe that they differ from one another in significant ways. The average environment, or the one designed for all teachers regardless of their differences, may be "too much" for some and "too little" for others. When a teacher educator approaches all teachers the same way—offers the same kind of support and provides the same kind of feedback—some teachers are likely to be overwhelmed, frightened, or angered by the teacher educator's apparent insensitivity. Other teachers, however, when faced with the same unvarying approach, may be bored, frustrated, or perhaps angered as well by what they perceive as the teacher educator's obtuseness. Fairness, then, may not be as much a matter of blindness to individual differences as it is one of sensitivity and responsiveness.

One of the most difficult ethical challenges that teacher educators face is identifying the ends of teacher development—the tasks in which teachers might engage and the behaviors they might demonstrate to be considered successful. Chapter 2 discussed a variety of activities that could be considered important for teachers to accomplish. Researchers have documented the importance of teachers keeping students actively involved in academic work and of avoiding severe criticism. Students suggest that teachers must listen to their concerns and involve them in decision making. Teachers recognize the need for being knowledgeable in their subject areas and coping with student apathy and misbehavior. Although we have tried to point out some statistically and educationally significant findings from which teacher educators might formulate objectives for teacher growth, we have defined no absolutes; neither have we identified activities that all teachers must perform in a prescribed fashion. Instead, we have suggested that the tasks teachers should undertake and the behaviors they should be expected to demonstrate must be determined by the evidence of task importance, the capabilities of the teacher, and the possibilities for providing a supportive environment.

Our reluctance to specify a common set of goals for teachers, however, does not mean that establishing some set of standards is either impossible for teacher development or antithetical to it. Many training programs have advocated minimum performance criteria for teachers. In some cases these standards reflect the interests and knowledge of various consortia composed of teachers, professors, parents, students, and state department of education representatives; these standards can thus be assumed to be fairly well founded and at least somewhat representative of the kinds of minimum expectations that might reasonably be set for teachers.[1]

Minimum criteria for teacher success can be established; but as recent teacher education history indicates, not without considerable difficulty. When commitments to "outcome floors," or absolute criteria, for the acceptability of performance are made, a few powerful treatments that reduce the effects of individual differences may need to be designed and administered (Gehlbach, 1979). For example, keeping pupils actively engaged in reading instruction is a task that might reasonably warrant a high priority for elementary school teachers. Such a task might be best accomplished by teachers creating interesting seatwork activities, providing immediate feedback to pupils about their progress, and conducting small group drill exercises. Given these "absolutes," teacher educators might usefully work to create one or two environments that require minimal adaptation to teacher differences in order to help teachers accomplish some tasks.

The Challenge of Building Teacher Educator Competence

To function effectively, teacher educators must continually refine and extend their own capabilities. They need to build their knowledge about teachers— how they learn, what they hope to accomplish, how they can be expected to perform—and organize such information into strategies for encouraging teacher growth. Because the needs of teachers can be expected to vary, teacher educators may frequently be required to adapt their support techniques. With a teacher who cannot make decisions quickly or effectively, for example, it may be eminently reasonable to tell the teacher what to do. But with a teacher who acts impulsively, the best course of action may be to encourage him or her to think more carefully before acting. Awareness of alternatives for supporting teachers, and when and how to use them, necessarily requires teacher educators to expand their sensitivities and skills.

Teacher educators can refine and extend their own abilities in a number of ways. But in teacher development, as in teaching, perhaps the best way to begin building one's competence is through practice—first in simple situations and then in more challenging ones. This might involve working initially with a single teacher on a fairly simple task. Consider, for example, the case of the inexperienced, anxious teacher whose problem is administering a stan-

---

[1] New York State's efforts to develop performance/compentency based teacher education called not only for the establishment of minimal competencies for teachers, but for a process of collaboration designed to identify these competencies.

dardized achievement test for the first time. In a pre-observation conference, the teacher educator could try proposing suggestions about procedures for preparing students, giving directions, or timing sections, and observe whether or not they were helpful to the teacher. Or the teacher educator might suggest ways of handling distracted or disruptive students—recommending such teacher behaviors as walking over to a child's desk and quietly describing desirable behavior or moving a child to a table at the back of the room. Joint planning of this nature, a subsequent visit to the teacher's classroom, and a follow-up discussion of the observational data are all activities with potential for increasing the competence of the teacher educator.

When working with only a single teacher, one can learn to ask probing questions, construct and use observational systems, summarize observational data, and give feedback to the teacher. Although necessarily limited, behaviors practiced in the context of the work environment with one teacher can provide a foundation for building greater expertise.

The teacher educator's competence may be increased by working with more teachers and undertaking more complex tasks. Interaction with a greater number of teachers will provide the teacher educator with diversity both in the types of instructional problems to be addressed and in the personalities and capabilities of teachers. Increasing the number of contacts with teachers should also help refine the teacher developer's adaptation skills. When a particular strategy fails to help a teacher satisfy a need (even though it may have been effective with another teacher who had a similar problem), the teacher educator must explore other methods. Perhaps this will mean learning about new resources, using different observational methods, or trying out a different management strategy. Responding to different teachers who have similar or different problems can thus expand a teacher educator's repertoire of skills.

As teacher educators encounter more complex situations, the challenges will increase but so will the opportunities for learning. Working with a variety of teachers allows teacher educators to learn from many people, each of whom may have different ideas, insights, and expertise. Exploring a teacher's knowledge of a topic may well be a learning experience for the teacher educator, too. In the same way, witnessing a teacher's effective demonstration of classroom skills may increase the skills of the teacher educator. Teachers and teacher educators who work as co-learners can help each other grow.

Higher levels of competence may also result as teacher educators begin to analyze patterns of behavior emerging from their work with various teachers. Although teachers may have different reactions to the same events, commonalities in their attitudes and behaviors can be informative. It may be apparent, for example, that teachers are unenthusiastic about scheduling conferences before school starts or that most respond favorably to weekly meetings or to suggestions about useful resources. Other patterns of teacher behavior may suggest what teacher educators should avoid: those who consistently show up late for observational sessions, for instance, should not be surprised when teachers become less cooperative and communicative.

Attacking complex problems may also encourage teacher educators to sharpen their skills in locating and using relevant resources. To illustrate, as a first step in working with a teacher who is excessively controlling, the teacher educator might identify another teacher who allows students more freedom. The second teacher could describe or model how a contract system can allow students to choose projects of interest and pursue them within a prescribed framework. To gain assurance that the students who use contracts are productive and well behaved, the controlling teacher might observe students as they work on their projects. Further, the teacher educator might supply the teacher with several well-chosen articles that point out why student autonomy is important and how students can be involved in making choices. Or, he or she might help the teacher construct a plan to help students increase the quantity and quality of their decisions.

As they gradually increase their workloads—conduct more conferences and observe more classrooms—teacher educators will necessarily learn how to manage their time effectively. They will learn how to keep a conference on task, record observational data efficiently, and schedule conferences that are convenient to themselves and the teachers with whom they work. Learning to manage time in the present helps teacher educators project reasonable workloads for the future.

To refine one's competence as a teacher educator it may also be useful to extend a working relationship over time. Ongoing work with a teacher or teachers may afford some unique opportunities for building teacher educator competence that are not available in short-term working relationships. With sufficient time, teacher educators can encourage teachers to accomplish more complex tasks that require the demonstration of many behaviors. By periodically observing and talking with a teacher, the teacher educator has opportunities to collect and organize different kinds of information, employ different kinds of support, and frequently assess the teacher's progress as well as his or her own.

A support group for teacher educators can also increase the possibilities for building competence. Two or more people working together on a set of protocols designed to teach an observation system can often make learning quicker and easier. By quizzing each other over category designators, discussing the intent of ground rules, and helping each other interpret data, there is less chance of misinterpretation and frustration. Furthermore, if members of the group share taped examples of their own conferences as well as the written notes or data they have collected during observations, they can critique each other's work, offer suggestions, and give positive reinforcement for a job well done. Teacher educators who provide one another with substantive direction and honest feedback—or form a support group in fact as well as name—can do much to develop their own individual competence.

Another obvious way to build competence in teacher development is to take formal course work. Unless teacher educators explore available college or university offerings, they may overlook genuine opportunities for improving their practice. If courses do no more than provide relevant readings, they still can help teacher educators build their own programs of study. In examining research, writing, and curricula pertinent to human growth and development, counseling, instructional design, delivery, and evaluation, teacher educators increase the resources they can offer teachers. Many courses also provide much more than readings; they are forums for the exchange of ideas, where one can test and refine one's own knowledge and beliefs. Although taking formal courses to obtain a higher degree may not be feasible or desirable, selecting even a few courses of particular interest may be extremely worthwhile to the teacher educator.

The Challenge of Organizing Resources

The costs of teacher development may be high, but few would disagree that the types of interventions suggested here, if implemented systematically over a reasonable period of time, could result in several positive gains. Teachers should grow as a result of their involvement with teacher developmental activities. They should learn new skills that enable them to design, deliver, and evaluate instruction more effectively and, at the same time, feel more valued as individuals because their needs and abilities have been recognized. Their responsibility for instructional improvement may well be expected to increase because they will have been partners in, rather than victims of, the process of change.

Students, too, should profit from teacher developmental activities. If their teachers become more satisfied, more competent, and more responsive, the learning environments created for students can be expected to improve. And those who work with teachers—the teacher educators—also stand to gain. By helping teachers solve problems, they may come to view themselves as contributing to, rather than simply judging, teacher competence.

Even in their most basic implementation, processes of teacher development can be time-consuming. They demand ongoing, systematic involvement in a professional relationship. Unlike teacher performance evaluations, which may occur only once or twice a year, systematic development of teacher capabilities requires frequent contact for cooperative planning and problem solving. Although the adage "two heads are better than one" may well apply to the quality of outcomes, joint planning is often less efficient than unilateral decision making. In addition, the necessity for providing support for teachers may require substantial investments of the teacher educator's time and energy to locate external resources or improve his or her own skills. With adequate financial resources, of course, the problem of time might easily be removed or substantially decreased. Additional personnel could be hired to serve as teacher educators or to lighten the responsibilities of others. But in the present period of retrenchment, there is little hope that new personnel will be added in public schools. Most likely what must happen is that existing staff members develop new opportunities for supporting teacher growth.

Administrative personnel, for example, may have to rearrange their priorities so that they can begin to devote more energy to working directly with teachers. No doubt many building principals experience frustration because they find so little time to work with teachers. They have been touted as "instructional leaders," but often principals express concern informally about their ability to fulfill this role. Finding time to visit each teacher's classroom more than once or twice a year is more than many think they can manage.

There are, of course, no easy ways to change one's priorities as a principal, but certain changes may help free up some additional time. For instance, a principal may delegate certain responsibilities to others, perhaps an assistant principal or a qualified secretary. These might include maintaining student personnel records, coordinating student transportation, or coordinating extracurricular activities. Or some interpersonally skilled teachers might work more closely with concerned parents. Although delegation of responsibilities means sharing authority, allowing others to help with typically administrative tasks does not necessarily translate into a surrender of control or an abdication of responsibility. Instead, it could mean that principals recognize the need to invest more of themselves in the lives of their teachers.

In addition to redefining the role of the building principal, individuals responsible for in-service training or staff development at the district level might redirect some of their energies in order to build supportive relationships with individual teachers. Group-oriented approaches to in-service (workshops, courses, conferences) may be beneficial, but many teachers need more personalized support to identify and remedy their classroom teaching problems. Yarger, Howey, and Joyce (1978), for example, found that less than one teacher in five was involved in regular in-service activities that specifically related to his or her work situation.

Other resource personnel in the district, such as curriculum specialists, could emphasize follow-through with teachers on new materials or methods. Rather than merely informing teachers about new materials and methods, or demonstrating their use, resource personnel could work more directly with teachers to integrate materials into their classrooms. The science specialist, for example, might help a teacher establish objectives and plan learning activities for a science unit and then observe how the lesson is taught. Following the observation, the specialist might serve as a resource for teacher skill improvement vis-à-vis the new materials.

Regardless of who assumes the role of teacher educator, whether it be a building principal, an administrative intern, a university professor, a member of the central office staff, or an in-service teacher, it is important to begin realistically. This means starting with one or two teachers instead of trying to work with every teacher in the entire school. It is not necessary for all teachers in a building, a department, or a grade level to be included in early teacher development efforts. In fact, these efforts might be doomed to failure if too much is taken on too quickly. Limiting oneself to working with a few carefully selected teachers in the beginning may increase the likelihood that early teacher developmental experiences will be successful.

The selection of teachers to work with initially can be guided by several criteria. Perhaps the most obvious of these is teacher need. Immediate instructional or personal teacher needs should be the logical beginning point for developmental activities. The teacher whose students are misbehaving, for example, must quickly learn classroom control management strategies. The advantage of using this kind of immediate teacher need as a guide for selection, of course, is that both teacher and teacher educator may enjoy relatively early results for their efforts.

Unfortunately, not all individuals who need help will seek it. Teacher educators might, therefore, select teachers to work with based on teacher willingness to participate. Although teachers who volunteer are likely to be open to change (because they understand that their classroom performance will be observed and critiqued), and some might earnestly want to improve their skills, others may regard such participation in teacher developmental activities as an opportunity to "get ahead" professionally. When selecting from among volunteers, then, the teacher educator may want to be particularly sensitive to teachers' underlying motivations for participation.

Another criterion for teacher selection in developmental activities may be the teacher educator's own needs. In their initial attempts to encourage teacher growth, some teacher educators will undoubtedly find that their own skills are also in need of improvement. For them, teacher development may represent a radically different philosophy toward working with teachers. These teacher educators should realize that feedback about their own performance is essential. A teacher with whom one has established a mutually open relationship might feel comfortable pointing out negative as well as positive aspects of the teacher educator's performance. In contrast, a new teacher or one who appears to be insecure may be unwilling or unable to provide such feedback. If reactions to one's own performance are especially important in the beginning, the teacher educator should carefully consider the possibilities of working with those teachers who are most capable of providing substantive direction.

In order to meet the demands of responding to teachers as individuals, new personnel may be hired or existing roles redefined, but even in the most optimistic moments, it is difficult to envision that "outsiders" alone can meet the needs of teachers. Perhaps, however, teachers may be able to do for themselves what others cannot do for them. When the major purpose of intervention is to improve instruction and enhance personal development, teachers may well be their own best resource.

Yarger, Howey, and Joyce (1978) found that in in-service activities within the work environment, teachers perceived other teachers as the most helpful instructors. The most credible teacher educators may well be those who are also teachers. Like their teacher partners, they too are struggling with the everyday problems of classroom teaching. Administrative personnel, whether they be principals, central office staff, or college or university supervisors, are more likely to be viewed by teachers as part of a different group. Blumberg (1974) captures the essence of the problem in his discussion of the reasons that teachers sometimes reject help from supervisors. Such rejection, he states,

> may be symbolic of the continuing battle that is waged in practically every organization between those who are "getting their hands dirty" and those whose job is managing, planning, organizing, training, and so forth.

In addition to the advantage of having a built-in credibility, teachers who serve as teacher educators may already know a great deal about the people with whom they will work. For example, when a member of an English faculty functions as a teacher educator, it may be assumed that he or she has already had extensive contact with others in the department. Teachers in the department will have struggled together to design and implement new curricula, collaborated on strategies for dealing with problem students, or shared moments of discouragement or elation. Having worked with others as colleagues, the teacher-as-teacher educator has a rich supply of information about fellow teachers' needs and abilities. In designing a teacher developmental environment to support a specific teacher, this kind of teacher educator may have an advantage over others who have less knowledge about their partners.

The idea that classroom teachers can work to assist each other has also been suggested in other contexts. Peer evaluation and supervision systems, for example, have been used in some schools (Blumberg, 1974). Similarly, Good, Biddle, and Brophy (1975) describe a program carried out by Martin and Kerman (Martin, 1973) in which the training goals were to make teachers aware of their nonproductive behaviors toward low-achieving students, and to change such behavior. In this program, teachers observed and coded the behaviors of their colleagues and then provided feedback. Not only did the teachers' behaviors toward these students improve, but so did the attitudes and reading performance of low-achieving students who worked with them.

For many teachers, the opportunities to help colleagues grow might provide a refreshing challenge. As Mosher and Purpel (1972) point out, teachers must be encouraged to grow in new directions:

> Typically and ironically, the ladder to success for a teacher has always been to leave teaching and enter administration, guidance, or higher education. School administrators as well as teachers are trying very hard to develop new roles which can combine teaching with other exciting and varied responsibilities.

Teachers as teacher educators might well find opportunities to take on new leadership roles and to learn how to share their own expertise with others—opportunities that undoubtedly will be welcomed by many.

The case for teachers serving as teacher educators seems strong, but it is not without problems. Teachers must, of course, find time for planning, conferences, and observing with their colleagues. In order to provide this time, the building principal might cover the teacher's class and free the teacher to observe and confer with a colleague. Or, for a modest cost, a part-time substitute teacher might be hired to cover a teacher's class several times a week. A one- or two-hour investment of time per week could mean that at least one new teacher-developmental relationship could be established. Other options may include combining two study halls once a week or rearranging schedules so that the two participants have the same free periods to confer. Or, perhaps, two teachers could serve as teacher educators in working with a single teacher so the amount of time and effort required of each is reduced.

If teachers are to serve as teacher educators, however, they must be given more than time. Teachers who are competent with pupils and interpersonally sensitive with adults may have the necessary but not sufficient skills to help their colleagues grow personally and professionally. Teachers will most likely need opportunities to increase their knowledge and skills if they are to provide genuine support for each other. Training in the form of in-service activities, workshops, courses, or the opportunity to work side by side with other teacher educators may be needed to ensure that teachers acquire such knowledge and skills.

The Challenge of Improving Knowledge

The teacher educator must be not only an applier of knowledge, but also a researcher—refining and extending what is already known about the development of teachers. The search for knowledge is just as important as immediate efforts to upgrade teaching. It is not that present knowledge is either nonexistent or so weak as to be useless; there is a considerable amount upon which teacher educators can base their practice. But only as teacher educators critically examine ideas about teaching and learning can existing knowledge be improved.

Conducting research on teacher development is similar to conducting research on any other type of human behavior. Whether teacher educators choose to examine the phenomena of teacher development in the field or in laboratory settings, or to conduct experimental or nonexperimental research, they face a number of challenges. Research questions or hypotheses must be formulated; research designs must be established and procedures specified; data must be collected, analyzed, and interpreted; and the results of different investigations must be integrated into an understandable whole.

Teacher educators can begin to respond to the challenges of improving knowledge about teacher development by asking relevant and important questions. As users of knowledge, they will necessarily be interested in problems of applied research—or research designed to assist in decision making in specific problem situations (Kerlinger, 1977). Any reasonably pragmatic person, for example, will be interested in determining how much the processes of supporting teacher growth cost, not only in terms of dollars, but in terms of time. Questions of cost-effectiveness can be stated in a variety of ways. If opportunities are created for teachers to work with one another on developmental activities, then to what extent are they used? Once teacher educators have worked with teachers in the context of their classrooms on specific activities, do changes in teaching behavior stand the test of time and do improvements carry over to other activities and other teachers? Are there barriers to teacher growth—such as teacher apathy, overwork, resistance to change—that can only be met and overcome by large expenditures of resources? These and similar questions of application may be good starting points for investigation.

Alone, the challenges of investigating problems of application could preoccupy almost any teacher educator; but if knowledge is to be improved on another level, teacher educators must also concern themselves with basic research, or research designed to study variables and their relationships (Kerlinger, 1977). The $B = (f)P,E,T$ conceptual scheme suggests the directions such basic research might take. There are potentially seven general sets of relationships that could be investigated in this scheme. These relationships and the types of questions they portend are listed in Table 8–1.

Some of these relationships have been studied for years and in considerable detail by researchers. As Cronbach (1957) has noted, correlationists have been concerned with the relationships between personal characteristics and behaviors; experimentalists have concentrated on the relationships of educational environments and learning outcomes; and interactionists have studied the combined effects of persons and environments on behavior. Much of the research on these relationships, though revealing, has concerned itself with these variables in terms of the education of children, not the education of teachers. Even in such relationships as those between teachers' personal characteristics and their teaching behavior (B:P) and teacher educational environments and teaching behaviors (B:E)—where a fairly extensive body of lit-

TABLE 8–1

Relationships Between and Among Teaching Behaviors (B), Teachers' Personal Characteristics (P), Teacher Developmental Environments (E), and Teaching Tasks (T).

(1) B:P—Do teachers' personal characteristics influence teacher behavior?
(2) B:E—Do teacher developmental environments influence teacher behavior?
(3) B:T—Do the tasks in which teachers engage influence teacher behavior?
(4) B:P × E—Are the behaviors of different teachers affected by different teacher developmental environments?
(5) B:P × T—Are the behaviors of different teachers affected by undertaking different tasks?
(6) B:E × T—Are some teacher developmental environments more effective in training teachers to perform some teaching tasks than other tasks?
(7) B:P × E × T—Are the behaviors of teachers influenced by a combination of teacher characteristics, teacher developmental environments, and teaching tasks?

erature exists—additional research may be warranted that focuses on yet relatively unexamined teacher characteristics (such as moral or ego development and conceptual level) and clinical environments of teacher development.

Ultimately, if teacher educators are to improve knowledge, they must be sensitive to the multivariate nature of teacher behavior. Investigating simple relations, such as those between teacher behavior and the training teachers receive, may yet provide useful information. But increasingly teacher educators will need to understand more complex relationships among variables. This demands that teacher educators concern themselves with the behavior of teachers in the context of educational environments as modified by the activities in which teachers engage and as influenced by the needs and abilities of the teachers. Questions designed to improve knowledge on teacher development must begin to reflect such complexity if we are to better understand the real world of teachers.

As questions are raised, teacher educators must face another set of challenges that deals with plans, strategies, or designs for conducting research. There are many possibilities for formulating valid, objective, and economical research designs; but whatever designs are selected or created, they must be carefully conceived so as to allow variables of interest to be controlled and measured, and the results of inquiry to be generalized to other situations. As Campbell and Stanley (1963) have emphasized in the case of experimental research, if one is to control and measure variables and apply findings to other problem situations with any degree of precision, it is imperative to formulate designs that protect against various threats to the validity of a study.

According to these researchers, in order to safeguard the *internal validity* of an experimental study—or the ability to determine whether or not an experimental treatment really makes a difference in the behaviors of subjects—researchers must try to reduce the influences of certain extraneous variables. Consider, for instance, a teacher educator who is interested in determining the effects of one type of clinical environment on the abilities of a group of teachers to perform an instructional task. The teacher educator should be aware that the behaviors of the teachers may be influenced not only by the planned clinical environment but by external events as well. Some of the teachers in the study may attend an outside workshop that offers new insights. Others may share an article that bears on the task in question. Such intervening events that are not planned parts of the study may jeopardize the teacher educator's ability to attribute behavioral outcomes to the effects of the clinical environment.

As Campbell and Stanley (1963) also point out, other threats to the internal validity of an experimental study emanate from the effects of maturation, testing, instrumentation, statistical regression, biases in selection, experimental mortality, and selection-maturation interaction. In many instances, these factors can be neutralized at least partially through the use of control groups and random assignment of subjects. Even these safeguards, however, are not always possible or even appropriate. If teacher educators remember that the first step to producing experimental results that are internally valid is a matter of controlling and measuring variables as carefully and completely as possible, they will be ready to take the second step—that of designing or getting help to design plans and strategies that control for such threats.

In addition to the challenge of safeguarding the internal validity of research, teacher educators must also select or create designs that protect the *external validity* of a study, or the generalizability of experimental results to other persons and other settings. Bracht and Glass (1968), building on the work of Campbell and Stanley (1963), discuss external validity in terms of selecting, describing, and managing experimental subjects and treatments in ways that allow research to approximate, as nearly as possible, persons and educational conditions as they exist in reality. Although at times the need to make research more generalizable may conflict with the need to control, attention to factors affecting the external validity of research, like those affecting internal validity, are extremely important.

Bracht and Glass (1968) discuss various threats to external validity, but Snow (1968) suggests that the biggest threat to the generalizability of research may come when the experiment does not fit the behavior being studied. He proposes that experimentation be "representative" (Brunswik, 1956) as opposed to the more "systematic" type of experimentation common in psychological research. By this he means that research may be designed so that experimenters allow subjects freedom to behave naturally by exerting only passive control—in other words, fitting research to human behavior, instead of trying to force human behavior to conform to the experiment.

According to Snow, several steps might be taken to create representative research designs. Specifically, he suggests that experiments be conducted in relevant contexts, such as school rooms; that they be imbedded in the normal flow of events; that they be replicated with different subjects; that subjects be observed within an experiment to determine how they perceive the treatment; and that experimental treatments be extended over time. Further, in order to conduct research that closely approximates real conditions, teacher educators may find it useful to conduct naturalistic studies as opposed to tightly controlled experimental ones. Such studies would try to observe and describe teachers as they go about teaching and learning in the context of their jobs and their outside activities. Snow (1968) and others note that informed observation of events as they occur in real life may yield a quality of information that laboratory experimentation in many cases has failed to provide.

Yet another set of challenges for the teacher educator as researcher is related to processes of analyzing and interpreting the results of research. Regardless of whether investigation is of an experimental or nonexperimental, field or laboratory variety, the job of analyzing and interpreting results can be formidable. Data must be organized, manipulated, and summarized according to predetermined design so that they may be intepreted. In some cases, interpretation must include examination of negative and inconclusive findings to determine what went wrong in a study. Positive results, too, may need to be scrutinized to provide greater understanding. That is, when relationships are shown to be statistically significant, they must be considered in terms of their strength as well (Barber, 1976). Conclusions and inferences must be drawn from results, and meaning derived by comparing results to other related research and to the propositions of theory.

But comparing and integrating one's own research with the research of others may offer special problems. Research methodology and variables of interest, although related, may differ considerably from study to study. Thus, integrating the results from various studies on teacher development into some understandable conceptual whole may present yet another challenge for teacher educators.

Glass (1976), however, lends direction for responding to such a challenge. He proposes that the diversity of findings from individual research studies be integrated by applying the procedures of what he refers to as "meta-analysis," or analysis of different but related analyses. In a meta-analysis of research on psychotherapy, Smith and Glass (1977) analyzed some 400 studies on the effects of psychotherapy. By relating the duration of therapy, experience of the therapist, diagnoses of subjects, type of therapy, and type of outcome, they were able to determine the size of the psychotherapy effect in each study. As teacher educators study or conduct research using various types of treatments involving different teachers under various conditions, they, too, may benefit from procedures of meta-analysis. The combined results of research in teacher development, teacher education, and adult growth and development may eventually provide direction for still further research and improved practice.

SUMMARY

Supporting the personal and professional growth of teachers is demanding work. Trying to do so with respect to the needs of individual teachers makes the work even more challenging. Among other things, teacher educators must formulate and adhere scrupulously to principles of conduct that protect the dignity of individuals. They must expand their own repertoire of skills in order to support a variety of teachers. Resources must be identified and allocated in ways that make sense for teachers and at the same time address the needs of children. And if that is not enough, teacher educators must be active learners in their own right—enlarging their knowledge about teachers and teaching and sharing that knowledge with others.

Although the challenges of teacher development are formidable, the future seems promising. As noted at the outset of the book, there are no magic methods for ensuring that all teachers, regardless of their needs and abilities, will succeed; nor are there likely to be in the near future. If teacher educators recognize what many teachers have already discovered, they might abandon the search for the best way to educate people and concentrate instead on varying their methods to meet individual needs. There are many risks to be taken and much to be learned through such a course of action. But the reward might just make teacher development worth the effort.

☟ References ☞

ACHESON, K. A., and M. D. GALL. *Techniques in the clinical supervision of teachers: Preservice and inservice applications.* New York: Longman, Inc., 1980.

AHANA, E. *A study on the reliability and internal consistency of a manifest anxiety scale.* Unpublished master's thesis, Evanston, Ill.: Northwestern University, 1952.

AHLGREN, A., and D. J. CHRISTENSEN. *Minnesota school affect assessment of Independent School District 196, Rosemount, Minnesota.* Minneapolis, MN: Center for Educational Development, University of Minnesota, 1972.

AHLGREN, A., D. J. CHRISTENSEN, and K. LUN. *Minnesota school affect assessment.* Minneapolis, MN.: Center for Educational Development, University of Minnesota, 1977.

ALLPORT, G. W. Attitudes. In C. A. Murchison (Ed.), *A handbook of social psychology.* Worcester, MA.: Clark University Press, 1935, 798–844.

AMIDON, E. J., and N. A. FLANDERS. *The role of the teacher in the classroom: A manual for understanding and improving teacher classroom behavior,* revised edition. St. Paul, MN.: Paul S. Amidon & Associates, 1971.

ANDERSON, H. H., and J. E. BREWER. Studies of teachers' classroom personalities, I. *Applied psychology monographs,* No. 8. Palo Alto, CA.: Stanford University Press, 1945.

———. Studies of teachers' classroom personalities, II. *Applied psychology monographs,* No. 11. Palo Alto, CA.: Stanford University Press, 1946a.

ANDERSON, H. H., J. E. BREWER, and M. F. REED. Studies of teachers' classroom personalities, III. *Applied psychology monographs,* No. 11. Palo Alto, CA.: Stanford University Press, 1946b.

BARBER, T. X. *Pitfalls in human research: Ten pivotal points.* Elmsford, N. Y.: Pergamon Press, Inc., 1976.

BELLACK, A. A., H. M. KLIEBARD, R. T. HYMAN, and F. L. SMITH. *The language of the classroom.* New York: Teachers College Press, 1966.

BERLINER, D. C., and L. S. CAHEN. Trait-treatment interaction and learning. In F. N. Kerlinger (Ed.), *Review of research in education.* Itaska, IL.: Peacock Publishers, 1973, 1: 58–94.

BERLINER, D. C., and W. TIKUNOFF. Ethnography in the classroom. In G. D. Borich, *The appraisal of teaching: Concepts and process.* Reading, MA.: Addison-Wesley Publishing Co., Inc., 1977, 280–291.

BERNIER, J. E., Jr. Psychological education intervention for teacher development (Doctoral dissertation, University of Minnesota, 1976). *Dissertation Abstracts International* (1977), **37:** 6266A–6267A. (University Microfilms No. 77–6932).

BLOOM, B. S. Mastery Learning. In J. Block (Ed.), *Mastery learning: Theory and practice.* New York: Holt, Rinehart and Winston, 1971.

BLOOM, B. S., M. B. ENGELHART, E. J. FURST, W. H. HILL, and D. R. KRATHWOHL. *Taxonomy of educational objectives. The classification of educational goals. Handbook I: Cognitive domain.* New York: Longmans Green, 1956.

BLUMBERG, A. A system for analyzing supervisor-teacher interaction. In A. Simon and E. G. Boyer (Eds.), *Mirrors for behavior,* III. Philadelphia, PA.: Research for Better Schools, Inc., 1970, 34.1-1-34. 1–15.

———. *Supervisors and teachers: A private cold war.* Berkeley, CA.: McCutchan Publishing Corporation, 1974.

BLUMBERG, A., and E. AMIDON. Teacher perceptions of supervisor-teacher interaction. *Administrator's Notebook* 14, No. 1 (September 1965).

BLUMBERG, A., and P. CUSICK. Supervisor-teacher interaction: An analysis of verbal behavior. *Education* (November 1970), 126–134.

BORG, W. R. *Protocol materials on classroom management.* Tampa, FLA.: National Resource and Dissemination Center, University of South Florida, 1974.

———. *Withitness: A classroom management concept related to effective teaching (student manual).* Tampa, FLA.: National Resources and Dissemination Center, University of South Florida, 1974.

BORG, W. R. GRE aptitude scores as predictors of GPA for graduate students in education. *Educational and Psychological Measurement* (1963), **23**: 379–382.

BORICH, G. D., and S. K. MADDEN. *Evaluating classroom instruction: A sourcebook of instruments.* Reading, MA.: Addison-Wesley Publishing Co., Inc., 1977.

BRACHT, G. H. Experimental factors related to aptitude-treatment interactions. *Review of Educational Research* (1970), **40**: 627–646.

BRACHT, G. H., and G. V. GLASS. The external validity of comparative experiments in educational and the social sciences. *American Educational Research Journal* (1968), **5**: 437–474.

BRANDT, R. *Studying behavior in natural settings.* New York: Holt, Rinehart and Winston, 1972.

BROPHY, J. Comments. In D. M. Medley, *Teacher competence and teacher effectiveness: A review of process-product research.* Washington, D.C.: American Association of Colleges for Teacher Education, 1977, pp. 117–118.

BROPHY, J. E., and T. L. GOOD. *Teacher-student relationships: Causes and consequences.* New York: Holt, Rinehart and Winston, 1974.

BRUNSWIK, E. *Perception and the representative design of psychological experiments.* Berkeley, CA.: University of California Press, 1956.

CAMPBELL, D. T., and J. C. STANLEY. *Experimental and quasi-experimental designs for research.* Skokie, ILL.: Rand McNally & Company, 1963.

CARROLL, J. B. A model of school learning. *Teachers College Record* (1963), **64**: 723–733.

CARTWRIGHT, C. A., and G. P. CARTWRIGHT. *Developing observation skills.* New York: McGraw-Hill Book Company, 1974.

CATTELL, R. B. *Abilities: Their structure, growth, and action.* Boston: Houghton Mifflin Company, 1971.

CLARK, C. M., and R. J. YINGER. Teachers' thinking. In P. L. Peterson, and H. J. Walberg (Eds.), *Research on teaching: Concepts, findings, and implications.* Berkeley, CA.: McCutchan Publishing Corporation, 1979, 231–263.

CLARK, R. J., Jr. Authoritarianism, educational progressivism, and teacher trainees' use of inquiry (Doctoral dissertation, Stanford University, 1970). *Dissertation Abstracts International* (1970), **30**: 2663A. (University Microfilms No. 70–1637).

COGAN, M. L. *Clinical supervision.* Boston: Houghton Mifflin Company, 1973.

COLLEGE ENTRANCE EXAMINATION BOARD. *A description of the College Board Scholastic Aptitude Test.* Princeton, N. J.: Educational Testing Service, 1956.

Cook, W. W., C. J. Hoyt, and A. Eikaas. Studies of predictive validity of the Minnesota Teacher Attitude Inventory. *Journal of Teacher Education* (1956), **7**: 167–172.

Cook, W. W., C. H. Leeds, and R. Callis. *The Minnesota Teacher Attitude Inventory.* New York: The Psychological Corporation, 1951.

Corrigan, D. C. Public law 94–142: A matter of human rights; a call for change in schools and colleges of education. In J. K. Grosenick, and M. C. Reynolds (Eds.), *Teacher education: Renegotiating roles for mainstreaming.* Reston, VA.: Council for Exceptional Children, 1978, 17–29.

Cronbach, L. J. Coefficient alpha and the internal structure of tests. *Psychometrika* (1951), **16**: 297–334.

————. The two disciplines of scientific psychology. *American Psychologist* (1957), **12**: 671–684.

————. Beyond the two disciplines of scientific psychology. *American Psychologist* (1975), **30**: 116–127.

Cronbach, L. J., and R. E. Snow. *Individual differences in learning ability as a function of instructional variables.* Final Report, 1969, School of Education, Stanford University, Contract No. OEC–4-6-061269-1217, U. S. Office of Education.

————. *Aptitudes and instructional methods: A handbook of research on interactions.* New York: Irvington, 1977.

Davis, O. L. Jr., and K. Yamamoto. Teachers in preparation: Professional attitudes and motivations. *Journal of Teacher Education* (1968), **19**: 365–369.

Della Piana, G., and N. Gage. Pupils' values and the validity of the Minnesota Teacher Attitude Inventory. *Journal of Educational Psychology* (1955), **46**: 167–178.

Dewey, J. Pedagogy as a university discipline. *University Record* (1896) 1(25, 26), 353–355, 361–363.

————. *The sources of a science of education.* New York: Liveright, 1929.

DiStafano, J. J. Interpersonal perceptions of field independent and field dependent teachers and students (Doctoral dissertation, Cornell University, 1969). *Dissertation Abstracts International* (1970), **31**: 463A–464A. (University Microfilms No. 70–11, 225)

Domino, G. Interactive effects of achievement orientation and teaching style on academic achievement. *Journal of Educational Psychology* (1971), **62**: 427–431.

Dowaliby, F. J., and H. Schumer. Teacher-centered versus student-centered mode of college instruction as related to manifest anxiety. *Journal of Educational Psychology* (1973), **64**: 125–132.

Dugan W. E. *A study of the Miller Analogies Test with graduate students in education.* Unpublished master's thesis, University of Minnesota, 1939.

Dunkin, M. J., and B. J. Biddle. *The study of teaching.* New York: Holt, Rinehart and Winston, 1974.

Eisner, E. W. Educational objectives: Help or hindrance? *School Review* (1967a), **75**: 250–266.

————. *Instructional and expressive educational objectives: Their formulation and use in curriculum.* Unpublished manuscript, Stanford University, 1967b.

Elam, S. M. (Ed.). *A decade of Gallup polls of attitudes toward education, 1969–1978.* Bloomington, IN.: Phi Delta Kappa, 1978.

Erickson, V. L. Education and women's development. Chapter section in R. C. Sprinthall and N. A. Sprinthall (Eds.), *Educational psychology: A developmental approach.* Reading, MA.: Addison-Wesley Publishing Co., Inc., 1974, 450–455.

Erlich, O., and G. Borich. *Measuring classroom interactions: How many occasions are required to measure them reliably?* Austin: University of Texas, the Research and Development Center for Teacher Education, Evaluation of Teaching Project. 1976.

Federal Register, *Proposed rules: Teacher centers program,* (Department of Health, Education, and Welfare, Office of Education) (1977), **42** (113): 30290–30293.

Feshbach, N. D. Student teacher preferences for elementary pupils varying in personality characteristics. *Journal of Educational Psychology* (1969), **60**: 126–132.

FESTINGER, L. *A theory of cognitive dissonance.* New York: Row Peterson, 1957.

FISHER, C. W., R. S. MARLIAVE, N. N. FILBY, L. S. COHEN, J. E. MOORE, and D. C. BERLINER. *A study of instructional time in grade 2 mathematics.* Technical report II–3, San Francisco: Far West Laboratory for Educational Research and Development, 1976.

FISKE, E. B. New York teachers are gaining in battle for professional status. *New York Times,* July 31, 1979, pp. A–1; C–4.

FLANDERS, N. A. *Teacher influence, pupil attitudes, and achievement. Final report, cooperative research project, number 397.* Minneapolis, Minn.: University of Minnesota, November 30, 1960.

——. *Analyzing teacher behavior.* Reading, MA.: Addison-Wesley Publishing Co., Inc., 1970.

FLANDERS, N. A., E. WERNER, R. A. ELDER, J. NEWMAN and M. K. LAI. *A minicourse on interaction analysis.* San Francisco: Far West Laboratory for Educational Research and Development, 1974.

FRENCH, E. G. Effects of the interaction of motivation and feedback on task performance. In J. W. Atkinson (Ed.), *Motives in fantasy, action, and society.* New York: D. Van Nostrand Company, 1958, 400–408.

FRENCH, J. W., and W. B. MICHAEL. *Standards for educational and psychological tests and manuals.* Washington, D.C.: American Psychological Association, 1966.

FRENCH, R. L., and C. M. GALLOWAY. *A description of teacher behavior: Verbal and nonverbal.* Columbus: Ohio State University, 1968. (ERIC Document Reproduction Service No. ED 028 134).

FULLER, F. F. Concerns of teachers: A developmental conceptualization. *American Educational Research Journal* (1969), 6(2): 207–226.

GAGE, N. L. *The scientific basis of the art of teaching.* New York: Teachers College Press, 1978.

GAGE, N. L., and P. E. WINNE. Performance-based teacher education. In K. Ryan (Ed.), *Teacher education,* The Seventy-fourth yearbook of the National Society for the Study of Education, Chicago: University of Chicago, 1975, 146–172.

GALLOWAY, C. *A description of teacher behavior: Verbal and nonverbal.* Unpublished doctoral dissertation, Ohio State University, 1968.

GALLOWAY, C. M. An exploratory study of observational procedures for determining teacher nonverbal communication. (Doctoral dissertation, University of Florida, 1962). *Dissertation Abstracts International,* 1962, 2310. (University Microfilm No. 6206529).

——. Nonverbal communication. *The Instructor* (April 1968), 37–42.

GARNER, J., and M. BING. The elusiveness of Pygmalion and differences in teacher-pupil contacts. *Interchange* (1973), 4(1): 34–42.

GEHLBACH, R. C. Individual differences: Implications for instructional theory, research, and innovation. *Educational Researcher* (1979), 8(4): 8–14.

GEORGE, A. Development and validation of a concerns questionnaire. Paper presented at the annual meeting of the American Educational Research Association, New York, 1977.

GLADING, J. C. *The Miller Analogies Test and its relationship to other tests and scholastic achievement at Springfield College.* Unpublished master's thesis, Springfield College, 1951.

GLASS, G. V. In M. C. Wittrock and D. C. Wiley (Eds.), *The evaluation of instruction: Issues and problems.* New York: Holt, Rinehart and Winston, 1970, 210–211.

——. Primary, secondary, and meta-analysis of research. *Educational Researcher* (1976), 10: 3–8.

GOLDHAMMER, R. *Clinical supervision: Special methods for the supervision of teachers.* New York: Holt, Rinehart and Winston, 1969.

GOOD, T. L., B. J. BIDDLE, and J. E. BROPHY. *Teachers make a difference.* New York: Holt, Rinehart and Winston, 1975.

GORDON, T. *T.E.T.—Teacher effectiveness training.* New York: David McKay Co., Inc., 1974.

GUILFORD, J. P. *The nature of human intelligence.* New York: McGraw-Hill Book Company, 1967.

HALL, G. E., GEORGE, A. and W. L. RUTHERFORD, Measuring stages of concern about the innovation: A manual for the use of the SoC Questionnaire. The University of Texas, Austin, Texas, 1979.

HALL, G. E., WALLACE, R. D., JR. and W. A. DOSSETT. A developmental conceptualization of the adoption process within educational institutions. Austin: Research and Development Center for Teacher Education, The University of Texas, 1973.

HARRIS, B. M. Limits and supplements to formal clinical procedures. *Journal of Research and Development in Education* (1976), **9:** 85–89.

HAUSER, S. T. Loevinger's model and measure of ego development: A critical review. *Psychological Bulletin* (1976), **83:** 928–955.

HARVEY, O. J., D. E. HUNT, and H. M. SCHROEDER. *Conceptual systems and personality organization.* New York: John Wiley & Sons, Inc., 1961.

HEATH, R. W., and M. A. NIELSON. The research base for performance-based teacher education. *Review of Educational Research* (1974), **44**(4): 463–484.

HERNDON, J. *The way it spozed to be.* New York: Bantam Books, Inc., 1968.

HILLS, J. R. Use of measurement in selection and placement. In R. L. Thorndike (Ed.), *Educational measurement*, 2nd ed., Washington, D.C.: American Council on Education, 1971.

HORN, J. L. Organization of abilities and the development of intelligence. *Psychological Review* (1968), **75:** 242–259.

HOUSTON, W. B. and R. B. HOWSAM, (Eds.), *Competency-based teacher education: Progress, problems, and prospects.* Chicago: Science Research Associates, Inc., 1972.

HUNT, D. E. *Matching models in education.* Monograph series No. 10. Toronto: Ontario Institute for Studies in Education, 1971.

————. *Person-environment interaction: A challenge found wanting before it was tried.* Address to the Division of Educational Psychology, American Psychological Association meeting, Montreal, Canada, August 28, 1973.

————. Person-environment interaction. *Review of Educational Research* (1975), **45**(2): 209–230.

————. Teachers' adaptation: 'Reading' and 'flexing' to students. *Journal of Teacher Education* (1976), **27**(3): 268–275.

HUNT, D. E. *Conceptions of persons, environments and behaviors (Exercises 1–3) and Manuals for scoring concepts of persons, environments and behaviors.* Unpublished manuscripts. Toronto: Ontario Institute for Studies in Education, 1976.

HUNT, D. E. Teachers are psychologists, too: On the application of psychology to education. *Canadian Psychological Review* (1976), **17:** 210–218.

HUNT, D. E., and B. E. JOYCE. Teacher trainee personality and initial teaching style. *American Educational Research Journal* (1967), **4:** 253–259.

HUNT, D. E., and E. V. SULLIVAN. *Between psychology and education.* New York: Holt, Rinehart and Winston, 1974.

HUNT, D. E., L. F. BUTLER, J. E. NOY, and M. E. ROSSER. *Assessing conceptual level by the paragraph completion method.* Toronto: Ontario Institute for Studies in Education, 1977.

JAMES, C. D. R. *A cognitive style approach to teacher-pupil interaction and the academic performance of black children.* Unpublished master's thesis. Princeton, N.J.: Rutgers University, 1973.

JOYCE, B., and M. WEIL. *Concepts of teacher centers.* Washington, D.C.: ERIC Clearinghouse on Teacher Education (Report ED 075 375), 1973.

————. *Models of teaching* (2nd ed.). Englewood Cliffs, N. J.: Prentice-Hall, Inc., 1980.

KERLINGER, F. N. *Foundations of behavioral research*, 2nd. ed. New York: Holt, Rinehart and Winston, 1973.

————. The influence of research on education practice. *Educational Researcher* (1977), **6**(8): 5–12.

KHAN, S. B., and J. WEISS. The teaching of affective responses. In R. M. W. Travers (Ed.), *Sec-*

ond handbook of research on teaching. Skokie, IL.: Rand McNally and Company, 1973, 759–804.

KING, A. Self-fulfilling prophecies in training the hard core: Supervisors' expectations and the underprivileged worker's performance. *Social Science Quarterly* (1971), **52:** 369–378.

KOEHLER, V. Comments. In D. M. Medley, *Teacher competence and teacher effectiveness: A review of process-product research.* Washington, D. C.: American Association of Colleges for Teacher Education, 1977, p. 122.

KONOPKA, G. *Young girls: A portrait of adolescence.* Englewood Cliffs, N. J.: Prentice-Hall, Inc., 1976.

KORAN, M. L., R. E. SNOW, and F. J. McDONALD. Teacher aptitude and observational learning of a teaching skill. *Journal of Educational Psychology* (1971), **62:** 219–228.

KORCHIN, S. J., and H. A. HEATH. Somatic experience in the anxiety state: Some sex and personality correlates of autonomic feedback. *Journal of Consulting Psychology* (1961), **25:** 398–404.

KOUNIN, J. S. *Discipline and group management in classrooms.* New York: Holt, Rinehart and Winston, 1970.

KRACHT, C. R., and I. P. CASEY. Attitudes, anxieties and student teaching performance. *Peabody Journal of Education* (1968), **45:** 214–217.

KRATHWOHL, D. R., B. S. BLOOM, and B. B. MASIA. *Taxonomy of educational objectives. The classification of educational objectives. Handbook II: Affective domain.* New York: David McKay, 1964.

KRATZ, H. E. Characteristics of the best teachers as recognized by children. *Pedagogical Seminary* (1896), **3:** 413–418.

KYTE, G. C. The effective supervisory conference. *California Journal of Educational Research* (1962), **13:** 160–168.

LEEDS, C. H. A second validity study of the Minnesota Teacher Attitude Inventory. *Elementary School Journal* (1952), **52:** 398–405.

LEWIN, K. *A dynamic theory of personality.* New York: McGraw-Hill Book Company, 1935.

LOEVINGER, J. The meaning and measurement of ego development. *American Psychologist* (1966), **21:** 195–206.

LOEVINGER, J., and R. WESSLER. *Measuring ego development* (Vol. 1). San Francisco: Jossey-Bass, 1979.

LOEVINGER, J. *Ego development.* San Francisco: Jossey-Bass, Inc., 1976.

LOEVINGER, J. R. WESSLER, and C. REDMORE. *Measuring ego development* (Vol. 2). San Francisco: Jossey-Bass, Inc., 1970.

LOREE, M. R. Shaping teachers' attitudes. In B. O. Smith (Ed.), *Research in teacher education: A symposium.* Englewood Cliffs, N. J.: Prentice-Hall, Inc., 1971, 99–118.

LORTIE, D. C. *School teacher: A sociological study.* Chicago: The University of Chicago Press, 1975.

LUCIO, W. H., and J. D. McNEIL. *Supervision: A synthesis of thought and action.* New York: McGraw-Hill Book Company, 1962.

MARK, J. H., and B. D. ANDERSON. Teacher survival rates—A current look. *American Educational Research Journal* (Summer 1978), **15**(3).

MARTIN, M. *Equal opportunity in the classroom ESEA, Title III: Session A Report.* Los Angeles: County Superintendent of Schools, Division of Compensatory and Intergroup Programs, 1973.

MEDLEY, D. M. Early history of research on teacher behavior. *International Review of Education* (1972), **18**(4): 430–439.

————. *Teacher competence and teacher effectiveness: A review of process-product research.* Washington, D.C.: American Association of Colleges for Teacher Education, 1977.

————. *The development and use of observation schedule and record, form 5V.* Charlottesville, VA.: University of Virginia, 1979 (Mimeograph).

MEDLEY, D. M., and H. E. MITZEL. A technique for measuring classroom behavior. *Journal of Educational Psychology* (1958), **49**(2): 86–92.

――――. Measuring classroom behavior by systematic observation. In N. E. Gage (Ed.), *Handbook of research on teaching*. Skokie, IL.: Rand McNally & Company, 1963, 247–328.

MILLER, W. S. *Manual for the Miller Analogies Test*. New York: The Psychological Corporation, 1970.

MITZEL, H. E. Teacher effectiveness. In C. W. Harris (Ed.), *Encyclopedia of educational research* (3rd ed.). New York: Macmillan Publishing Co., Inc., 1960, 1481–1486.

MORINE, G. *Entry module: An introduction to observing classroom interaction* (discussion format). San Francisco: Bay Area Teacher Training Complex, Far West Laboratory for Educational Research and Development, 1973. (Mimeographed.)

MOSHER, R. L., and N. A. SPRINTHALL. Psychological education in secondary schools. *American Psychologist* (1970), **25**; 911–924.

MOSHER, R. L., and D. E. PURPEL. *Supervision: The reluctant profession*. Boston: Houghton Mifflin Company, 1972.

MOSKOWITZ, G., and J. L. HAYMAN. Interaction patterns of first year, typical and "best" teachers in inner city schools. *Journal of Educational Research* (1974), **67**(5): 224–230.

McGUIRE, C. H. The evaluation of teachers and teaching effectiveness. In G. E. Millers and T. Fulop (Eds.) *Education strategies for the health professions*. Geneva: World Health Organization, 1974, 67–79.

McLACHLAN, J. F. C., and D. E. HUNT. Differential effects of discovery learning as a function of student conceptual level. *Canadian Journal of Behavioral Science* (1973), **5**: 152–160.

McNEIL, J. D., and W. S. POPHAM. The assessment of teacher competence. In R. M. W. Travers (Ed.), *Second handbook of research on teaching*. Chicago: Rand McNally Publishing Company, 1973, 218–244.

McNERGNEY, R. F. Investigating the training needs of preservice and inservice teachers in cooperative teaching centers. *Improving Human Performance Quarterly* (1978), 236–243.

McNERGNEY, R. F., R. BENTS, and J. BURCALOW. *Effects of training on teachers' abilities to generate constructs*. Paper presented to the Midwestern Educational Research Association, Kalamazoo, Michigan, March 23, 1979.

McNERGNEY, R. F., C. A. CARRIER, L., LEONARD, and B. HAROOTUNIAN. *Teacher development: An interactive approach*. Paper presented to the American Educational Research Association annual meeting, San Francisco, CA., April 12, 1979.

NATIONAL INSTITUTE OF EDUCATION. Violent schools—Safe schools. *Executive summary: The safe school study report to the Congress*. (U.S. Department of Health, Education, and Welfare, 1978).

NEWLOVE, B. *The 15 minute hour*. Austin: The University of Texas, 1966, 3 pp. (Mimeo).

NUTHALL, G., and I. SNOOK. Contemporary models of teaching. In R. M. W. Travers (Ed.), *Second handbook of research on teaching*. Chicago: Rand McNally Publishing Company, 1973, 47–76.

OJA, S. N. *A cognitive-structural approach to adult ego, moral, and conceptual development through inservice education*. Paper presented at the annual meeting of the American Educational Research Association, San Francisco, April 1979.

OJA, S. N., and N. A. SPRINTHALL. Psychological and moral development for teachers: Can you teach old dogs? In N. A. Sprinthall and R. L. Mosher (Eds.), *Value development: The aim of education*. Schenectady, N.Y.: Character Research Press, 1978, 117–134.

OLWEUS, D. A critical analysis of the modern interactionist position. In D. Magnusson and N. S. Endler (Eds.), *Personality at the crossroads*. New York: John Wiley & Sons, Inc., 1977, 221–233.

OSBORNE, M. D. *The influence of teacher expectancy of anxiety on teacher behaviour and pupil performance*. Bachelor's thesis, University of Sydney, 1973.

OSTROM, T. M. The emergence of attitude theory: 1930—1950. In A. G. Greenwald, T. C.

Brock, and T. M. Ostrom (Eds.), *Psychological foundations of attitudes*. New York: Academic Press, Inc., 1968, 1–32.

PARSONS, J. S. *Anxiety and teaching competence*. Unpublished doctoral dissertation, Stanford University, 1970.

———— *Assessment of anxiety about teaching using the Teaching Anxiety Scale: Manual and research report*. Austin, Tex.: Research and Development Center for Teacher Education, The University of Texas, 1973.

PECK, R. F., and J. A. TUCKER. Research on teacher education. In R. M. W. Travers (Eds), *Second handbook of research on teaching*. Chicago: Rand McNally Publishing Company, 1973, 940–978.

PETERSON, P. L. Aptitude × treatment interaction effects of teacher structuring and student participation in college instruction. *Journal of Educational Psychology* (1979), **71**(4): 521–533.

PETRUSICH, M. M. Separation anxiety as a factor in the student teaching experience. *Peabody Journal of Education* (1967), **14**: 353–356.

POLANYI, M. *Personal knowledge*. New York: Harper & Row, Publishers, 1958.

POPHAM, W. J. *Educational evaluation*. Englewood Cliffs, N. J.: Prentice-Hall, Inc., 1975.

RATHBONE, C. Teachers' information handling behavior when grouped with students by conceptual level (Doctoral dissertation, Syracuse University, 1970). *Dissertation Abstracts International* (1971), **32**: 798A. (University Microfilms No. 71–18, 505).

REAM, M. A. *Status of the American public school teacher, 1975–76* (Research report). Washington, D. C.: National Education Association, 1977.

REST, J. R. *Manual for the Defining Issues Test: An objective test of moral judgment*. University of Minnesota, 1974a.

REST, J. R. New approaches in assessing moral judgment. In T. Lickona (Ed.), *Man and morality*. New York: Holt, Rinehart andWinston, 1974b.

———— The cognitive developmental approach to morality: The state of the art. *Counseling and Values* (1974b), **18**(4): 64–78.

REST, J. R., D. COOPER, D. R. COOPER, J. MASANZ, and D. ANDERSON. Judging the important issues in moral dilemmas—An objective measure of development. *Developmental Psychology* (1974), **10**: 491–501.

ROBERTSON, M., and W. NIELSEN. The Graduate Record Examination and selection of graduate students, *American Psychologist* (1961), **16**: 648–650.

ROSENSHINE, B., and N. F. FURST. Research on teacher performance criteria. In B. O. Smith (Ed.), *Research in teacher education*. Englewood Cliffs, N. J.: Prentice-Hall, Inc., 1971, 37–72.

ROSENSHINE, B. and M. MEYERS. Staff development for teaching basic skills. *Theory into Practice* (1978), **17**(3): 267–271.

ROSENTHAL, R. The Pygmalion effect lives. *Psychology Today* (September 1974), 56–63.

ROSENTHAL, R., and L. JACOBSON. *Pygmalion in the classroom: Teacher expectation and pupils' intellectual development*. New York: Holt, Rinehart and Winston, 1968.

RYAN, C. *The testing maze*. Chicago: The National PTA, 1979.

RYAN, K., K. NEWMAN, G. MAGER, J. APPLEGATE, T. LASLEY, R. FLORA, and J. JOHNSTON. *Biting the apple: Accounts of first year teachers*. New York: Longman, Inc., 1980.

RYANS, D. G. *Characteristics of teachers*. Washington, D. C.: American Council on Education, 1960.

SALOMON, G. Heuristic models for the generation of aptitude-treatment interaction hypotheses. *Review of Educational Research* (1972), **42**(3): 327–343.

SCHMIEDER, A. A., and S. J. YARGER. Teacher/teaching centering in America. *Journal of Teacher Education* (1974), **25**(1): 5–12.

SCHRODER, H. M., M. J. DRIVER, and S. STREUFERT. *Human information processing*. New York: Holt, Rinehart and Winston, 1967.

SERGIOVANNI, T. J. Toward theory of clinical supervision. *Journal of Research and Development in Education* (1976), **9:** 20–29.

SEWALL, G., D. SHERMAN, and E. D. LEE. Chasing ghosts. *Newsweek* (August 27, 1979), p. 44.

SHOWS, W. D. Psychological differentiation and the A-B dimension: A dyadic interaction hypothesis (Doctoral dissertation, Duke University, 1967). *Dissertation Abstracts International* (1968), **28:** 3885B. (University Microfilms No. 68–2744).

SIMON, E. G., and A. BOYER. (Eds.). *Mirrors for behavior III: An anthology of observation instruments*. Wyncote, PA.: Communication Materials Center, 1974.

SMITH, L. M., and W. GEOFFREY. *The complexities of an urban classroom*. New York: Holt, Rinehart and Winston, 1968.

SMITH, M. L., and G. V. GLASS. Meta-analysis of psychotherapy outcome studies. *American Psychologist* (1977), **32:** 752–760.

SNOW, R. E. Brunswickian approaches to research on teaching. *American Educational Research Journal* (1968), **5:** 475–489.

———. Representative and quasi-representative designs for research on teaching. *Review of Educational Research* (1974), **44**(3): 265–292.

SOAR, R. S. An integration of findings from four studies of teacher effectiveness. In G. D. Borich, *The appraisal of teaching: Concepts and process*. Reading, MA.: Addison-Wesley Publishing Company, 1977, 96–103.

SPAULDING, R. L. *An introduction to the use of coping analysis schedule for educational settings (CASES) and the Spaulding teacher activity rating schedule (STARS)*. Durham, N. C.: Education Improvement Program, Duke University, 1967.

SPEARMAN, C. *The abilities of man*. London: Macmillan & Company, Ltd., 1927.

STAFFORD, J. W. The prediction of success in graduate school. *American Psychologist* (1951), **6:** 298–307.

STERN, G. G., J. MASLING, B. DENTON, J. HENDERSON, and R. LEVIN. Two scales for the assessment of unconscious motivations for teaching. *Educational and Psychological Measurement* (1960), **20:** 9–29.

STINNETT, T. M. *A manual on standards affecting school personnel in the United States*. Washington, D.C.: National Education Association, 1974.

STONE, M. K. The role of cognitive style in teaching and learning. *Journal of Teacher Education* (1976), **27**(4): 332–334.

STRICKER, G., and J. J. HUBER. The Graduate Record Examination and undergraduate grades as predictors of success in graduate school. *Journal of Educational Research* (1967), **60:** 446–448.

SUEDFELD, P. Attitude manipulation in restricted environments: Conceptual structure and response to propaganda. *Journal of Abnormal and Social Psychology* (1964), **68:** 242–247.

TAYLOR, J. A. A personality scale of manifest anxiety. *Journal of Abnormal and Social Psychology* (1953), **48:** 285–290.

TAYLOR, J. A., and K. W. SPENCE. The relationship of anxiety to performance in serial learning. *Journal of Experimental Psychology* (1952), **44:** 61–64.

TENNYSON, R. D., and W. ROTHEN. Pre-task and on-task adaptive design strategies for selecting number of instances in concept acquisition. *Journal of Educational Psychology* (1977), **64:** 586–592.

TERKEL, S. *Working*. New York: Avon Books, 1972.

TERMAN, L. M. *The measurement of intelligence*. Boston: Houghton Mifflin Company, 1916.

THURSTONE, L. L. The measurement of social attitude. *Journal of Abnormal and Social Psychology* (1931), **26:** 249–269.

TOBIAS, S. *Research strategy in the effect of individual differences on achievement from programmed instruction*. Paper presented at the meeting of the American Psychological Association, Washington, D.C., September 1969.

————. Achievement-treatment interactions. *Review of Educational Research* (1976), **46:** 61–74.

TOBIAS, S., and T. INGBER. Achievement treatment interactions in programmed instruction. *Journal of Educational Psychology* (1976), **68**(1): 43–47.

TOMLINSON, P. D., and D. E. HUNT. Differential effects of rule-example order as a function of conceptual level. *Canadian Journal of Behavioural Science* (1971), **3:** 237–245.

TRAVERS, R. M. W., and others. *Measured needs of teachers and their behavior in the classroom.* Provo, UT.: University of Utah, 1961.

TYLER, L. E. *Individual differences: Abilities and motivational directions.* Englewood Cliffs, N. J.: Prentice-Hall, Inc., 1974.

WASHBURNE, C., and L. N. HEIL. What characteristics of teachers affect children's growth? *School Review* (1960), **68:** 420–426.

WEAVER, W. T. Educators in supply and demand: Effects on quality. *School Review* (August 1978), **86**(4): 552–593.

WELLER, R. H. *Verbal communication in instructional supervision: An observational system for research study of clinical supervision in groups.* New York: Teachers College Press, 1971.

WHITE, G. Indian dropouts tell why they left school. *Minneapolis Tribune,* June 4, 1970; Indian pupils were paid to attend classes, *Minneapolis Tribune,* June 5, 1979; Special schools cater to Indian students, *Minneapolis Tribune,* June 6, 1979.

WIRT, F. M., and M. W. KIRST. *The political web of American schools.* Boston: Little, Brown and Company, 1972.

WIRTH, A. G. *John Dewey as educator: His design for work in education (1894–1904).* New York: John Wiley & Sons, Inc., 1966.

WITHALL, J. Development of a technique for the measurement of socioeconomic climate in classroom. *Journal of Experimental Education* (1949), **17:** 347–361.

WITKIN, H. A.; P. K. OLTMAN, E. RASKIN, and S. A. KARP. *A manual for the Embedded Figures Test.* Palo Alto, Ca.: Consulting Psychologists Press, 1971.

WITKIN, H. A., C. A. MOORE, D. R. GOODENOUGH, and P. W. COX. Field-dependent and field-independent cognitive styles and their educational implications. *Review of Educational Research* (1977), **47**(1):1–64.

WU, J. J. Cognitive style and task performance—A study of student teachers (Doctoral dissertation, University of Minnesota, 1967). *Dissertation Abstracts International* (1968), **29:** 176A. (University Microfilm No. 68–7408).

YANKOLOVICH, D. *The new morality: A profile of American youth in the 70s.* New York: McGraw-Hill Book Company, 1974.

YARGER, S. J., K. R. HOWEY, and B. R. JOYCE. *Inservice teacher education.* Palo Alto, in press.

ZIEGLER, H., H. J. TUCKER, and L. A. WILSON. Communication and decision making in American public education: A longitudinal and comparative study. In J. D. Scribner (Ed.), *The politics of education,* The Seventy-sixth yearbook of the National Society for the Study of Education, 1977, 218–254.

✦ Index ✦